Anti-Anabaptist Polemics

Anabaptist and Mennonite Studies (New Series)

Edited by Maxwell Kennel

Volume 1. Gary Waite, *Anti-Anabaptist Polemics: Dutch Anabaptism and the Devil in England, 1531-1660*. Thunder Bay: Pandora Press, 2023. 265 pp.

Volume 2. Cornelius J. Dyck, *Hans de Ries: A Study in Second Generation Dutch Anabaptism*. Introduction by Mary S. Sprunger. Thunder Bay: Pandora Press, 2023. 370 pp.

Volume 3. Edmund Pries, *Anabaptist Oath Refusal: Basel, Bern, and Strasbourg, 1525-1538*. Thunder Bay: Pandora Press, 2023. 485 pp.

Anti-Anabaptist Polemics
Dutch Anabaptism and the Devil in England, 1531-1660

Gary K. Waite

PANDORA
PRESS

Library and Archives Canada Cataloguing in Publication

Title: Anti-Anabaptist polemics: a study in second generation Dutch Anabaptism / Gary K. Waite.
Names: Waite, Gary K., 1955- author.
Description: Series statement: Anabaptist and Mennonite studies (New series); volume 1 | Includes bibliographical references.
Identifiers: Canadiana 20230228259 | ISBN 9781926599991 (softcover)
Subjects: LCSH: English literature—Early modern, 1500-1700—History and criticism. | LCSH: Religion and literature—England—History—17th century. | LCSH: Anabaptists—Netherlands—History. | LCSH: Polemics.
Classification: LCC PR428.R46 W35 2023 | DDC 820.9/38209032—dc23

Author: Gary K. Waite, FRSC. Professor Emeritus, Department of History, University of New Brunswick.

Book design, cover, and editing by Maxwell Kennel

The author and publisher gratefully acknowledge the financial support for this title provided by the Department of History at the University of New Brunswick and the Acadia Centre for Baptist and Anabaptist Studies. The present book is an expansion of the 2021 Zeman Lecture delivered on September 20, 2021 and hosted by the Acadia Centre for Baptist and Anabaptist Studies.

ANTI-ANABAPTIST POLEMICS
ISBN: 978-1-926599-99-1

Copyright © 2023 Pandora Press
Published by Pandora Press
All rights reserved.
www.pandorapress.com

Praise for *Anti-Anabaptist Polemics*

"The Anabaptists demolished the conventions of early modern Europe – in theology, in politics and in socio-economic affairs. Although few and foreign in England, their reputation for breaking with traditional ways provoked outspoken denunciation there. Gary Waite has analysed the English writers who wrote against Dutch and German Anabaptism between 1531 and 1660, bringing out their habitual concentration on the horrors of the violence, communism, and polygamy of the outbreak at Münster in 1533-35. The English polemicists were eager to blacken the image of Separatists at home by drawing spurious parallels. The effect was to arouse anxiety among adherents of the established Church of England but also, paradoxically, to give ideas to some of those who created new religious movements in the 1640s. Because this study is so revealing about the nature and consequences of hate literature inspired by religion, it holds dismaying relevance for the twenty-first century."

— Dr. David Bebbington, Emeritus Professor of History, University of Stirling

"Meticulously researched and brilliantly written, this engaging and timely book opens up a fascinating and neglected subject in ways that will interest anyone who looks at religion in early modern England. Essential for those working on English Baptist history, it also offers rich new insights for researchers interested in the intersections of religion, politics, polemic, and the supernatural in the early modern world."

— Dr. Andrew Crome, Senior Lecturer in Early Modern History, Manchester Metropolitan University

"This compellingly written book surveys anti-Anabaptist polemics in England from the Reformation to the Restoration. Waite deftly analyzes a wide range of printed texts to reveal the English attitude toward and caricature of "radical" reform movements in continental Europe. Yet this book is about much more than the use of Anabaptism as a rhetorical cudgel carved for various purposes over the course of the sixteenth and seventeenth centuries. Instead, what Waite offers is a new window into the power— and unintended consequences—of fear, paranoia, and print in an age of demonization as much as reformation. *Anti-Anabaptist Polemics* is essential reading for scholars interested in the early modern polemics of hate and how they speak to our own moment of polarization and extremism."

— Dr. Michelle D. Brock, Associate Professor of History, Washington and Lee University

"Historians have long wrestled with the question of the relationship between the continental Radical Reformation of the sixteenth century and the religious explosion during the English Civil War in the middle of the seventeenth. Was the latter the final flourishing of the former as some scholars have claimed? Gary Waite brings a novel approach and new insights to this debate. Rather than focusing on the pedigree of the ideas of so-called religious radicals, he turns his attention to how they were represented in the polemics of their opponents and concludes that the anti-Anabaptist propaganda produced in England actually helped to foster radical religion there. In the process, he also contributes to our understanding of major events and trends in early modern Europe, including the development of religious tolerance and the evolution of perceptions of witchcraft and the devil."

— Dr. Geoffrey Dipple, Professor of History, University of Alberta

"Gary Waite provides a fascinating and thorough overview of interpretations of Anabaptism in sixteenth- and seventeenth-century England. This book is laden with treasures from the archives and will enrich scholarly understanding of the era."

— Dr. Melody Maxwell, Associate Professor of Christian History at Acadia Divinity College and Director of the Acadia Centre for Baptist and Anabaptist Studies

Table of Contents

List of Figures	xi
Series Editor's Preface	xiii
Acknowledgements	xiv

Introduction — 1
Charitable Hatred — 4
Amsterdamnified! and Polemics — 7

Chapter 1.
Anabaptists in the Dutch and English Reformations
The Dippers Dipt… — 13
Were there Anabaptists in England? — 16
Historiography — 18
Historians and Polemical Categorization — 24
"Anabaptist" in Early English Books Online — 26
English Anxieties and Dutch Anabaptism — 27
Dutch Anabaptism: The Historical Record — 30
The English Reformation and Anabaptism — 35

Chapter 2.
Anti-Anabaptist Polemics 1531-1560
William Barlow's A dyaloge, 1531 — 42
Thomas More and Henry VIII on Anabaptism — 43
They "thinke that the payne … of deuylles…" — 45
Anti-Anabaptist Works under King Edward VI — 48
William Turner and the Disease of Heresy — 51
English Polemics and Tudor Policy — 53
The Translation of Johannes Sleidanus' Chronicle — 55

Chapter 3. Anti-Anabaptist Polemics, 1562-1640
Anabaptists, "an vnquyetouse kynde of men" 59
"Howling Anabaptists" & "Hell-maisters" 64
"Certaine rash-pates and giddy-headed preachers" 65
Error on the Right and Left 66
John Smyth's Self-Baptism in 1609 68
Leonard Busher's Religions Peace, 1614 72
Polemics in the lead up to the Civil War 75

Chapter 4.
Anabaptism and Interregnum Polemics, 1640-1650: The Era of the Heresiographers
Thomas Edwards' Gangraena, 1646 81
Ephraim Pagitt's Heresiography, 1645 84
Daniel Featley's 1645 The Dippers Dipt 89
Robert Baillie 101
The Rabid Puritan, William Prynne 106
Anabaptists as Secret Jesuit Agents 108
Prynne: Punishment and Polemics 112
Demonizing Diversity: Prynne and the Quakers 121
Prynne's Sources 124

Chapter 5.
Anti-Anabaptist Polemics and English Witch-hunting, 1600-1660
Matthew Hopkins and the East Anglia Witch Hunts 130
Demonizing Rhetoric and Witchcraft in England 134
Byfield on Witches, Libertines, and Anabaptists 135
Renunciation of Infant Baptism & Demonic Witches 138
Thomas Hall on Pacts with the Devil, 1652 140
John Eachard on the Devil and Baptism, 1646 142
Devilish Dreams, Anabaptist Enthusiasm, Witchcraft 145
Diabolical Sedition, Spiritual Sorcery, and Atheism 148
Accusations of Witchcraft against Baptists & Quakers 151
Quakers and Witchcraft Accusations 152
A Large Meeting of Witches… 155

Chapter 6.
Anti-Anabaptist Propaganda, 1650-1660
William Prynne and the Jews   159
Alexander Ross's Pansebeia, 1655   167
Blome, The Fanatick History, 1660   171
The Monster of Munster, 1660   182

Conclusion
Polemics and Repression   186
"Anabaptism" as a Polemical Tool   187
Polemics and Unintended Consequences   188
"Anabaptism" and Malleable Religious Identity 191
Polemics Then and Now   194
Hate Literature and Violence   198

Bibliography   199

Index of Proper Names   234

List of Figures

Figure 1: Engraved frontispiece to Daniel Featley, 'Katabaptistai kataptysoi. The Dippers Dipt, or, The Anabaptists Duck'd and Plung'd over Head and Eares' (London, Nicholas Bourne, 1645). Courtesy of the Cambridge University Library, F.3.117. (page 13)

Figure 2: Jan van Leiden, Portrait of Jan van Leiden by Christoffel van Sichem (I), after Jan Cornelisz. van 't Woudt, in *Warhaffte Abbildung des königs von Munster/ genant [genamt] Johan Bochholds seines Hanttwercks ein Schneider/ geboren zu Leyden in Hollant/ welcher in seine Zitel gfuhrt hatt diese wort.* (Amsterdam: Christoffel von Sichem, 1606), Courtesy of the Rijksmuseum, Amsterdam, RP-P-1918-1733, cropped. (page 31)

Figure 3: Image of Anabaptists attacking the Amsterdam City Hall, 1535; from Lambertus Hortensius, *Van den oproer der weder-dooperen* (Enkhuizen: J.L. Meyn, 1614), p.20. After a lost painting by Barend Dircksz. Courtesy of the Rijksmuseum, Amsterdam, RP-P-AO-28-11. (page 33)

Figure 4: Featley, *Dippers Dipt*, cropped, figure of the demon. Courtesy of the Cambridge University Library, F.3.117. (page 41)

Figure 5: Anabaptists walk naked through the Dam at Amsterdam, 1535, by Jan Lucas van der Beek, after a drawing by Bernard Picart, 1723-1818. Courtesy of the Rijksmuseum, Amsterdam, RP-P-1911-2920. (page 92)

Figure 6: Anonymous engraver, after lost original 1536 painting by Barend Dircksz, in Lambertus Hortensius, *Van den oproer der weder-dooperen* (Enkhuizen: J.L. Meyn, 1614), 18. Courtesy of the Rijksmuseum, Amsterdam, RP-P-AO-28-5-1(R). (page 93)

Figure 7: Featley, *The Dippers Dipt*, closeup of titlepage. Courtesy of the Cambridge University Library, F.3.117. (page 96)

Figure 8: *Wenceslaus Hollar, portrait of William Prynne, The Wenceslaus Hollar Collection, Hollar-k-1216, courtesy the Thomas Fischer Rare Book Room, University of Toronto,* https://iiif.library.utoronto.ca/presentation/v2/hollar:Hollar_k_1216/manifest. (page 109)

Figure 9: *A Catalogue of the Severall Sects and Opinions in England and other Nations: With a briefe Rehearsall of their false and dangerous Tenents,* broadsheet, 1647; pub domain, https://commons.wikimedia.org/wiki/File:Catalogue_of_Sects.GIF (page 110)

Figure 10: Diederick Snyder, leader of the Naaktloopers, by Van Sichem, in Haestens, *Historische beschrijvinge ende affbeeldinge der voorneemste hooft ketteren* (Amsterdam: C. Claesz, 1608), plate 11. Courtesy of the Rijksmuseum, Amsterdam, RP-P-1907-3379. (page 177)

Figure 11: The Quaker and Schwaermer Witchcraft, in Johann Friedrich Corvinus, *Anabaptisticum Et Enthusiasticum Pantheon*, in German translation of Blome, *The fanatick history*, 38. Courtesy of Münchener Digitalisierungs Zentrum, https://mdz-nbn-resolving.de/urn:nbn:de:bvb:12-bsb11205321-0. (page 181)

Series Editor's Preface

The Anabaptist and Mennonite Studies series was first published by Pandora Press between 2000 and 2010, and sponsored by the Institute of Anabaptist Mennonite Studies at Conrad Grebel University College. Its titles included landmark works in the history of Anabaptism like *Bernhard Rothmann and the Reformation in Münster, 1530-35*, by Willem de Bakker, Michael Driedger, and James Stayer (Pandora Press, 2009), and essential texts in Mennonite theology like A. James Reimer's anthology *Mennonites and Classical Theology: Dogmatic Foundations for Christian Ethics* (Pandora Press, 2000). As the new Director of Pandora Press, it is my distinct pleasure to re-launch the series as an independent venture, guided by our editorial board and our growing list of authors.

The series begins with the present volume by Gary Waite, which substantially expands upon his 2021 Jarold K. Zeman Lecture at the Acadia Centre for Baptist and Anabaptist Studies (ACBAS). It will be followed by the first published edition of a dissertation written by Mennonite historian Cornelius J. Dyck on the Dutch Anabaptist figure Hans de Ries, and a comprehensive study of Anabaptist oath refusal by Edmund Pries. Future volumes in the series will include a second edition of J. Lawrence Burkholder's *Mennonite Ethics* and an expanded edition of Linda Hubert Hecht's *Women in Early Austrian Anabaptism*. Beyond these first five titles, several translation projects are underway, and submissions to the series are open and welcome.

— Dr. Maxwell Kennel
Series Editor and Director of Pandora Press
Thunder Bay, Ontario.

Acknowledgements

I write these acknowledgements in the Winter of 2022/2023 in the shadow of extreme political polarization across the world, and the recent infusion of religious antagonisms into political discourse, escalated by the anxieties arising from the global Covid-19 pandemic. In a May 16, 2022, column in the *Washington Post*, religion reporter Michelle Boorstein commented on the growing power of Christian nationalism in the United States in the leadup to the 2022 mid-term elections. She observed that scholars on American religion were remarking on how "many conservative Republican leaders seem in recent years to be using more exclusionary and sharper religious language," especially in some branches of charismatic churches, "where life is about a real, daily battle between Satan and God." She then quotes historian John Fea who provides some examples: "Things like: 'You are the devil, you don't belong in this country and I'm going to elect people who are on God's side.'" Fea comments that such "rhetoric is incapable of discourse. There is no distinction between political argument and spiritual warfare. That is new," he concludes.[1] I have been observing similarly disturbing trends in the rise of uncivil discourse in my own country and province.

---

[1] Michelle Boorstein, "Christian nationalism is shaping a Pa. primary — and a GOP shift" *Washington Post*. May 16, 2022. https://www.washingtonpost.com/religion/2022/05/16/mastriano-pennsylvania-republican-christian-nationalism/.

I have been reading, writing, and teaching about religious conflict and demonizing rhetoric over a career spanning some four decades, so for me, none of this is new. What is disturbing, however, is that much of the rhetoric that I have become accustomed to while studying the early-modern sources has returned, with comparable zeal and even some of the specific content. The devil is suddenly front and centre in political and civic discourse, and his agents identified and attacked. Specific ideas and language drawn from the violent history of Antisemitic mythmaking, which includes the global conspiracy and ritual murder accusations, have been revived, as have specific elements drawn from the sixteenth and seventeenth-century witch-hunts. The kind of polarizing language that we are witnessing now, as I write this, is frighteningly similar to that which dominated the sixteenth-century Reformation and which led to a century of religious conflict and bloodshed. The subject of this book has therefore become far more pertinent and contemporary than I could ever have imagined just a few years ago. Witnessing this religious and political polarization in real time has sharpened my focus on the subject of this historical work on the anti-Anabaptist polemics of sixteenth and seventeenth-century England. When I presented a much shorter draft of this research to a virtual audience at the Acadia Centre for Baptist and Anabaptist Studies in September 2021, I was asked by one participant if the works I was discussing were not hate literature. I had to agree, and seeing how some people are picking up the old demonizing canards used against Jews, persecuted Anabaptists and Quakers, and supposed witches, and using them in their own hate-filled tirades, I was inspired to dig deeper into this subject. And this book is the result.

What I seek to do in this monograph is to focus attention on a fairly narrow sub-section of early-modern religious history – polemical publications printed in England targeting continental Anabaptism – and to use that as a lens to peer at broader attitudes toward religious dissent, toleration, witchcraft, and God and the devil, among other things. While the number of publications that I have examined here is relatively small compared to the thousands of printed works that made reference to "Anabaptist," I have been reading comparable publications from the Netherlands and Germany over the course of my career. Turning my sights on the English scene, I did a test run of sorts with an analysis of the reaction to the life and ideas of one of the most controversial figures of the sixteenth century, the artist, Anabaptist messiah, and Spiritualist David Joris (1501-1556). That exercise involved only about 140 printed works, allowing me to be more comprehensive in my analysis that I can be here. It also gave me a sense of the relationship English writers had with continental sources, which was, to put it mildly, narrow and quite selective.[2]

That article and this book are, in fact, part of the "Amsterdamnified!" research program led by Michael Driedger (Brock University) and me. Together with a wonderful team of research collaborators, we have organized colloquia and in 2021 produced a special double journal issue in *Church History and Religious Culture* on the subject of Spiritualism in early modern Europe.[3] Our research goal is

---

[2] "The Devil of Delft in England: the Reception of the Dutch Spiritualist David Joris in 17th-Century English Polemics," *Church History and Religious Culture* 101/4 (2021), 429-95, https://brill.com/view/journals/chrc/101/4/article-p429_1.xml.

[3] *Church History and Religious Culture* 101/2-3 (2021). The introduction and several of the essays are Open Access: https://brill.com/view/journals/chrc/101/2-3/chrc.101.issue-2-3.xml. I am deeply grateful to the other contributors to this collection, most of whom presented drafts of their essays at the "Spiritualism and Freethinkers Symposium," Vrije Universiteit Amsterdam, July 10-11, 2019. I am also thankful for the excellent work of the other editors: Michael Driedger, Francesco Quatrini, and Nina Schroeder.

to explore the "radical religious" roots of the Early Enlightenment, with a particular focus on dissenter or nonconformist networks, publications, and ideas in the Dutch Republic and England. One of our many findings to date is that polemical literature which intended to inspire fear, disgust, and anger over the religious other, often had unanticipated effects – something that will be made very clear here. We are also exploring how the ideas of our Dutch and English nonconformists – especially those Spiritualists who depreciated religious externals in favour of a religion of the heart – contributed to the reshaping of thought not just on matters religious, but also in social, economic, political, and philosophical affairs. Famed philosophers René Descartes, John Locke, and Baruch Spinoza lived in the culturally rich environment of the Dutch Republic where Spiritualism circulated widely. Amsterdamnified! is revealing how much these thinkers absorbed several of their key ideas from these spiritualistic currents flowing freely in the Republic. Their contribution was to knit these ideas together into coherent philosophies. Instead of seeing seventeenth-century religion and philosophy as being essentially at odds, we see them as interlinked in efforts to rethink society and the cosmos.

Here I approach the subject of English writings as a relative outsider, for most of my work has focused on continental religious dissenters, especially Anabaptists and Spiritualists. This background, however, provides me with the ability to see the relative accuracy of English assertions about Anabaptism and the distortions that polemicists deemed important to get their messages across. The goal here, which will be reached from several angles, is to see how the polemical literature condemning continental Anabaptism helped to formulate stereotypes of religious dissenters that were intended to inspire revulsion and fear, mostly by association with the demonic. We will see that at particular moments, especially in the mid 1640s, such demonizing rhetoric intersected with, and in fact shaped, attitudes toward witches, especially the stereotype of sects of witches worshipping Satan and plotting against Christendom, a version promoted by the Witchfinder General Matthew Hopkins that was at odds with traditional English witchcraft.[4]

The religious conflicts among Puritans, Episcopalians, recusant Catholics, and Independents, were critical in creating attitudes of suspicion and fear toward the devil's agents. For example, prior to writing his famous 1584 attack on witch beliefs, *The Discoverie of Witchcraft*, the gentleman Reginald Scot had attended the trial of the accused witch, Margaret Simons, in Rochester. Scot laid her predicament clearly at the feet of the credulous vicar, John Ferrall, who believed that his hoarseness had been caused by Simons' curse, confirming (in his mind) his neighbours' complaints about her witchcraft. Scot thought that Protestant godly efforts to purify the land of such blasphemies as sorcery and Catholicism were causing community divisions. As Peter Elmer notes, Scot cited several examples from his home county of Kent in which "witch-hunting and puritanism" came together.[5] Such coalescence of Puritanism's zeal to

---

[4] For an excellent overview, see Malcolm Gaskill, "Witchcraft Trials in England," *The Oxford Handbook of Witchcraft in Early Modern Europe and Colonial America*, Brian P. Levack, ed. (Oxford, 2013), 283-99.

[5] Peter Elmer, *Witchcraft, Witch-Hunting, and Politics in Early Modern England* (Oxford, 2016), 18-32, especially 19-20. Elmer further discovered that prior to composing *The discouerie*, Scot had switched his allegiance from Puritanism to support of the ecclesiastical hierarchy of John Whitgift who became archbishop in 1583. See also Reginald Scot, *The discouerie of witchcraft, Wherein the lewde dealing of witches and witchmongers is notablie detected, the knauerie of coniurors, the impietie of inchantors, the follie of soothsaiers, the impudent falsehood of cousenors, the infidelitie of atheists, the pestilent practises of Pythonists, the curiositie of figurecasters, the vanitie of dreamers, the beggerlie art of*

reform religion and morality and fears over witchcraft reached its peak of intensity during the chaos of the 1640s.

In the meantime, whether intended or not, attacks on Anabaptism added specific elements to the demonic witch stereotype in England – elements already commonplace on the continent.[6] And, of course, such polemics had intended to make life difficult for religious dissenters such as Baptists and Quakers, and such efforts worked. Whereas the Restoration returned England to centralized, monarchical rule in 1660, many of the forces and ideas unleashed during the Civil War and Interregnum periods remained in muted form, helping to shape discourse on questions of religious diversity and tolerance thereafter. My analysis here, it must be pointed out, is not comprehensive nor exhaustive. It is instead intended to provoke discussion and further research into the subject of polemics and demonizing rhetoric, in both the past and present.

As mentioned, an earlier, and considerably shorter, version of this study was presented as the 2021 Jarold K. Zeman Lecture at the Acadia Centre for Baptist and Anabaptist Studies at Acadia University, Wolfville, Nova Scotia, on September 20, 2021. Due to Covid-19, the lecture was delivered virtually.[7] My thanks go to Dr. Melody Maxwell and her team at ACBAS for making this virtual visit possible. I had the great pleasure of meeting Dr. Zeman in

---

Alumystrye, The abhomination of idolatrie, the horrible art of poisoning, the virtue and power of natural magike, and all the conueiances of Legierdemaine and iuggling are deciphered: and many other things opened, which haue long lien hidden, howbeit verie necessarie to be knowne. Heervnto is added a treatise vpon the nature and substance of spirits and diuels, etc (London: [Henry Denham for] William Brome, 1584), 5-6; and Gaskill, "Witchcraft Trials," 291.

[6] See Gary K. Waite, *Eradicating the Devil's Minions: Anabaptists and Witches in Reformation Europe, 1535-1600* (Toronto, 2007).

[7] It is available here: https://acadiadiv.ca/acbas/event/zeman-lecture-2021/.

1995 when I delivered the Simpson lecture at Acadia a quarter century earlier, and I am honoured to have celebrated his career as a meticulous scholar and true gentleman in the field.

Researching and writing has been one of the great pleasures of my career as a professor and colleague in the History Department of the University of New Brunswick. For several reasons, over the years I did more than my share of administrative service, including several years as chair or acting chair, with the last two years of my tenure during the Covid-19 outbreak and the sudden shift to working and teaching virtually. Despite many challenges, I have enjoyed teaching thousands of students, and have learned a great deal from them; they have inspired me to continue asking questions and look for different angles to comprehend the past. So too have many colleagues, both at UNB and around the world, whom I must now thank.

I am extremely grateful to the Social Sciences and Humanities Research Council of Canada which in 2015 provided funding for the Amsterdamnified! research program. From these funds we were able to conduct research in both Amsterdam and England, hire research assistants for various projects, organize two fascinating symposia in 2019, one in Toronto and the other in Amsterdam, and to disseminate our findings at various conferences. I wish to thank all of our supportive colleagues who have at various times been part of Amsterdamnified!: those who were contributors to the formulation of the research program at the start – Ruben Buys, Mirjam van Veen (the local organizer of the 2019 Amsterdam symposium), Hans de Waardt, and David Wootton – as well as those who joined us in extremely productive ways along the way – Sebastien Drouin (the local organizer for the Toronto 2019 symposium), Matthew Milner, Francesco Quatrini, Nina Schroeder, and Nigel Smith. And both Mike and I are profoundly grateful to our honorary member and source of advice, inspiration, hospitality, and decades-long friendship Piet Visser. Our research assistants Kelsey Bodechon (UNB), Brookelnn Cooper (Brock), Ace Gammon-Burnett (Brock), Kapri MacDonald (UNB), John Raimondo (Brock), Andrew Taber (UNB), and Jarrett Weston (UNB) have not only produced significant results from their work for us, but also important insights. Taber's 2018 UNB MA Thesis, "'You May Be What Devil You Will:' Depictions of Dutch Religious Plurality in English Print, 1609-1699," has been an inspiration and model for my own research into English polemical works. Working with Mike and our other scholar friends has been inspiring and a great joy. Conversations at conferences and colloquia with many others, such as Andreas Pietsch, Anselm Schubert, and Nicholas Terpstra, to name just a few, have resulted in new ideas or reconsideration of old ones. And such conversations have been also one of the great pleasures of this profession.

I must also express my thanks for the support of my own institution, the University of New Brunswick, and especially the Department of History which was my work home for so many wonderful years. Colleagues past and present have listened patiently when I have described my research ideas and approaches and have offered helpful insights that have shaped this current work in numerous ways. And, I have to say, we have had a great deal of fun, along with challenges and frustrations, along the way. My thanks must also go to past and present department chairs, most recently Lisa Todd, for providing very practical support and encouragement, including a small subvention that, along with one from ACBAS, has made the production of this book possible. I have had the enormous pleasure of working with Lisa on another project, a text reader of primary sources on the long history of European racism. This work, and our many discussions on the subject, have significantly shaped my thinking about conspiratorial reasoning and hate literature in ways that I hope are obvious here.[8] And I am thankful to the Director of Pandora Press, Maxwell Kennel, not only for his excellent editing and production skills and advice, but also for encouraging me to turn a paper presentation into a book. While it was originally intended to be a short book, one thing led to another in the way that scholarship often does. And this is the result.

Having recently sorted through the detritus of my academic career as I packed up my university office, I had the opportunity to reflect on the path that brought me to this point and to acknowledge those mentors who assisted me along the way. In particular I need to thank my graduate supervisors who played the greatest role in shaping me as an historian: my MA supervisor Walter Klaassen and my PhD supervisor Werner O. Packull, who were both at Conrad Grebel University College at the University of Waterloo. Werner was a thorough critic of my writing who taught me how to be a careful and thoughtful scholar of Anabaptist history; he was even more a mentor, supporter, and friend. Unfortunately, he was forced to retire early due to early onset Alzheimer's disease and died in 2018. I dedicate this book to him and to his beloved partner Karin Packull.

There are so many others that I could mention, but space will not allow more than a few. I do need to express my gratitude to James M. Stayer of Queen's University who acted as external examiner on my PhD defence and who has remained a scholarly critic, advisor, and friend throughout my career. And thank you to all of my other academic friends around the world whose conversations and advice have proven so formative in all of the various research subjects that I have pursued: Anabaptism; Spiritualism (thanks again to Mirjam van Veen and Benjamin Kaplan for so many

---

[8] Lisa M. Todd and Gary K. Waite, eds, *European Racism: A History in Documents*. In preparation for the Broadview Press Sources Series.

wonderful discussions); the life and thought of David Joris (and here I must mention Samme Zijlstra, whose life was tragically cut short in 2001); the Chambers of Rhetoric (thanks especially to Elsa Strietman); demonology and the witch-hunts (thanks especially to Hans de Waardt again); attitudes toward Jews and Muslims in European discourse; and of course Amsterdamnified! These have all offered great challenges for me, and I could not have completed the research in these fields without the help of so many others.

I wish also to thank the President and Fellows of Clare Hall, Cambridge, who in 2001 admitted me as a Visiting Fellow, then as a Life Fellow, and who provided such an inspiring environment for scholarly pursuits and a wonderfully supportive one also for Kate and our girls. Subsequent stays proved similarly stimulating and refreshing. My thanks go also to the staff of the Cambridge University Library, as well as to the staff of the Library of the University of Amsterdam and its rare book unit, the Allard Pierson, where I spent so many wonderful days. I was introduced to this amazing collection by its former Curator, Piet Visser, an incredible guide into the labyrinthine world of old books, and supported too by his successor Adriaan Plak. Of course, the hard-working staff at the Harriet Irving Library at UNB deserve high praise for their efforts, and success, in finding for me some of the most obscure publications that I'm sure they have ever had to search for. And I am grateful to the library's leadership for investing in digital databases like Early English Books Online that made this project possible.

My deepest gratitude, of course, goes to family. My spouse Kate Hayward and I have been partners for the bulk of my career, and she has been and continues to be a bulwark support and loving companion through challenges, sorrows, and joyful moments, the greatest of which has been helping our daughters Jessica and Eleanor become the absolutely wonderful adults that they are now. And enjoying the company of Jessica's darling daughters, Callie and Georgia, allows us to experience just a bit of this pleasure again. I am thankful to Kate for filling in the many gaps in the household activities when I was away on research and conference trips, and for also putting up with my writing activities which continue to absorb a significant portion of my day-to-day life, despite retirement. She too shares profound concern over the religious extremism and conspiracy theories raging around us, something we discuss on a daily basis, and those conversations have shaped my thinking on the subject of this book in ways even she is probably unaware of. It was her earlier research into Holocaust denial that got me interested in pursuing the history of Antisemitism, something that has obviously shaped my recent scholarship, including this book. I cannot express adequately my gratitude to Kate, but I will keep trying. In the meantime, we will continue to do what we can to bring reason and a historical perspective to conversations on such problems.

Thank you all.

Introduction

Even today, the image of Dutch and German Anabaptism that dominates the popular imagination remains that of the theocratic kingdom led by the tailor and actor Jan van Leiden that in 1534-35 mandated polygamy, enforced community of goods, and spread the news of Christ's imminent arrival to the city by force of arms. Since its spectacular fall to its besiegers on June 25, 1535, its story has been used as a cautionary tale among nearly all Christian denominations ever since.[1] Yet it must be noted that while the Anabaptists may have gone to some extremes in their efforts to prepare for the apocalyptic return of Jesus Christ to earth, most of their contemporaries – Catholic, Lutheran, Reformed – were just as motivated by eschatological anxieties and religious zeal as were the Anabaptists. For example, the major German Reformer Martin Luther saw himself as living in the Last Days when the devil raged against the godly before the Last Judgement.[2] The vicious persecution of Anabaptists and other religious dissidents by Catholic and Protestant governments long after Münster can only be explained as the effect of a powerful, even visceral, fear of the

---

[1] See for example, the best-selling historical fiction Luther Blissett (pseudonym), *Q* (Mariner Books, 2005), which sensationally describes the events of the early Reformation from the perspective of an Anabaptist and a Catholic spy. See also the research website of Michael Driedger, "Dutch Dissenters," especially on Anabaptist Münster: http://dutchdissenters.net/wp/page/3/

[2] See, for example, Heiko A. Oberman, *Luther: Man between God and the Devil* (New Haven, 1989).

wrath of God and the raging of Satan in the Last Days. I have explored this theme on the continent in my other works.[3]

But here in this study my focus is on how English observers interpreted Dutch and German Anabaptism. We will observe that English writers of polemical books, tracts, and pamphlets – like their counterparts on the continent – could not resist using Dutch Anabaptism as a cautionary tale, but they did so in ways that even further distorted the continental narrative to fit the English scene. For example, in 1605 the learned Anglican rector Oliver Ormerod weighed into the debate over whether separatists from the Church of England should be tolerated, and in so doing, he questioned how "Protestant" the Anglican Church should be. His contribution was entitled *The picture of a puritane: Or, A relation of the opinions, qualities, and practises of the anabaptists in germanie, and of the puritanes in england Wherein is firmely prooued, that the puritanes doe resemble the anabaptists, in aboue fourescore seuerall things.*

To win over the masses, Ormerod composed this work as a dialogue, "in a moste plaine and familiar manner," between an "Englishman" and a "Germaine" who on some eighty different points of theology and religious practice compared contemporary English Independents or Separatists to the Anabaptists of the previous century, especially those who infamously turned the German city of Münster into the kingdom of God on earth for a few years. Despite the spectacular stories that the Germaine recounts to his friend, the Englishman finds ways to portray his dissenters as even worse, even on salacious topics as "lustfull carnalitie and

---

[3] See Gary K. Waite, *Eradicating the Devil's Minions: Anabaptists and Witches in Reformation Europe, 1535-1600* (Toronto, 2007), and *Heresy, Magic and Witchcraft in Early Modern Europe* (Basingstoke, 2003).

vncleannes," or on following visions to disastrous results.⁴ In order to reveal English Puritans as equal to, or worse than, the German Anabaptists, Ormerod indulges in fabrication, inuendo, and distortion on both fronts. Some of this was a feature of Ormerod's principal source, the anti-Anabaptist treatise of the sixteenth-century Swiss Reformed leader Heinrich Bullinger, to which we will return below.

On the continent there were numerous such polemical works intended to persuade the authorities to attack Anabaptists and other heretics as dangers to civil order and to incurring the wrath of God. Some of these publications were intended to bring to the reader's mind the 1486 witch-hunting manual of the German Inquisitor Heinrich Kramer, the *Malleus Maleficarum* (*The Hammer of Witches*), by using a similar title: *Malleus Haereticorum* (*The Hammer of Heretics*), different versions of which were produced by the German Catholic humanist jurist Johann Faber in 1527, the German Catholic humanist and jurist Georg Eder in 1580, and the Dutch Reformed pastor Carolus Gallus in 1606, the last entitled *Malleus Anabaptistarum* (*The Hammer of Anabaptists*).⁵

Similarly, Ormerod's goal was to inspire fear among the English populace about the insurrectionary danger of

---

⁴ Oliver Ormerod, *The picture of a puritane: Or, A relation of the opinions, qualities, and practises of the anabaptists in germanie, and of the puritanes in england Wherein is firmely prooued, that the puritanes doe resemble the anabaptists, in aboue fourescore seuerall things … wherunto is annexed a short treatise, entituled, puritano-papismus: Or a discouerie of puritan-papisme* (London: Edward Allde for Nathaniel Fosbroke, 1605), 75. All of the English publications cited here were accessed on Early English Books Online.

⁵ See their entries in Global Anabaptist Mennonite Encyclopedia Online: https://gameo.org/index.php?title=Faber,_Johann_(1478-1541)
https://gameo.org/index.php?title=Eder,_Georg_(1523-1586)
https://gameo.org/index.php?title=Gallus,_Carolus_(1530-1616). I am thankful to Michael Driedger for this information.

separation from the state church. Written decades before the wild fluorescence of new religious groups during England's Civil War and Interregnum (1642-1660), Ormerod's dialogues may have succeeded in escalating anxiety, or alternately in inspiring interest and imitation, or simply been taken as humorous entertainment. Or all three.

In this study I examine a number of such polemical works printed between 1531 (when the first known treatise on Anabaptism was printed in England) and 1660 (when the Restoration brought back royal control over religion after the Interregnum) to gauge how continental Anabaptism was understood, polemically distorted, and utilized as a weapon in the debates over religious diversity in England. In the process I suggest that some of the weaponized elements of Dutch and German Anabaptism that were hurled about in thousands of hate-filled pamphlets and treatises over the century inadvertently offered the discontented a number of innovative ideas to draw from, helping in fact to inspire the surge in new religious movements of the 1640s, even though the intention of the authors was to suppress, not encourage, dissent.

Charitable Hatred

In many respects the material that we are exploring here can be described as hate-literature because the writers' goal was to describe the Anabaptists in such a way as to cause their readers revulsion at the horrors of such religious dissent.[6]

---

[6] The polemical literature against English dissenter groups is vast. See, among others, David Loewenstein, *Treacherous Faith: The Specter of Heresy in Early Modern English Literature and Culture* (Oxford, 2013), and *Representing Revolution in Milton and His Contemporaries: Religion, Politics, and Polemics in Radical Puritanism* (Cambridge, 2001); and Nigel Smith, *Perfection Proclaimed: Language and Literature in English*

This general point has been made by others, most especially in Alexandra Walsham's 2006 book *Charitable Hatred: Tolerance and Intolerance in England, 1500-1700*, which critiques the popular myth that England transitioned from a persecutory to a tolerant society along a fairly straight, if bumpy, linear path. Instead, Walsham reveals that hatred for the religious opponent coexisted with, and shaped the debates over, toleration throughout the early modern period. In most cases when it was granted, toleration was grudging and hedged about by conditions and restrictions and could quickly return to persecution under a variety of circumstances. Some groups were tolerated more than others, and hostility toward the Quakers seems to have been particularly endemic, as we shall see. Walsham suggests that forbearance was the most that was on offer for a majority of English writers and authorities.[7] This was certainly the case elsewhere in Europe, including the Dutch Republic, where, despite its reputation as a place of toleration, animosity between Protestants and Catholics could break out into name calling or fisticuffs at any time, and where Catholic and Mennonite services had to be conducted behind private façades.[8] That said, the Dutch Republic was a far better place

---

Radical Religion, 1640-1660 (Oxford, 1989), and *Literature and Revolution in England, 1640-1660* (New Haven, 1997).

[7] Alexandra Walsham, *Charitable Hatred: Tolerance and Intolerance in England 1500-1700* (Manchester, 2006). See also John Coffey, *Persecution and Toleration in Protestant England, 1558-1689* (Harlow, 2000).

[8] See in particular Benjamin J. Kaplan, *Reformation and the Practice of Toleration: Dutch Religious History in the Early Modern Era* (Leiden, 2019); on Catholics, see Christine Kooi, "Paying off the Sheriff: Strategies of Catholic Toleration in Golden Age Holland," in *Calvinism and Religious Toleration in the Dutch Golden Age*, R. Po-Chia Hsia and Henk van Nierop, eds (Cambridge, 2002), 87–102, and *Calvinists and Catholics during Holland's Golden Age: Heretics and Idolaters* (Cambridge, 2012); Charles H. Parker, *Faith on the Margins: Catholics*

for religious dissenters than most anywhere else in Europe at the time.⁹ In all regions, the rhetoric used by preachers significantly influenced whether the toleration of religious difference was likely or not. Even in the Dutch Republic the anti-dissenter language used by Calvinist Reformed ministers could be strong indeed, and the Regents found it necessary to pass laws shaped by that rhetoric to appease their ministers. Yet, they often proved lax in enforcing them.

To demonize one's enemy made dialogue and respect far more difficult to achieve. If continental Anabaptism, with its well-known excesses around the kingdom of Münster (1533-1535) and its immediate aftermath, was associated with the devil, then all polemicists needed to do to make toleration toward a particular group unpalatable was to compare it with Anabaptism. Like so much political rhetoric today, it did not matter to these writers that there was no real connection or comparison between seventeenth-century English Baptists and sixteenth-century Dutch/German Anabaptists; they knew that by repeating claims of influence and similarity, they could persuade at least some of their readers and, they hoped, the authorities, not to give the Baptists and other dissenters room to survive or prosper. As we shall see, some writers believed it was possible to hate the heresy while stopping short of calling for the eradication of the heretics. Even so, looking carefully at their rhetoric suggests that, even though they intended to provide a position of moderation on the question of religious persecution, their fiery and demonizing language often had the opposite effect.

---

and Catholicism in the Dutch Golden Age (Cambridge, MA, 2008); and Judith Pollmann, *Catholic Identity and the Revolt of the Netherlands, 1520-1635* (Oxford, 2011).

⁹ For an excellent treatment of how and why the Reformation took such divergent courses in the various Netherlandic Provinces, and why the Northern provinces developed its unusual approach to confessional identity, see Christine Kooi, *Reformation in the Low Countries, 1500-1620* (Cambridge, 2022).

In some of these publications, it is unclear how far the writer would be willing to go to oppose Anabaptist ideas. But as we will see below, some of them openly called for the removal of anyone espousing anything close to Anabaptist ideas from England.

Amsterdamnified! and Polemics

The discussion here arises from a broader research program analyzing changing attitudes toward religious identity and diversity in the early-modern period that I and my colleagues in Amsterdamnfied! have been pursuing for the last few years.[10] Our focus is on the Dutch Republic and England, and the cross-Channel relations between them. This was a dynamic and fluid space with merchants, artisans, and religious refugees travelling between the two realms with regularity. Ships often carried cargoes of clandestine publications, usually produced by Dutch printers for the English readership. Depending on the level of heresy prosecution at home, dissenters and Protestants of all sorts (and at times Catholics too) travelled across the Channel, discovering what the other's society was like. Religious refugees in the Dutch Republic found themselves in a culture that was unusual, and certainly fascinating to them. They also observed that the Mennonites, who were the heirs of the Anabaptist tradition, were as wary of their Anabaptist past as were their Catholic and Protestant neighbours.

Religious exiles certainly appreciated the informal tolerance of diversity that the Dutch magistrates practised, and it was the interaction among so many diverse groups of people that gave that realm its intense atmosphere of

---

[10] See our website: http://amsterdamnified.ca/project/; as well as the excellent international collaboration of EMoDiR: https://emodir.hypotheses.org/ which is similarly pursuing analysis of "religious differences, conflicts and plurality in Europe."

cultural, economic, and technological innovation. English writers often complained that by allowing ordinary artisans to debate theology and philosophy in public places, the Dutch were allowing their society to go literally to hell.[11] Yet, it was here where several of the leading figures in the dramatic shifts in thought known as the Enlightenment lived as they wrote their works – including René Descartes, Baruch Spinoza, and John Locke – and their innovations bear the marks of having resided in this rich culture of vernacular rationalism and religious diversity.[12] It was here where the groundwork was laid for new appraisals of religion, philosophy, and of the entire supernatural world.

Much of that groundwork was prepared by the religious nonconformists inhabiting this Dutch-English community. As they reacted against the infamy of their Anabaptist forebears, Mennonites reimagined religious communities devoid, for the most part, of authoritarian claims or the eschatological or demonological fixations still prominent among many of their neighbours. More liberal Mennonites, who called themselves *Doopsgezinden* – meaning "baptism-minded folk" – were a small but influential group residing mostly in urban Holland. They interacted with other

---

[11] See, for example, J. Taylor, *Religions Enemies: With a Brief and Ingenious Relation, as by Anabaptists, Brownists, Papists, Familists, Atheists and Foolists, Sawcily Presuming to Tosse Religion in a Blanquet* (London, 1641); it was he (p. 5) who coined the term "Amsterdamnified" to describe the audacity of ordinary folk to debate intellectual and religious matters.

[12] Ruben Buys, *Sparks of Reason: Vernacular Rationalism in the Low Countries, 1550–1670* (Hilversum, 2015); Jonathan Israel, *Radical Enlightenment: Philosophy and the Making of Modernity, 1650-1750* (Oxford, 2001); and John Marshall, *John Locke, Toleration and Early Enlightenment Culture* (Cambridge, 2006). I have learned a great deal about what Descartes may have picked up from his Dutch residency from the Master's thesis by Jacob Powning, "'The Rippling Stream': Dutch Influences in Descartes' Concept of Self," Master's of Interdisciplinary Studies, University of New Brunswick, 2022.

dissenter groups, such as the Remonstrants who were forced out of the Reformed Church after the Synod of Dort in 1618, or the Polish Socinians in exile in the Republic for their rationalistic approach to scripture, or the Iberian conversos (Jewish converts to Catholicism) who reverted to their ancestral faith once in safety in Amsterdam, or English Separatists in exile from their home.

In the process, many of the Doopsgezinden redefined their theology in interesting new ways, some of which foreshadowed Enlightenment shifts in thought. Meanwhile, some of these Doopsgezinden joined expelled Remonstrants to create the fascinating Collegiant movement, an informal network who met without clergy to worship and discuss scripture and theology. Over the seventeenth century those conversations about theology encompassed other matters subject to rational analysis, and they became important vehicles for the development of new approaches to philosophy.[13] Spinoza was deeply immersed in this culture, frequently meeting with Collegiants and discussing his ideas with them. Several Doopsgezinden, moreover, assisted him in disseminating and translating his controversial works, such as his first important study of religion and philosophy,

---

[13] On the Collegiants, see Andrew Fix, *Prophecy and Reason: The Dutch Collegiants in the Early Enlightenment* (Princeton, 1991), and "Mennonites and Collegiants in Holland, 1630-1700," *Mennonite Quarterly Review* 64 (1990), 160-77; and most recently, Francesco Quatrini, *Adam Boreel (1602–1665): A Collegiant's Attempt to Reform Christianity* (Leiden, 2021); and Maxwell Kennel, *Postsecular History: Political Theology and the Politics of Time* (Cham, 2022), esp. chapter 3: "Postsecular History and the Seventeenth-Century Dutch Collegiants," 56-83, and "Postsecular History: Continental Philosophy of Religion and the Seventeenth Century Dutch Collegiant Movement." *Studies In Religion/ Sciences Religieuses* 56 (2017), 406-32. I am thankful to Maxwell Kennel for sending me copies of his fascinating work.

the *Tractatus Theologico-Politicus* of 1670.[14] Reading this work in conjunction with the previous and contemporaneous writings of Collegiants and Doopsgezinden reveals that Spinoza fed from a long tradition of nonconformist Christian ideas, and some scholars have even suggested that he was far more comfortable in the Christian nonconformist world than he was in his Jewish context.[15] While many of his Christian friends may not have gone as far as Spinoza in reframing the natural and supernatural worlds, Spinoza owed a debt of gratitude to them. Indeed, the polemical debates over the new philosophies became part of these

---

[14] On this, see Piet Visser, "'Blasphemous and pernicious': the role of printers and booksellers in the spread of dissident religious and philosophical ideas in the Netherlands in the second half of the seventeenth century," *Quaerendo* 26 (1996), 303-26, and Piet Visser, "Mennonites and Doopsgezinden in the Netherlands, 1535-1700," in *A Companion to Anabaptism and Spiritualism, 1521-1700*, John D. Roth and James M. Stayer, eds. (Leiden, 2007), 299-345. See also Jonathan Israel, ed., *Spinoza: Theological-Political Treatise* (Cambridge, 2007), viii; Israel, *Radical Enlightenment*; Leszek Kolakowski, "Dutch Seventeenth-Century Anticonfessional Ideas and Rational Religion: the Mennonite, Collegiant and Spinozan Connections," trans. James Satterwhite, *Mennonite Quarterly Review* 64 (1990), 259-97 and 385-416; Graeme Hunter, *Radical Protestantism in Spinoza's Thought* (Aldershot, 2005), 1-6; Michael Driedger, "Response to Graeme Hunter: Spinoza and the Boundary Zones of Religious Interaction," *The Conrad Grebel Review* 25 (2007), 21-28; Steven Nadler, *Spinoza: A Life* (Cambridge, 1999), 166-70; and Ruben Buys, "'Without thy self, O man, thou hast no means to look for, by which thou maist know God': Pieter Balling, the Radical Enlightenment, and the Legacy of Dirck Volckertsz Coornhert," *Church History and Religious Culture* 93 (2013), 363–83. For a discussion of religious nonconformism and the Enlightenment in Germany, see Andrew Weeks, *The Radical Enlightenment in Germany: A Cultural Perspective*, ed. Niekerk (Leiden, 2018).

[15] Israel, *Radical Enlightenment*, 275-85; see also Piet Visser, "Stad van verdraagzaamheid? Amsterdam als vrijhaven voor andersdenkenden," in *Spinoza als gids voor een vrije wereld*, Cis van Heertum, ed. (Amsterdam, 2008), 19-39, and the other essays in that volume.

intellectual transformations, as opponents of Descartes and Spinoza forced the philosophers and their supporters to refine and reconsider some elements of their innovations. Anti-innovation polemics may also have inadvertently helped disseminate these new ideas, but that is a topic for a separate study; we need to return to our Anabaptists!

One point needs to be made first: English writers seem, on the whole, to have been ignorant of, or simply ignoring, these fascinating developments within the Dutch Mennonite world. Instead, they were fixated upon the Anabaptists' militant past of the 1530s, for that moment of radicalism when thousands were caught up in apocalyptic excitement served English writers the best for polemical purposes.

However, many of these polemicists were vaguely aware of one of the most important developments in the Dutch religious scene after the fall of the Anabaptist kingdom in 1535: the rise of Spiritualism. Some of those Anabaptists whose disillusionment with their own failed apocalyptic expectations and need to hide from their persecutors led them to develop an approach to religious identity that focused on the inner person and depreciated external confessions and rites that were behind so much of the religious violence they experienced. Foremost among these was the artist David Joris (1501-1556) who, in the immediate aftermath of the fall of Münster, was proclaimed by many of his coreligionists to be the spiritual successor to king Jan van Leiden, but whose interpretation of scripture was already quite allegorical or spiritualistic. His supporters believed that he would be revealed as the new messianic king on December 25, 1538. But this too proved to be an abysmal failure, and over the next few years Joris turned his allegorical approach into full-bore Spiritualism.

In his later career as a Spiritualist, Joris transformed his religious identity into a purely internal matter and dismissed external confessions and rites. He went beyond many other

Spiritualists of his generation by relegating supernatural beings – in particular, angels and demons – to the inner conscience. In fact, he became the first vernacular writer to remove demons and angels from the natural world, publishing this idea by around 1540, and responding to critics by saying simply that belief in an external devil was only for the spiritually immature. He reasoned that if the devil were real, he could appear tangibly before Joris to prove his existence.[16] Joris's demonology proved prescient, for it would become a major feature of Enlightenment thought to restrict the devil to the inner world. Eventually Joris even fused the Holy Spirit to the inner conscience of the enlightened. These ideas, along with his strong pleas for an end to religious persecution, were further developed by later Spiritualists and the Collegiants. They were then carried over across the Channel in polemical works to English writers, who were as disturbed by the implications of such innovation as were their continental brethren.[17] In what follows we will examine in closer detail one vital and influential element of these intriguing developments: the role of English polemical writings against Anabaptism in the wider debates over theology, religious difference, toleration, and society.

---

[16] Gary K. Waite, "'Man is a Devil to Himself': David Joris and the Rise of a Sceptical Tradition towards the Devil in the Early Modern Netherlands, 1540-1600," *Nederlands Archief voor Kerkgeschiedenis / Dutch Review of Church History*, 75 (1995), 1-30.

[17] Gary K. Waite, "The Devil of Delft in England: the Reception of the Dutch Spiritualist David Joris in 17th -Century English Polemics," *Church History and Religious Culture* 101/4 (Winter 2021), 429-95, Open Access, https://brill.com/view/journals/chrc/101/4/article-p429_1.xml.

Chapter 1
Anabaptists in the Dutch and English Reformations

The Dippers Dipt or the Anabaptists Duck'd and Plung'd over Head and Eares

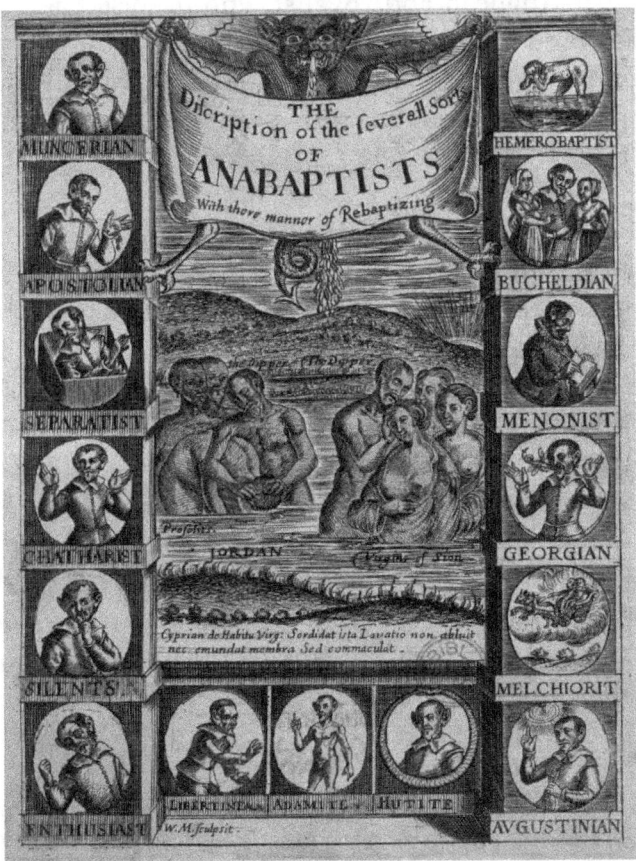

Figure 1: Engraved frontispiece to Daniel Featley, 'Katabaptistai kataptysoi. The Dippers Dipt, or, The Anabaptists Duck'd and Plung'd over Head and Eares' (London, Nicholas Bourne, 1645). Courtesy of the Cambridge University Library, F.3.117.

Let us therefore begin the formal analysis with Figure 1, the title page from Daniel Featley's *The Dippers Dipt, or the Anabaptists Duck'd and Plung'd over Head and Eares* of 1645. This was one of hundreds of English publications using continental Anabaptism to condemn the rise of new religious groups in England during the first half of the seventeenth century. As is evident from this scandalous image, English Separatists who split from the Church of England were of particular concern to Featley (1582-1645), who himself was a Calvinist Anglican and royalist who despised any and all alternatives to the state church. It must however be pointed out that the other 14 Anabaptist groups that he identified were not from England but were located across the Channel. Yet Featley was right to discern a cross-Channel interaction among these groups.

Among the English Separatists who Featley was thinking of was John Smyth (c. 1554-1612), who in 1608 moved to Holland where he was supported and influenced by liberal Dutch Mennonites –*Doopsgezinden* or baptism-minded folk – as he took the step toward adopting believer's baptism.[1] It seems they could not baptize him unless he joined their fellowship, so in 1609 Smyth baptized himself. He soon regretted that controversial move and applied to join his fellowship with that of the Doopsgezinden, but this did not transpire until shortly after Smyth's death in 1612. In the meantime, a branch of Smyth's congregation led by Thomas Helwys had split from Smyth and returned to London, where they established the first Baptist congregation in 1612

---

[1] More scholarship will be cited below, but for a particularly fascinating analysis of the interrelations among Smyth, his fellow English Baptists, the Doopsgezinden, and the other English residents in Amsterdam, centred on the major building where they interacted, see Keith Sprunger and Mary Sprunger, "The Church in the Bakehouse: John Smyth's English Anabaptist Congregation at Amsterdam, 1609-1660," *Mennonite Quarterly Review* 85 (2011), 219-58.

in Spitalfields.² The relationship between the continental dissenters and their English versions is thus a complex and vexed question, although John Coffey has recently concluded that the English Baptist movement was largely an indigenous one.³ The discussion here is intended to add another element to this debate, for while Coffey is doubtless correct in suggesting that the interactions among continental and English dissenters were not in themselves formative for the Baptist movement in England, the ways in which English writers portrayed Dutch Anabaptism to their readers provided them with many intriguing ideas to consider. Sure, the writers' sole goal was to deter people from any hint of Anabaptism, but that does not mean that all readers followed the intended aim of the writer as they absorbed the material.

By 1640, the anti-Anabaptist polemics had become a commonplace of religious discourse, as writers assumed readers had sufficient knowledge of events and individuals associated with Anabaptism to avoid explanations. Most of the stories told were distorted versions of real Anabaptist beliefs and practices, and some were even imagined out of whole cloth. Yet, these polemical works provided another source of cross-Channel influence that we need to examine carefully, and with an eye to their intended and unintended consequences.

---

² See Joe Early, Jr., *The Life and Writings of Thomas Helwys* (Macon, GA, 2009), esp. 15-50.

³ John Coffey, "'The Last and Greatest Triumph of the European Radical Reformation'? Anabaptism, Spiritualism and Anti-Trinitarianism in the English Reformation," in *Radicalism and Dissent in the World of Protestant Reform*, Bridget Heal and Anorthe Kremers, eds. (Göttingen, 2017), 201-24, here 215, and the literature he cites. On Smyth and the Mennonites, see James R. Coggins, *John Smyth's Congregation: English Separatism, Mennonite Influence and the Elect Nation* (Scottdale, PA, 1991); and Jason Lee, *The Theology of John Smyth: Puritan, Separatist, Baptist, Mennonite* (Macon, GA, 2003).

Were there Anabaptists in England?

As for those actual connections, they were significant too, as several groups of Dutch and Flemish Anabaptists lived in refuge in England. These groups faced periodic prosecution but they also interacted with English residents.[4] There was also a brisk printer network and cross-Channel business between the Netherlands and England during the time.[5]

---

[4] See Irvin B. Horst, *The Radical Brethren: Anabaptism and the English Reformation to 1558* (Nieuwkoop, 1972); Alastair Duke, "Martyrs with a Difference: Dutch Anabaptist Victims of Elizabethan Persecution," *Dutch Review of Church History / Nederlands Archief Voor Kerkgeschiedenis* 80 (2000), 263–81; and now Carrie Euler, "Anabaptism and anti-Anabaptism in the Early English Reformation: Defining Protestant Heresy and Orthodoxy During the Reign of Edward VI," in John Marshall and David Loewenstein, eds., *Heresy, Literature and Politics in Early Modern English Culture* (Cambridge, 2006), 40-58. The Protestant Bishop Hugh Latimer referred to the burning of continental Anabaptists in England, critiquing their supposed intrepidness in the face of the flames as a false martyrdom; unfortunately, Latimer would face the same fate in 1555 under Queen Mary. Hugh Latimer, *The seconde [seventh] sermon of maister hughe latimer which he preached before the kynges maiestie [with?]in his graces palayce at westminster, ye xv. day of marche [-xix daye of apryll]*, M.ccccc.xlix (London: John Day and Wyllyam Seres, 1549), fol. Mi^r; see also Euler, "Anabaptism and anti-Anabaptism," 40-41. The tribulations of several of the Dutch/Flemish refugees are recorded in the Mennonite *Martyrs Mirror* of 1660, Thieleman J. van Braght, *Martyrs Mirror: The Story of Seventeen Centuries of Christian Martyrdom, from the Time of Christ to A.D. 1660*, trans. Joseph F. Sohm (Scottdale, PA, 1938), 1008, 1012, 1019-24.

[5] On the various cross-Channel nonconformist networks, see Michael Driedger et al., eds., *Spiritualism in Early Modern Europe*, special double issue of *Church History and Religious Culture* 101/2-3 (2021), https://brill.com/view/journals/chrc/101/2-3/chrc.101.issue-2-3.xml, especially Michael Driedger and Gary K. Waite, with contributions from Francesco Quatrini and Nina Schroeder, "From 'the Radical Reformation' to 'the Radical Enlightenment'?: The Spectre and Complexities of Spiritualism in England, Germany, and the Low

Also of great concern to Anglican writers were translations of the works of the spiritualistic Family of Love, a group which had begun in the maelstrom of Dutch Anabaptism in the 1530s but whose leader, Hendrik Niclaes, emphasized an inner transformation of the individual, of being "godded with God," rather than the correct practice of baptism, and who allowed his followers to pretend to be orthodox (Nicodemism) to avoid detection. The Familists maintained a secretive presence in England into the era of the Civil War.[6]

However, as Coffey has noted, no explicitly Anabaptist works, such as those by prominent leaders Melchior Hoffman, David Joris, or Menno Simons, were translated into English, so there was little chance of English dissenters getting their information on Anabaptism directly from the source.[7] We will return to the subject of actual Dutch and Flemish Anabaptists in England below, but first we need to

---

Countries," 135-166; William Cook Miller, "Theodora Wilkin's *Wandering Soul*: Spiritual Adaptation in an Anglo-Dutch context," 357-75; and Nigel Smith, "To Network or Not to Network: Art, the Literary, and 'Invention' in Early Modern European Radical Religion," 376-98. For a broader overview of English-Dutch relations that includes the activities of merchants, artisans, and printers, see Hugh Dunthorne, *Britain and the Dutch Revolt, 1560-1700* (Cambridge, 2013). See also Sjoerd Levelt, Esther van Raamsdonk, and Michael Rose, eds., *Anglo-Dutch Connections in the Early Modern World*, (Abingdon, 2023). On Protestant Dutch exiles in England more generally, see Ole Peter Grell, *Calvinist Exiles in Elizabethan and Stuart England* (Abingdon, 1996).

[6] Alastair Hamilton, *The Family of Love* (Baden-Baden, 2003); Christopher W. Marsh, *The Family of Love in English Society, 1550-1630* (Cambridge, 1994); and David R. Como, "The Family of Love and the Making of English Revolutionary Religion: The Confession and 'Conversions' of Giles Creech," *Journal of Medieval and Early Modern Studies* 48 (2018), 553-598. See also David R. Como, *Blown by the Spirit: Puritanism and the Emergence of an Antinomian Underground in Pre-Civil-War England* (Stanford, 2004); and the essays in Marshall and Loewenstein, *Heresy, Literature and Politics*.

[7] Coffey, "'The Last and Greatest Triumph'," 214, 217.

turn to a brief historiographical overview of research into English polemical discourse.

Historiography: Polemics and Unintended Consequences

My focus here is on how polemical attacks on Anabaptism shaped the discourse on English nonconformist groups. To date very little attention has been paid to English anti-Anabaptist polemics, as noted by Carrie Euler in 2006: "scholarship on anti-Anabaptism is virtually nonexistent."[8] Similarly, in 2022 Andrew Crome published an article on the use of Anabaptist Münster by English anti-dissent writers in the Restoration era, commenting that "[h]istorians have often recognized that the incident [of Anabaptist Münster] was used to attack English Baptists in the seventeenth century, but there has been little systematic exploration of the processes behind this."[9] He argues, convincingly, that by the Restoration (1660), the polemical use of Münster as a comparative with English dissenter groups had become so commonplace that it could be "invoked as shorthand for political chaos and the dangers of religious dissent" without mentioning the actual groups and disturbances of the Civil War era, for with the 1660 Act of Indemnity and Oblivion, Charles II had commanded a national act of forgetting of the conflict. In this way, writers could simply raise the spectre of Münster, and readers would understand the word to encompass all of the religious and political upheaval of recent decades without having to name them. Münster also served as "a cultural symbol that helped to define the limits of

---

[8] Euler, "Anabaptism and anti-Anabaptism," 41.
[9] Andrew Crome, "The Münster Rising, Memories of Violence, and Perceptions of Dissent in Restoration England," *The Historical Journal* 65 (2022), 946-68, here 946. See also Walsham, *Charitable Hatred* and Loewenstein, *Treacherous Faith*.

acceptable religious practice."[10] While Crome provides some examples of how Anabaptism was manipulated by English conformist writers in the century before the Restoration, his goal is to show how modern studies of consensus memory help historians better understand the English appropriation of a moment in continental religious history and how by 1660 it had become a lens through which the English could interpret their own contested history.[11]

This present study is intended to fill this significant gap in our understanding of the development and impact of polemical publications against Anabaptism in England leading up to the Restoration. Here I am building on the work of Euler, Coffey, David Como, Nigel Smith, and David Loewenstein, among others, who have examined closely what unconventional works were being read sympathetically by English writers. Coffey, Michael Driedger, Ann Hughes, and others are also examining the heresiographers – those writers who sought to categorize and compare the various heresies as a means of condemning their contemporary variants of dissent.[12] Nina Schroeder is also exploring the shifting perspectives and meanings of the many images produced for such publications by artists.[13]

---

[10] Crome, "The Münster Rising," 947.
[11] Crome, "The Münster Rising," 949-50.
[12] Coffey, "'The Last and Greatest Triumph'"; Michael Driedger, "Against 'the Radical Reformation': On the Continuity between Early Modern Heresy-Making and Modern Historiography," in Heal and Kremers, *Radicalism and Dissent*, 139-61; and Ann Hughes, *Gangraena and the Struggle for the English Revolution* (Oxford 2004). See also Walsham, *Charitable Hatred*.
[13] Nina Schroeder, "Heretics and Martyrs: Picturing Early Anabaptism in Visual Culture of the Dutch Republic," (Ph.D. diss., Queen's University, 2018), and "Art and Heterodoxy in the Dutch Enlightenment: Arnold Houbraken, the Flemish Mennonites, and Religious Difference in *The Great Theatre of Netherlandish Painters and Painteresses* (1718–1721)," *Church History and Religious Culture*, 101 (2021), 324-56.

My own perspective is to examine how such propaganda inspired anxiety among mainstream Protestants who sought to keep England a unitary Protestant realm free of Catholic remnants and divisive heresy. For these writers, Dutch Anabaptism was not just an historical curiosity of religious enthusiasm run amok, but it was the logical consequence of separating from the true church. They wrote as if the Dutch Anabaptist experience was being replayed on English soil. And to some extent they were correct, for, as Crome argues, conformist writers so successfully overlaid the infamous history of Münster onto the English memory of their own religious events that there was something of a fusion. Yet, English polemicists seemed largely unaware that their own rhetorical efforts could become a self-fulfilling prophecy, as the image of Anabaptism crafted by Featley and hundreds of other English writers caught the imagination of some readers in unanticipated ways. For as these polemicists sought to dissuade their audience from adopting any hint of Anabaptist errors, they described these errors in sensational detail, and naively assumed that readers would follow their critique as intended. Instead, for some readers, the ideas portrayed in the controversial pamphlets and books proved attractive rather than repulsive; as noted by Hughes, in the heresiographers' treatises, the errors they were attacking "were publicized through the attack itself."[14]

This process was observed at the time by opponents of the heresiographers. In 1647, for example, John Saltmarsh, an unconventional minister who served as chaplain in Oliver Cromwell's New Model Army and who was a strong promoter of religious toleration, critiqued Thomas Edward's *Gangraena* of the year before by suggesting that his detailed

---

[14] Hughes, *Gangraena*, 89. She also notes the naiveté of writers such as Thomas Edwards to assume that "the mere process of describing error was sufficient to defeat it" (ibid., 94).

descriptions of the errors of heretics actually helped create the groups he was assailing:

> Whether the design which *Mr Edwards* pretends in setting forth his Book, *viz.* to make the *blasphemies and errours of the times* (as he calls them) *to be detested*, is not rather a farre contrary design, *viz.* to spread poyson, infect many souls who by this shall come to the knowledge of such things as they never heard before, having provided no *Antidote*, nor any Answer of *Scripture* or *reason* against them, but meerely contradictions, and ill words; it was observed that some books set forth for the discovery of *Witch-craft*, made many *Witches*; and so who knows how many *hereticks* he may make by this his *pretended design* against them; sure either some of the *heresies* or diseases were so above his *cure* or *remedy*, or he had a counter design to make *Hereticks* or the *wisdome* of his design was turned into *folly*, making *Hereticks* by writing against *them*.[15]

Saltmarsh's astute observation was built on a long-standing complaint made against the writers of works skeptical of witchcraft, such as the *De praestigiis daemonum* by the Dutch physician Johan Wier (Weyer) of 1563 and *The Discoverie of*

---

[15] John Saltmarsh, *Groanes for liberty presented from the presbyterian (formerly non-conforming) brethren, reputed the ablest and most learned among them, in some treatises called smectymnuus, to the high and honorable court of parliament in the yeare 1641, by reason of the prelates tyranny. now awakened and presented to themselves in the behalf of their now non-conforming brethren. with a beam of light, discovering a way to peace. also some quæres for the better understanding of mr edwards last book called gangræna. with a parallel betweene the prelacy and presbytery* (London: for Giles Calvert, 1646); on Edwards and Saltmarsh, see Hughes, *Gangraena*. A good summary of Saltmarsh's life is https://en.wikipedia.org/wiki/John_Saltmarsh_(priest)

Witchcraft by the English Gentleman Reginal Scot of 1584, both of whom provided detailed descriptions of magical practices as a means of showing how ridiculous traditional demonology and witch-hunting were.

They were, however, criticized for including so much detail since many readers might miss the satire and take the scandalous stories at face value, and in fact be drawn into the devil's clutches as a result.[16] Saltmarsh turns that critique on Edwards' long and salacious diatribe against religious difference because he (Saltmarsh) was more open and agreeable to alternative religious perspectives than many of his fellows, and did not fear diversity, as is clear in his *Groanes for liberty*. He asked, for example, "Whether is Independency, Anabaptism, Brownism, Seekers, of more evil report now, then Lutheranism, Calvinism, Zuinglianism formerly?"[17] His comment nicely sets up our discussion of the impact of anti-Anabaptist polemics in England.

That controversial works could elicit a response different from that intended has been observed for other places and movements. Alan C. Kors, for example, has argued that the detailed attacks on atheism in late seventeenth-century and eighteenth-century France helped create the very monster that polemicists were assailing. He wrote, "[t]heologians and philosophers indeed took with utmost gravity their

---

[16] This was a point made by Jean Bodin in his *On the Demon-Mania of Witches* of 1584, when he angrily critiqued Wier's detailed descriptions of magical recipes and witchcraft stories; see Jean Bodin, *On the Demon-Mania of Witches*, Jonathan L. Pearl, ed., Randy A. Scott, trans. (Toronto, 1995), 27. This did not stop Bodin from using Wier's anecdotes uncritically as evidence of the reality of witchcraft, despite Wier's sceptical approach. See Jan Machielsen, *Martin Delrio: Demonology and Scholarship in the Counter-Reformation* (Oxford, 2015), 259. On demonology in general, the best work remains Stuart Clark, *Thinking with Demons: The Idea of Witchcraft in Early Modern Europe* (Oxford, 1997).

[17] Saltmarsh, *Groanes for liberty*, 2.

responsibility to provide indubitable proofs and to assail those that they found dubious. They may have inhibited some potential atheists by this endeavor. The evidence suggests very strongly, however, that they brought others into being."[18] Similarly, Martin Mulsow's study of the rise of the radical Enlightenment in Germany reveals how "a mixture of joking, suspicion, and serious doubt, sometimes ironic or even borrowing words from an opponent, came to be elaborated and taken seriously, thus appearing as statements fully in favor of much more radical Enlightenment."[19]

Earlier research into how ordinary people understood Martin Luther's reform slogans, sermons, and writings has also shown that there could often be a significant divergence between intended meaning and received interpretation. Luther was certainly shocked in 1525 to see how the commoners applied his spiritual teaching to their prosaic world, inspiring them to fight for an end to serfdom during the Peasants' War of 1525. In response, he composed his infamous *Against the Robbing, Murdering Horde of Peasants*, thereby losing the support of the commoners as he turned his Reformation fully to the princes.[20] Such examples of

---

[18] Alan C. Kors, *Atheism in France, 1650-1729*, vol. 1, *The Orthodox Sources of Disbelief* (Princeton, NJ, 1990, 2016), 296.

[19] Martin Mulsow, *Enlightenment Underground: Radical Germany, 1680-1720*, trans. H. C. Erik Midelfort (Charlottesville, 2015), 1-2. I am thankful to Erik Midelfort for these references.

[20] Peter Blickle, *The Revolution of 1525: The German Peasants' War from a New Perspective*, trans. Thomas A. Brady, Jr., and H.C. Erik Midelfort (Baltimore, 1981); Martin Luther, *Against the Robbing, Murdering Hordes of Peasants*, http://zimmer.csufresno.edu/~mariterel/against_the_robbing_and_m urderin.htm. See also Robert W. Scribner, *For the Sake of Simple Folk: Popular Propaganda for the German Reformation* (Cambridge, 1981), and *Popular Culture and Popular Movements in Reformation Germany* (London, 1988), and other of his brilliant studies.

creative misunderstandings or reinterpretations could be multiplied many times.

Closer to (English) home, Alexandra Walsham and Ann Hughes have both noted how the polemical terms used about dissenters helped to shape their own self-awareness and religious identity. Hughes astutely observes the impact of having one's name appear in a heresiographer's work, for an "appearance in Edwards's books, however, was a sure sign of intensifying fame, and it was through being named and described in print that some sectaries acquired an inescapable notoriety throughout the country."[21] Walsham notes that this process was comparable to those employed by late medieval inquisitors who used checklists of ancient heresies to form the leading questions they put to the accused, which "had the consequence of enhancing the unity of the assortment of individuals who were interrogated, thereby providing the incentive for even more systematic efforts to eradicate heresy," ultimately confirming their suspicions of a diabolical plot against Christendom, and leading to the infamous witch hunts.[22] This is a point I have made elsewhere in some detail.[23] Such studies reveal the importance of exploring the polemical literature, however distasteful, for potential impact, both positive and negative, intended and unintended.

Historians and Polemical Categorization

Also of interest here is how historians have taken up the polemical characterizations of early-modern dissidents but

---

[21] Hughes, *Gangraena*, 310.
[22] Hughes, *Gangraena*, 11; Walsham, *Charitable Hatred*, 27-28.
[23] Gary K. Waite, *Eradicating the Devil's Minions: Anabaptists and Witches in Reformation Europe, 1535-1600* (Toronto, 2007), and *Heresy, Magic and Witchcraft in Early Modern Europe* (Basingstoke, 2003), among others.

turned them into positive narratives of an alternative stream of reform. The clearest example of this pattern is found in the magisterial work by George H. Williams, *The Radical Reformation* of 1962.[24] Lumping together a dizzying array of dissenter voices from outside of orthodox Catholicism, Lutheranism, and Calvinism into a single coherent category of reform was problematic enough, but in doing so Williams adopted the category of radical reform or Anabaptism as devised by sixteenth-century mainstream churchmen, potentially maintaining the negative perspectives of the polemicists and blurring or distorting the incredible variety among the dissenters.[25] Such categorization, moreover, can make it difficult to observe the significant shifts in thought of individual nonconformists, some of whom moved from one reform approach to another, or developed idiosyncratic variations in interpretation. The example of David Joris offers a case in point, for to describe him as an Anabaptist forgets his earlier reform activity as a Dutch Evangelical or Sacramentarian and his evolution into a Spiritualist, one that encompassed a phase as a spiritualistic Anabaptist but ended as a creative Spiritualist influenced by his humanist friends.[26] But here our purpose is to look carefully at the polemical characterizations made against Anabaptism as a way of seeing just how distorted a view English writers

---

[24] George H. Williams, *The Radical Reformation*, 3rd ed. (Kirksville, MO, 1992).
[25] Driedger, "Against 'the Radical Reformation'"; and Mirjam van Veen, "Dutch Anabaptist and Reformed Historiographers on Servetus' Death: Or How the Radical Reformation Turned Mainstream and How the Mainstream Reformation Turned Radical," in Heal and Kremers, *Radicalism and Dissent*, 162-72. See also Driedger and Waite, "From 'the Radical Reformation' to 'the Radical Enlightenment'"?
[26] Gary K. Waite, "Spiritualism and Rationalism in Early Modern Europe: The Case of David Joris," in Driedger et al., *Spiritualism in Early Modern Europe*, 263-285, and "Sixteenth-Century Spiritualists," in the *T&T Clark Handbook of Anabaptism*, Brian C. Brewer, ed. (London, 2021), 543-58, esp. 543-44.

offered to their readers, and the possible effects of that presentation, both negative and positive.

"Anabaptist" in Early English Books Online

I make no pretence here of examining all of the polemics referencing Anabaptism. In Early English Books Online, the database of all English works printed up to 1700, a 2022 search for the term "Anabaptist" uncovered 3,463 works citing the term between 1530 and 1660. Of course many, perhaps most, of these are incidental references that would contribute very little to our analysis. By contrast, in my analysis of references to the Dutch Anabaptist/Spiritualist David Joris in English writings over the same period I had to deal with only 140 works cited, and these I could analyze with a degree of comprehensiveness not possible here.[27]

In this study I examine a number of works at particularly important moments in the history of the dissenter movements in England, while following EEBO's relevance algorithms to prioritize those publications which cited the term Anabaptist the most, but even then, I have not read all of the relevant titles. I turned to some of the works here because other authors, both modern and contemporary, cited them and considered them to be important.

So, again, this study is not a comprehensive overview, but merely a preliminary analysis of key works on the subject, and one that I hope will inspire further research. I believe that this selection of works has provided me with a good, if not comprehensive, sense of how relevant polemical writers portrayed Dutch Anabaptists in their battles to oppose

---

[27] Gary K. Waite, "The Devil of Delft in England: the Reception of the Dutch Spiritualist David Joris in 17th -Century English Polemics," *Church History and Religious Culture* 101/4 (2021), 429-95, https://brill.com/view/journals/chrc/101/4/article-p429_1.xml.

English dissenter groups, and the degree to which the characterizations of continental Anabaptism were distorted.

English Anxieties and Dutch Anabaptism

Our polemicists had good reason to be concerned, for some English folk adopted and adapted Anabaptist ideas from Flemish refugees, most famously Joan Boucher, or Joan of Kent, who was burned at the stake in 1550 for clinging to the Dutch Anabaptist doctrine that Christ had brought his human flesh from heaven and hence avoided sharing his mother's sinful humanity; this is called the Celestial Flesh of Christ, or the Melchiorite Incarnation doctrine after its proponent, the Anabaptist prophet Melchior Hoffman.[28]

Polemicists certainly wrote as if this were a popular idea. In 1549 the Protestant preacher of London, John Hooper, wrote to the Swiss Reformed theologian Heinrich Bullinger that "Anabaptists" were flocking to his sermons to challenge him on the question of the "incarnation of the Lord;" and while these may have been Flemish-speaking members of the Strangers' Church of London, some were likely English folk attracted to the Anabaptist Incarnation doctrine.[29]

Another major target for polemicists was Anabaptism's sectarianism. Most writers labelled any form of English Independence or Separatism as Anabaptist in order to dissuade readers from following suit. Authors also feared the popularity of the practice of community of goods, which the Anabaptists of Münster had made mandatory in 1534 due to the privations of the siege. It did have, moreover, New Testament precedents, especially in Acts 2:42-45, and many of the early Swiss Brethren and South German Anabaptists

---

[28] On Joan of Kent see Williams, *The Radical Reformation*, 1197. On the Incarnation doctrine, see Sjouke Voolstra, *Het Woord is Vlees Geworden: De Melchioritisch-Mennniste Incarnatieleer* (Kampen, 1982).
[29] Williams, *The Radical Reformation*, 1198.

adopted a form of common fund or voluntary community of goods as part of their practice. However, when interrogated, they denied ever wanting to apply this economic practice to society at large. Anabaptists in refuge in Moravia were the first to adopt community of goods on a large scale, beginning in 1528 but really not becoming formalized until the mid 1530s, among both the Münsterites in the North and the Hutterites in the East.[30] English writers were largely unaware of these Anabaptist forms of community of goods until the spectacular events of Münster. Such teachings obviously worried them, perhaps because they knew that community of goods was indeed practised by some within the early church and could therefore inspire imitation.

Their concerns were frequently justified. For example, in 1549 a rebellion in Norfolk – a region with a noticeable presence of Flemish Anabaptists – against the enclosure of pasturage was led by Robert Kett who wrote a defence of community of goods, and his group contained many who identified as Anabaptists, both immigrant and native.[31] In response, King Edward VI's government turned to Hooper and the Scottish Calvinist John Knox to write against such pernicious Anabaptist ideas, and their tracts influenced many other later polemicists.[32] In his writing, Hooper was

---

[30] C. Arnold Snyder, *Anabaptist History and Theology: An Introduction* (Kitchener, 1995), 62, 237-52; James M. Stayer, *The German Peasants' War and Anabaptist Community of Goods* (Montreal and Kingston, 1991); and Werner O. Packull, *Hutterite Beginnings: Communitarian Experiments during the Reformation* (Baltimore, 1999).

[31] Williams, *The Radical Reformation*, 1199. But see Euler, "Anabaptism and anti-Anabaptism," 50, who observes that "Historians now know that there was no direct relationship between the 1549 uprisings and radical evangelical religion." Yet, there may have been a direct relationship between the anti-Anabaptist polemics against community of goods and the 1549 events.

[32] Williams, *The Radical Reformation*, 1199. John Hooper, *A godly confession and protestacion of the christian fayth, made and set furth by*

deeply concerned that the Anabaptists had "resuscitated" ancient errors that would, thanks to the devil's inspiration, lead to the destruction of the country, as well as theological heresy. He wrote:

> now in our time to the great trouble and unquietness of many common wealths, in Europe, the Anabaptists hath resuscitated, and revived the same errors. Which is an argument and token of the devils great indignation against civil policy and order. for he knoweth where such errors and false doctrines of political orders be planted: two great evils necessarily must needs follow, the one is sedition, that bringeth murders, bloodshedding and dissipations of realms: the other is blasphemy against Christs precious blood, for those sects think they be able to save them selves, of & by themselves.[33]

The story of the Dutch Anabaptist movement, with its intense apocalyptic expectations, prophetic predictions, and efforts to establish the kingdom of Christ on earth by force, was used to great effect by learned English writers. Here we will briefly survey the history of Dutch Anabaptism,

---

ihon hooper, wherin is declared what a christia[n] manne is bound to beleue of god, hys kyng, his neibour, and hymselfe (London: John Daye, 1550); John Knox, *An answer to a great number of blasphemous cauillations written by an anabaptist, and aduersarie to gods eternal predestination. and confuted by iohn knox, minister of gods worde in scotland. wherein the author so discouereth the craft and falshode of that sect, that the godly knowing that error, may be confirmed in the trueth by the euident worde of god* (Geneva: John Crespin 1555). On Protestant polemics during this period more broadly, see Catharine Davies, *A Religion of the Word: The Defence of the Reformation in the Reign of Edward VI* (Manchester 2003).

[33] Hooper, *A godly confession*, fols. Cviij^v-Di^r.

focusing on the events that English writers found most useful for their polemics, followed by a similarly brief overview of the Reformation in England, which determined how the continental Reformation would be regarded. Then we can turn to a largely chronological analysis of tracts and treatises that were composed by polemicists who were seeking to oppose religious diversity in England.

Dutch Anabaptism: The Historical Record

Dutch Anabaptist history is filled with plenty of material for polemicists seeking to condemn their opponents. While in the early 1520s several Reformers, such as Thomas Müntzer and Andreas Bodenstein von Karlstadt had critiqued infant baptism, it was not until the circle around Conrad Grebel performed the first baptism of adult believers in Zurich in January 1525 that there was an actual Anabaptist (rebaptized) movement.

This event occurred during the major uprising of the German commoners, called the Peasants' War, and with the defeat of the peasants by May, 1525, some of the rebels' reform preachers, like Hans Hut, a veteran in Müntzer's Thuringian band, reinterpreted the defeat in apocalyptic terms, turning away from political action to await the eschatological deliverance from above. For both the Swiss and South-German Anabaptists, their goal was comparable to that of the major Protestant Reformers, especially Ulrich Zwingli of Zurich, to be faithful to the gospels and to pursue the reform of the church to its complete end. Seeing that Zwingli had reformed the Mass into the Lord's Supper and rejected the Real Presence of Christ in the bread and wine, Grebel pushed him to take next logical step by replacing infant baptism with adult or believer's baptism. When Zwingli refused, Grebel's group baptized themselves.³⁴

Figure 2: Jan van Leiden, Portrait of Jan van Leiden by Christoffel van Sichem (I), after Jan Cornelisz. van 't Woudt, 1606, in *Warhaffte Abbildung des königs von Munster/ genant [genamt] Johan Bochholds seines Hanttwercks ein Schneider/ geboren zu Leyden in Hollant/ welcher in seine Zitel gfuhrt hatt diese wort* (Amsterdam: Christoffel von Sichem, 1606), plate 8. Courtesy of the Rijksmuseum, Amsterdam, RP-P-1918-1733, cropped.

---

³⁴ See the excellent overviews in John D. Roth and James M. Stayer, *A Companion to Anabaptism and Spiritualism, 1521-1700* (Leiden, 2007), especially Hans-Jürgen Goertz, "Karlstadt, Müntzer and the Reformation of the Commoners, 1521-1525," 1-44; C. Arnold Snyder, "Swiss Anabaptism: The Beginnings, 1523-1525," 45-82; and James M. Stayer, "Swiss-South German Anabaptism, 1526-1540," 83-118.

As the authorities saw Anabaptism as something organically associated with the German Peasants War and Thomas Müntzer, they heavily prosecuted Anabaptist heresy.[35] This intensified their eschatological expectations, leading Anabaptist prophets like Melchior Hoffman to predict Christ's coming to earth in 1533. When Hoffman was imprisoned in Strasbourg – the city he believed would become Christ's capital – his successor, Dutch Anabaptist Jan Matthijs, moved the locale to Münster in Westphalia, and the date to Easter, 1534. Thousands of Anabaptists moved to the city, or tried to, in hopes of witnessing the blessed event. The resident Anabaptists soon managed to win the city council elections in 1533, leading the Bishop of Münster to lay siege to what he regarded as his city (jurisdictional disputes had long festered in the region). In 1534, in the wake of the siege, the Anabaptists mandated community of goods. On Easter Day, Matthijs, perhaps worried that Christ would not descend to his kingdom unless the prophet made a symbolic act of faith, marched out of the city and was cut to pieces. The tailor and actor Jan van Leiden took up his prophet's mantle, then in September was declared king of the New Jerusalem (figure 2). Seeing that a majority of the city's population were women unsupervised by husbands, he soon ordered all to be married, leading to polygamy. Van Leiden stirred up unrest also in Amsterdam, Groningen, and Friesland, with several notorious events, such as the 't Zandt affair in January 1535 in which a gathering of hundreds of Anabaptists on a farm in northeast Groningen organized by one of his emissaries was taken over by Harmen Schoenmaker who declared himself God the Father. In February the naked walkers (*naaktloopers*) of Amsterdam abandoned clothing to preach the naked truth

---

[35] See the essays in the note above, and Brad S. Gregory, "Anabaptist martyrdom, Imperatives, Experience, and Memorialization," in Roth and Stayer, *A Companion to Anabaptism*, 467-506.

to the residents. Then in March, a group of 300 Anabaptists captured the Friesland monastery of Oldeklooster, only to be defeated in a pitched battle days later. And in May a group of Anabaptists attacked and captured Amsterdam's city hall, killing one of the burgomasters in the process, and being themselves killed or captured the next day (figure 3).[36]

Figure 3: Image of Anabaptists attacking the Amsterdam City Hall, 1535; from Lambertus Hortensius, *Van den oproer der weder-dooperen* (Enkhuizen: J.L. Meyn, 1614), p. 20. After a lost painting by Barend Dircksz. Courtesy The Rijksmuseum, Amsterdam, RP-P-AO-28-11.

---

[36] For a recent overview, see Ralf Klötzer, "The Melchiorites and Münster," in Roth and Stayer, *A Companion to Anabaptism and Spiritualism*, 217-56; see also Willem de Bakker, Michael Driedger, and James M Stayer, *Bernhard Rothmann and the Reformation in Münster, 1530-35* (Kitchener, ON, 2009); Samme Zijlstra, *Om de ware gemeente en de oude gronden: Geschiedenis van de dopersen in de Nederlanden 1531-1675* (Hilversum, 2000), 83-147; and Stayer, *The German Peasants' War*.

Münster itself fell to its besiegers on June 25, 1535, and Anabaptists soon abandoned their end-times predictions in favour of either the biblicism of Menno Simons (which sought to ensure purity on a congregational, rather than society-wide scale), or the Spiritualism of Joris who turned religion into an entirely inward matter. Joris's turn to Spiritualism did not occur until after his expectations to be revealed as the "third David," the messianic successor to Jan van Leiden, were then crushed when governmental officials arrested dozens of his supporters who had gathered in Delft, Holland, in December 1538 to witness the dramatic moment – which was to transpire on December 25, exactly two and a half years after Münster's fall, in accordance with the "time, and times, and half a time" of Revelation 12:14 (KJV).[37] After that moment, Joris's movement toward complete Spiritualism that thoroughly internalized the supernatural – including demons and angels – within the individual, moved apace. None of these leaders wished to be associated with their Anabaptist past, and rarely referred to Münster.

With the start of the Dutch Civil War around 1568, its Reformed rebels ended heresy prosecution. In their 1579 Union of Utrecht they also did not require membership in the public Reformed Church. Dissident groups, including Catholics and Mennonites, could now worship in churches hidden behind the doors of private businesses, and tolerance of religious diversity became a hallmark of the Dutch Republic. In this environment several new groups arose, such as the Remonstrants who opposed strict Calvinism and the Collegiants who met without clergy and who allowed all members, both women and men and from whatever denomination, to participate in their informal services. For

---

[37] Willem de Bakker and Gary K. Waite, "Rethinking the Murky World of the Post-Münster Dutch Anabaptist Movement, 1535-1538: A Dialogue between Willem de Bakker and Gary K. Waite," *Mennonite Quarterly Review* 92 (2018), 47-91.

their part, in their quest to maintain congregational purity, Mennonites used the ban to discipline the wayward, in the process dividing into several groups over the practice's severity, from the liberal Waterlanders or *Doopsgezinden* of Holland to the strict Frisians.

The Doopsgezinden were influenced by spiritualistic currents which emphasized the inner meaning of scripture over the letter and promoted love of God and neighbour over confessional precision. Some of them participated in the Collegiant meetings and met with other nonconformists, such as the Polish Socinian refugees who emphasized rational interpretation of scripture that led them to deny the doctrine of the Trinity. The Doopsgezinden were clearly influenced by this interaction, and it was with these particular Mennonites that the English Separatist John Smyth would meet in Holland.[38]

The English Reformation and Anabaptism

While most English writers did not read Dutch, they often cited translations of continental works, especially those translated during King Edward's reign, to stop the spread of Anabaptism in England: Calvin's *A Short Instruction for to Arme all Good Christian People* in 1549, and most especially Bullinger's *An Holsome Antidotus or Counterpoysen against the Anabaptists* of 1548, as well as his defence of infant baptism, translated in 1551.[39] English writers used these to

---

[38] For a good analysis of the unusual form of toleration developed by the Dutch, see Willem Frijhoff, "Religious Toleration in the United Provinces: From 'Case' to 'Model,'" in *Calvinism and Religious Toleration in the Dutch Golden Age*, Ronnie Po-Chia Hsia and Henk van Nierop, eds. (Cambridge, 2002), 27-52; and Kaplan, *Reformation and the Practice of Toleration*.

[39] John Calvin, *A short instruction for to arme all good christian people agaynst the pestiferous errours of the common secte of anabaptistes*

suppress any desire to take religious reform to the extreme of separating from the Church of England. Not surprisingly, England's rulers maintained a formal state church, from Henry VIII's Catholic Church divorced from the pope, to Edward VI's Protestant church, to the return of Catholicism under Queen Mary, and finally to Elizabeth I's compromise of a theologically Protestant Church with a traditional hierarchical ecclesiology and some of the Catholic ritual.[40] Strict Puritans (Calvinists) decried any residual Catholic elements.

Like "Protestant" or "Anabaptist," the term "Puritan" encompasses a wide range of reform-minded individuals and groups, all of whom shared their opposition to Catholicism, but this attitude did not result in any real sense of unity. Some Puritans were strict Calvinists, while others allowed for some measure of free will within salvation (so-called Antinomians), and others emphasized the movement of the Spirit within; William Lamont's study of Puritanism focuses on three very different examples: William Prynne, Richard Baxter, and Lodowicke Muggleton; the first two would

---

(London: John Daye and William Seres, 1549); Heinrich Bullinger, *A most necessary & frutefull dialogue, betwene [the] seditious libertin or rebel anabaptist, & the true obedient christia[n] wherin, as in a mirrour or glasse ye shal se [the] excellencte and worthynesse of a christia[n] magistrate: & again what obedience is due vnto publique rulers of all th[os]e [that] professe christ yea, though [the] rulers, in externe & outward thinges, to their vtter dampnatyon, do otherwyse then well: Translated out of latyn into englishe, by iho[n] veron senonoys* (Worcester: John Oswen, 1551); and Heinrich Bullinger, *A moste sure and strong defence of the baptisme of children, against [the] pestiferous secte of the anabaptystes. set furthe by that famouse clerke, henry bullynger: & nowe translated out of laten into englysh by ihon veron senonoys* (Worcester: John Oswen, 1551). On these see also Euler, "Anabaptism and anti-Anabaptism."

[40] For recent studies, see Peter Marshall, *Heretics and Believers: a History of the English Reformation* (New Haven, CT, 2017); and Eamon Duffy, *Fires of Faith: Catholic England under Mary Tudor* (New Haven, CT, 2009).

certainly want nothing to do with the third, nor possibly with each other.⁴¹ Some Puritans decided therefore to separate from the Church of England, beginning with Robert Browne (c.1550-1633) in Norfolk, who in 1581 moved his congregation to Middelburg in the Dutch Republic. Even so, Browne denied having been influenced by Anabaptists per se, although George Williams observes that in the years preceding Browne's move, his Cambridge mentor Thomas Cartwright became engaged in a print debate with the Bishop of Lincoln, John Whitgift, over whether Cartwright's views were akin to Anabaptism. Williams observes: "While Cartwright's actual position was *not* so close as Whitgift assumed, it appears that Whitgift's published charges against Cartwright must have called at least these Anabaptist tenets to the attention of the reading public. Certainly among those readers would have been Cartwright's student, Browne."⁴² We will see many other possible examples of how such propaganda against a particular idea or group, such as Anabaptism, could have the reverse effect than that intended by the writer.⁴³

---

⁴¹ William M. Lamont, *Puritanism and Historical Controversy* (Montreal, 1996) See also the works by Peter Lake and David Como cited above.
⁴² Williams, *The Radical Reformation*, 1207-08. He draws this from the study by Donald J. McGinn, *The Admonition Controversy* (New Brunswick, NJ, 1949). See John Whitgift, *The defense of the aunswere to the admonition against the replie of T.C. by iohn Whitgift doctor of diuinitie. in the beginning are added these. 4. tables. 1 of dangerous doctrines in the replie. 2 of falsifications and vntruthes. 3 of matters handled at large. 4 A table generall* (London: Henry Binneman, 1574).
⁴³ This was the case with Joris's denial of the devil, which English writers only became aware of in the late 1640s. They turned it into a cause célèbre, increasing discussion about it just as England was experiencing its worst witch panic in East Anglia; some dissenter groups seem to have adopted and adapted Joris's demonology; see Waite, "David Joris in England," esp. 472-76.

After Queen Elizabeth's death in 1603, Puritans feared a restoration of Catholicism especially when Charles I sought to enforce the Anglican hierarchy and high church policies on Presbyterian Scotland, leading to the Civil War between Parliament and the king, and his execution in 1649. Since Parliament's New Model Army was filled with Puritans and Independents, its leader, Oliver Cromwell, ended central control over religion and the press; the result was a surge in unorthodox publications and new religious groups such as the Ranters and Quakers. Some of these had socially revolutionary platforms, others, such as the Quakers, developed a Spiritualist's transformational doctrine for the inner person, as had the Familists before them.[44] David Como has recently commented that, despite being the preserve of small groups of "separatists and Anabaptists" before 1640, the

> sudden removal of episcopal oversight, coupled with the furiously contested conditions of civil war, allowed these tiny groups to pour their ideas into the public domain with evangelical zeal. The result was fierce controversy, but also the rapid spread of these doctrines and practices outward into the broader godly community; once again, the ideas and impulses were decoupled from their original carriers, who were forced to watch (sometimes in horror) as enthusiasts carried treasured doctrines in new directions, splicing them together with alien traditions or influences …[45]

---

[44] Coffey, "'The Last and Greatest Triumph'," 201-202.
[45] Como, "The Family of Love and the Making of English Revolutionary Religion," 584. See also Peter Lake, *The Boxmaker's Revenge: "Orthodoxy", Heterodoxy' and the Politics of the Parish in Early Stuart*

In this context, the Baptists were no longer under threat of prosecution, and were just one of many alternatives to the Anglican Church. Those alternatives caused considerable distress among both Anglican traditionalists and Calvinist Puritans, both of which groups sought to have instead a single, state-sponsored church for the realm. The sudden rise of several new religious groups in the 1640s was, as we have noted, heralded by the earlier dissenters such as the Baptists and Familists, not to mention the Seekers. What we will explore in the next two chapters is how the anti-Anabaptist propaganda helped prepare the ground for the religious explosion during the Civil War. Chapter 2 will begin this examination with works produced contemporaneous with Dutch Anabaptism and in the three decades after Münster, for their narratives provided the core elements of subsequent ones.

London (Manchester, 2009). There are many other studies of English dissenter groups; see, for example, Kenneth L. Campbell, *Windows into Men's Souls: Religious Nonconformity in Tudor and Early Stuart England* (Lanham, MA, 2012). The classic work remains Christopher Hill, *The World Turned Upside Down: Radical Ideas During the English Revolution* (London, 1972).

Chapter 2
Anti-Anabaptist Polemics 1531-1560

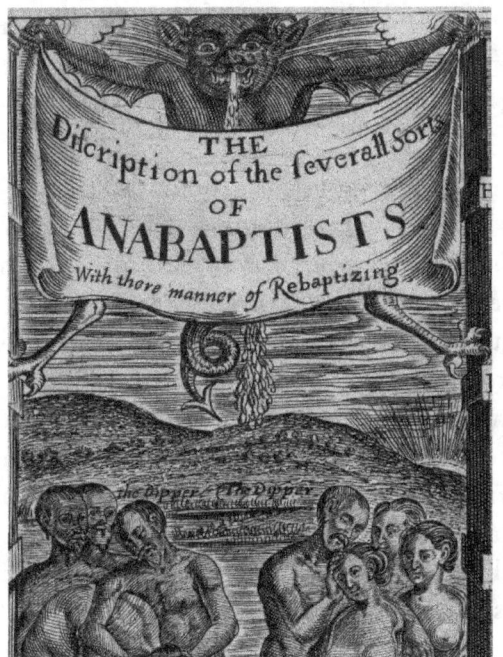

Figure 4: Featley, *Dippers Dipt*, cropped, figure of the demon. Courtesy of the Cambridge University Library, F.3.117.

Supporters of a single state church were clearly terrified of the prospect of confessional disunity and religious diversity that they believed that Anabaptism was promoting, and they escalated their fear mongering enormously. They had plenty of precedent with which to work. By 1560, English writers had demonized Dutch Anabaptist ideas such as rejection of infant baptism; the Celestial Flesh doctrine; polygamy; community of goods; and of course, Anabaptist sectarianism, pacificism, and rejection of civic offices for true Christians. These polemicists argued that even one of these heresies would necessarily lead to diabolical sedition and a

Münsterite destruction of morality. That this was an unfair reading of continental Anabaptism, and even of Anabaptist Münster, was neither here nor there for these propagandists, and these writers played freely upon the monster/Münster alliteration, as seen in Featley's demon-serpent (Figure 4).

William Barlow's *A dyaloge*, 1531

The first known surviving anti-Anabaptist work included in EEBO was Canon Sir William Barlow's 1531 *A dyaloge describing the originall grou[n]d of these lutheran faccyons, and many of theyr abusys*, a Catholic warning that Protestant reforms would lead to extreme sectarism and heresy, such as Anabaptism.[1]

Anabaptists, he asserted, are "twice christened" and refuse to accept as brethren anyone not "rebaptized again," opposing infant baptism and possessing "many straunge opynyons," including that it was impossible for rulers to be Christian, that believers should not resist their enemies, that Anabaptists have a great show of outward piety, and are constantly reading scripture, but that these were mere covers for their real nature. He even notes that Anabaptists are "redye to helpe theyr nedy brotheren, vsyng theyr goodes in comone."[2] Barlow believed that his summary of Anabaptism would horrify readers. Yet, some of these practices, such as believer's baptism, supporting fellows in practical ways, opposing violence in personal relationships, and criticizing

---

[1] William Barlow, *A dyaloge describing the originall grou[n]d of these lutheran faccyons, and many of theyr abusys, compyled by syr wyllyam barlow chanon* (London: William Rastell, 1531).

[2] Barlow, *A dialogue*, fols. G3ᵛ-G4ʳ. He then tells a story of a Swiss Anabaptist who allegedly beheaded his own brother at the command of God; this was in fact an idiosyncratic individual, Thomas Schugger, whose relationship with Anabaptism is disputed; see Harold S. Bender, "St. Gall (Switzerland)," GAMEO: https://gameo.org/index.php?title=St._Gall_(Switzerland)

secular and religious leaders for hypocrisy, were not in themselves unattractive ideas and seem to have provoked positive attention.

Thomas More and Henry VIII on Anabaptism

Similarly, two years later, in 1533, Sir Thomas More, Henry VIII's Chancellor, used Anabaptism as an example of where Protestants, such as William Tyndale, would take England if allowed. After listing the "sins" of Protestant sects, he points to Anabaptism as the logical extension of Protestantism, because Anabaptists use vernacular scripture to say that "baptysynge of chyldren is voyde," that "there ought to be no rulers at all in crystendome," "that no man shold haue any thynge proper of his owne, but that all landes and all goodes ought by goddes lawe to be all mennys in comen," and "that all women ought to be comen to all men, as well the nexte of kynne as the farthest straunger, & euery man husbande to euery woman, and euery woman wyfe vnto euery man." And finally, they taught that Christ was "but onely man and not god at all."

All of these teachings were "brethed and blowen into the brothels brestes, by the spyryt of dyscorde, debate, and dyssencyon the deuyll."[3] More's diatribe predates the Münsterite community of goods by a year, and while earlier Anabaptists taught the value of supporting fellow believers in need, and some saw the practice as an ideal, there really was no full, mandated community of goods practiced among them prior to Münster, nor any real polygamy. Similarly, rejecting the divinity of Christ was not taught by most Anabaptists. Instead, More cobbled together an image of

---

[3] Thomas More, *The second parte of the co[n]futacion of tyndals answere in whyche is also confuted the chyrche that tyndale deuyseth. and the chyrche also that frere barns deuyseth. made by syr thomas more knyght* (London: William Rastell, 1533), fols. cclxix and Cccciii.

Anabaptism from various heterodox elements – ancient communitarian heresies, the peasant rebels, Thomas Müntzer, idiosyncratic prophets, and anything distasteful he could find.[4]

Concerned about the influx of Dutch Anabaptists fleeing Habsburg persecution, in 1535 King Henry VIII issued a decree against them, commenting that these people,

> in contempte of the holye sacramente of baptisme soo gyuen and receyued, they haue of theyr owne presumption and auctorite, latelye rebaptised theym selfes: and ouer and besyde that, they denye the moste blessed and holy sacrament of the aulter to be really the very body of our lord Iesu Christ: And yet farther, they kepe holde and teche other dyuers and sondry pestilent herysies agaynste god and his holy scriptures, to the great vnquyetnesse of christendome.[5]

Missing are Hoffman's Celestial Flesh doctrine, millenarian expectations, or Münster's community of goods, polygamy, or use of the sword, so it appears that news of the kingdom of God had not yet reached the court.

Only one contemporary newssheet on the subject of Anabaptist Münster seems to have survived: an anonymous 1535 work entitled *A treuue nyeuu tydyinges of the wonderful worckes of the Rebaptisers of Munster in Westuaell*. It was printed in Antwerp and must have appeared after June 25 when the city fell to the besiegers and the king was captured.[6]

---

[4] On More, Henry VIII, and heresy, see also Loewenstein, *Treacherous Faith*, 23-68.

[5] Single page broadsheet: England, Sovereign (Henry VIII), *A proclamation concerninge heresie* (London: Thomas Berthelet, 1535).

[6] *A treuue nyeuu tydynges of the wo[n]derfull worckes of the rebaptisers of mu[n]ster in westuaell how the cete haethe bene wo[n]ne and in what mannar the kinge is taeken, and all their deades and intencyons haethe*

Here the author cites various newssheets recounting how the Anabaptists took over the city, and describing the many battles the combatants endured, while focusing on the city's fall and the capture of Jan van Leiden. Despite the heretical king's insistence on complete loyalty from his people and their property, the famine in the city seriously weakened the defenders, some of whom let the besiegers in. When the besiegers entered the city, they discovered that Van Leiden had hoarded wine, grain, and meat that could have easily fed his people.[7] Such stories contributed to the image of ordinary Anabaptists being misled by unscrupulous charlatans. This was an assumption made in fact by court officials when dealing with women Anabaptists in particular, and explains why a smaller proportion of women were executed for heresy compared to male Anabaptists.[8] At the same time, as in many such populist movements, it was often the rank-and-file members of the movement who pushed their leaders in particular directions.

They "thinke that the payne … of deuylles shal haue an ende: Translations of German Anti-Anabaptist Polemics

Over the following few years there were further elaborations on alleged Anabaptist teachings. For example, in a 1536 translation of the Lutheran Augsburg Confession of Faith, readers would have learned that Anabaptists believed that

---

taeken an ende [et]c. iohu[n] of ley a kinge of nyew iherusalem and of the hoole vniuerall worlde beynghe in the aege of. xxvi. years. aetatis 26 (Antwerp: M. de Keyser, 1535).

[7] *A treuue nyeuu tydyinges*, fol. Bij^r.

[8] Gary K. Waite, "Sixteenth Century Religious Reform and the Witch-Hunts," in *The Oxford Handbook of Witchcraft in Early Modern Europe and Colonial America*, Brian P. Levack, ed. (Oxford, 2013), 485-506, here 498.

the Holy Spirit comes to people without "any externe or outwarde worke / by their owne preparations and workes," which struck the Lutherans as a quasi-Catholic position. They damned Anabaptists for disallowing the baptism of children and teaching that it was possible for Anabaptists to become spiritually perfect so that "they can nat synne."[9] Anabaptists are further condemned for forbidding civic offices to Christians. Most unorthodox is the purported teaching of Anabaptists who "thinke that the payne of euyl men / and of deuylles shal haue an ende."[10] This was an exaggerated depiction of the spiritualistic teaching of the South German Anabaptist Hans Denck (d.1527), whose universalism was never that explicit, but almost all continental polemicists had accused him, and by extension all Anabaptists, of holding to the ultimate salvation of the devil and his minions, to the ending of hell. These English writers grabbed at this profound unorthodoxy to defame all Anabaptists as holding to "wicked and madde opinions."[11]

In 1538 a German Lutheran writer called Erasmus Sarcerius (1501-1559) suggested that Anabaptist heresy led ultimately to "To deny that the euil spirites do togither lye in a wayt of al the creatures of god. To deny that witchcraft

---

[9] *The confessyon of the fayth of the germaynes exhibited to the moste victorious emperour charles the. v. in the councell or assemble holden at augusta the yere of our lorde. 1530. to which is added the apologie of melancthon who defendeth with reasons inuincible the aforesayde confesyon translated by rycharde tauerner at the commaundeme[n]t of his master thomas cromwel chefe secretarie to the kynges grace* (London: Robert Redman, 1536), fols. 6r-8v.
[10] Ibid., fol. 9ᵛ.
[11] Ibid., fol. Jiijʳ. On Denck's universalism, see Morwenna Ludlow, "Why was Hans Denck Thought to be a Universalist?" *Journal of Ecclesiastical History* 55 (2004), 257-74; and Geoffrey Dipple, "The Spiritualist Anabaptists," in Roth and Stayer, *A Companion to Anabaptism and Spiritualism*, 357-97.

is of any strength by the power of the devyll."¹² When Sarcerius' treatise was published, there was no Anabaptist who denied the reality of the devil, although David Joris would do so in the following years.¹³ One likely source for Joris's demonology were the unpublished manuscripts of the Strasbourg Spiritualist Clemens Ziegler, whom Joris surely met when he visited that city in June 1538. However, Ziegler did not publish his manuscripts describing an entirely internalized, and ultimately impotent, devil. Sarcerius seems instead to be extrapolating from previous heresies to predict developments in current ones. Perhaps such polemical exaggeration gave Joris the encouragement he needed to push his internalizing motif to its ultimate conclusion?

In other words, it is possible that descriptions of the heresy of denying the devil (such as Sarcerius') added impetus to Joris taking it up after his presumed conversation with Ziegler. Then, with the profound disillusionment of the prophetic predictions in December, Joris abandoned any form of external religiosity and began publishing the concept of an internalized devil in 1539/1540.

With an increased number of Dutch Anabaptist refugees by 1538, Henry VIII's government again issued a new decree against those who printed books by "sundry straunge persones called Anabaptistes and sacramentaries whiche be lately commen into this realme" with their superstitious, rash, erroneous, and "fantasticall opinions, bothe in their

---

[12] Erasmus Sarcerius, *Co[m]mon places of scripture ordrely and after a co[m]pendious forme of teachyng set forth with no litle labour, to the gret profit and help of all such studentes in gods worde as haue not had longe exercyse in the same ... translated in to englysh by rychard tauerner* (London: John Byddell, 1538), fol. xxxiiʳ.

[13] See Gary K. Waite, "Knowing the Spirit(s) in the Dutch Radical Reformation: From Physical Perception to Rational Doubt, 1536-1690," in *Knowing Demons, Knowing Spirits in the Early Modern Period*, Michelle D. Brock, Richard Raiswell, and David R. Winter, eds. (Basingstoke, 2018), 23-54.

preachinges and familyar communications, whereby dyuers and many of his louyinge symple subiectes, haue ben enduced and encouraged, arrogantly and superstitiousely" to "dispute in open places, tauernes, and alehouses," attacking the blessed sacraments. These Anabaptists and sacramentaries "lurk secretly in dyuers corners and places" stirring the king's subjects to their errors. They must be apprehended and expelled.[14] By this year, then, English writers were identifying Anabaptists as teaching community of goods, the denial of baptism for children, the rejection of the Real Presence in the sacrament, millenarian extremism, and the ultimate salvation of demons, with a hint that some might in fact deny the power of demons altogether.[15]

Anti-Anabaptist Works under King Edward VI (1537-53)

Throughout the 1540s English writers kept up these calls for the eradication of Anabaptist errors, being assisted by the translation of both Bullinger's and Calvin's treatises on the subject. The Heavenly Flesh of Christ doctrine, which was still maintained by most Dutch Anabaptists and Mennonites throughout the sixteenth century, seems to have been a particular point of concern for writers such as Miles Coverdale, who composed a dialogue on the subject in

---

[14] Single page broadsheet, England and Wales, Sovereign (Henry VIII), *The kynges most royall maiestie being enfourmed* (London: Thomas Berthelet, 1538).

[15] See, for examples, *The original [and] sprynge of all sectes [and] orders by whome, wha or were they beganne. translated out of hye dutch in englysh* (London: James Nicolson, 1537); and *The institution of a christen man conteynynge the exposytion or interpretation of the commune crede, of the seuen sacramentes, of the .x. commandementes, and of the pater noster, and the aue maria, iustyfication [and] purgatory* (London: Thomas Berthelet, 1537).

1541.¹⁶ Other works, like George Joye's 1545 translation of Lutheran interpretations of the book of Daniel, lumped Anabaptists together with a variety of Spiritualist leaders, including Joris and Michael Servetus, the Spanish physician who was believed to have denied the Trinity and who would be burned for such in Calvin's Geneva in 1553.¹⁷ Other works, such as the translation, again by George Joye, of the Lutheran Andreas Osiander's work on conjectures over the end of the world, printed in Antwerp in 1548, linked Anabaptists with English papists, followers of Thomas Müntzer, the David Georgians, and various high church Anglicans, in a grand plot by Satan to destroy the gospel.¹⁸

Similarly, in 1547 appeared a translation of Herman van Wied's treatise on what a true reformation should look like. The author was the reform-minded Catholic Archbishop of

---

[16] Miles Coverdale, *A confutacion of that treatise, which one iohn standish made agaynst the protestacion of D. barnes in the yeare. M.D.XL. wherin, the holy scriptures (peruerted and wrested in his sayd treatise) are restored to their owne true vnderstonding agayne* (Zurich: C. Froschauer, 1541). See also T. Becon, *The iewel of ioye* (London: John Daye and William Seres, 1550), fol. Miii^r.

[17] G. Joye, *The exposicion of daniel the prophete gathered oute of philip melanchton, iohan ecolampadius, chonrade pellicane [and] out of iohan draconite. [et] c. by george ioye. A prophecye diligently to be noted of al emprowrs [and] kinges in these laste dayes* (Antwerp: A. Goinus, 1545).

[18] Andreas Osiander, *The coniectures of the ende of the worlde, translated by george ioye* (Antwerp: S. Mierdman, 1548), fol. Bviij^r. This linkage of Servetus with the Anabaptists and Libertines became a commonplace; see Thomas Edwards, *The first and second part of gangræna, or, A catalogue and discovery of many of the errors, heresies, blasphemies and pernicious practices of the sectaries of this time, vented and acted in england in these four last years also a particular narration of divers stories, remarkable passages, letters: An extract of many letters, all concerning the present sects: Together with some observations upon and corollaries from all the fore-named premisses* (London: T.R. and E.M. for Ralph Smith, 1646), fol. Ci^r. On the reception of Servetus' death, see Van Veen, "Dutch Anabaptist and Reformed Historiographers on Servetus' Death."

Cologne who summarized the core teaching of Anabaptists to be the denial of original sin; refusal to baptize children; reliance on their own suffering as a good work to achieve righteousness; and renunciation of the outward ministry of the church in favour of "private illuminations and visions." They also separate from the church and consider the sacraments "only outward signs."[19] Some Anabaptists, he warns, hold to even worse beliefs, such as those who "invaded the city Monster," setting up a new tyranny, all inspired, of course, by Satan, who maintains them in their madness. They allegedly also allowed for easy divorce and regarded holding private property as a sin. These "errors be seditious" and must, Van Wied concludes, be restrained through preaching and persuasion and, failing that, through the civic office.[20]

Other chronicles and newssheets through the century recounted Anabaptist Münster's most spectacular excesses. A translation of J. Carion's account that was written in the immediate aftermath of the kingdom's fall, appeared in English in 1550, highlighting how the simple Anabaptists had conquered the city (which was not true), selected Jan van Leiden as king, created so much chaos that "all the people of Westphalia did rise against them" (again, untrue), were forced to eat leather book covers in their last days, and without any shame not only enjoyed polygamy, but also

---

[19] Herman von Wied, *A simple, and religious consultation of vs herman by the grace of god archebishop of colone, and prince electour. [et] c. by what meanes a christian reformation, and founded in gods worde, of doctrine, administration of the deuine sacramentes, of ceremonies, and the hole cure of soules, and other ecclesiastical ministeries may be begon among men committed to our pastorall charge, vntil the lorde graunt a better to be appoynted either by a free, and christian cou[n]sayle, general, or national, or elles by the states of the empire of the natio[n] of germanie, gathered together in the holye gost* (London: John Daye, 1547), fol. Tv^r.
[20] Van Wied, *A simple*, fols. Tv^r-Tvii^r.

strode about the city completely naked (an exaggeration).[21] The tortured end of the pretended king in 1536 and his associates was just desserts for the Anabaptist tumult. A bit later the chronicle turns to the case of Joan of Kent, rightfully burned, according to our author, for following seditious Anabaptist teaching, especially the heavenly flesh of Christ doctrine.[22]

William Turner and the Disease of Heresy

Some polemicists also used medical terminology to warn readers away from Anabaptism, such as the work by the medical doctor William Turner (d.1568). He lumped together various continental heretics into a seven-headed "monstere of our tymes": Anabaptists, Adamites, Loykenistes (Loyists), Libertines, Swenckfeldians, Davidians, and "the spoylers" (whoever they were). While Turner advocates for fighting against these descendants of the fifth-century Pelagius with "the sworde of goddes word" rather than with the papists' fire, he also uses medical terminology to frighten readers already on the alert for outbreaks of the plague: "rotting moisture," "raging plague,"

---

[21] J. Carion, *The thre bokes of cronicles, whyche iohn carion (a man syngularly well sene in the mathematycall sciences) gathered wyth great diligence of the beste authours that haue written in hebrue, greke or latine wherunto is added an appendix, conteynyng all such notable thynges as be mentyoned in cronicles to haue chaunced in sundry partes of the worlde from the yeare of christ. 1532. to thys present yeare of. 1550. gathered by iohn funcke of nurenborough. whyche was neuer afore prynted in englysh* (London: S. Mierdman, 1550), fols. CCi^v-CCii^r, CCvij^v-CCviij^v.

[22] Carion, *The thre bokes*, fol. CClxxvij^r; see also E. Becke, *A brefe confutatacion of this most detestable, [and] anabaptistical opinion, that christ dyd not take hys flesh of the blessed vyrgyn mary nor any corporal substaunce of her body for the maintenaunce whereof ihone bucher otherwise called ihone of kent most obstinately suffered and was burned in smythfyelde, the .ii day of may. anno domini M.D.L* (London: John Day and William Seres, 1550).

"cruel pestilence," and even "bewitched thaughtis," all from Satan. These would have provoked an emotional response of anxiety, perhaps even anger, that some malicious people would join such a pestilential crowd.[23] Turner is correct to notice some inter-relations among the Anabaptists and the Spiritualists, as Joris was engaged in both worlds and had met with the Spiritualistic Loyists of Antwerp and the Schwenckfeldians, followers of the Silesian Spiritualist Caspar von Schwenckfeld.[24] Dutch Libertines were indeed Reformed preachers who were seeking a softened Calvinist theology that would allow Catholics to remain within an inclusive Reformed Church, and many of these were influenced by the spiritualistic ideas of Joris, Niclaes, and Dirck Volckertsz Coornhert.[25] Turner's sensational stories about Münster imply that Anabaptism leads to sedition: "I may a great dele be lesse ashamed of my poore, and innocente infantes, then ye maye be, to defende the doctryne of your sedytions, and mourderynge Anabaptistes," which destroyed noble Münster, revolted against Amsterdam's magistrates, and came close to destroying Groningen. These "factious catabaptistes" he fumes, "baptysed so many deuilishe and reprobat persones of your sect" that they could set up a king who had 16 wives and murdered and despised God's ministers of the "elect chyrche." Such "swarmes of

---

[23] William Turner, *A Perseruatiue, Or Triacle, Agaynst the Poyson of Pelagius Lately Renued, ... by the Furious Secte of the Annabaptistes ...* (London, S. Mierdman, 1551), fol. Aiij^v.

[24] See Waite, "Sixteenth-Century Spiritualists"; and Dipple, "The Spiritualist Anabaptists."

[25] See Benjamin J. Kaplan, *Calvinists and Libertines: Confession and Community in Utrecht, 1578-1620* (Oxford, 1995); and Ruben Buys, "'Without Thy Self, O Man, Thou Hast No Means to Look for, by Which Thou Maist Know God': Pieter Balling, the Radical Enlightenment, and the Legacy of Dirck Volckertsz Coornhert," *Church History and Religious* Culture 93 (2013), 363–383, and *Sparks of Reason.*

Anabaptistes of your sect" were baptized as adults "and afterwarde committed hordom robry and shamefull murder"; were these the "chosen ones" of God?[26]

English Polemics and Tudor Policy: Queens Mary and Elizabeth I

Catholic writers similarly linked believer's baptism with community of goods,[27] and promoted judicial action to suppress such dissent. For example, in 1556 Miles Huggarde approvingly cited harsh treatment of English Anabaptists who denied the baptism of infants, "whereof some were burnt in Smythfielde."[28] So too was Joan of Kent, "a great pratler of diuinite" who believed that "Christe toke no fleshe of the blessed virgin Mary, and was worthely burned in Smythfielde," as was a "duche man" who denied the divinity of Christ.[29] Puritan writers may have opposed such violent judicial treatment of dissenters, but their language against both Catholicism and Anabaptism was just as extreme. In his rebuttal to John Knox's *The Monstrous Regiment of Women* of 1558 which had attacked Queen Mary's persecution of Puritans by denying that women had any right to rule at all, the Anglican bishop John Aylmer (1521-

---

[26] Turner, *A Perseruatiue*, fols. Fi^v-Fij^v.
[27] R. Smith, *A bouclier of the catholike fayth of christes church conteynyng diuers matters now of late called into controuersy, by the newe gospellers. made by richard smith, doctour of diuinitee, [and] the quenes hyghnes reader of the same I her graces vniuersite of oxford* (London: Rychard Tottell, 1554), fol. 12^r.
[28] Miles Huggarde, *The displaying of the protestantes, [and] sondry their practises, with a description of diuers their abuses of late frequented newly imprinted agayne, and augmented, with a table in the ende, of all suche matter as is specially contained within this volume. made by myles huggarde seruant to the quenes maiestie* (London: Robert Caly, 1556), fol. 18^v.
[29] Huggarde, *The displaying*, fols. 18^v-19^r.

1594) advocated loyalty to Queen Elizabeth, but seethed with fury over the "vgglie monsters and brodes of the deuils brotherhead," such as the Anabaptists and "infinite other swarmes of Satanistes."[30] As I have argued, this demonizing language not only worried readers about Anabaptists, but also unintentionally intensified anxiety about the Devil's traditional minions – witches – leading to the revival of large-scale witchcraft trials, a subject to which we will return to below.[31]

Queen Elizabeth I almost immediately took action, and her edict reflected Turner's language of disease, citing foreigners "infected with certain dangerous and pernicious opinions, in matters of religion," such as Anabaptists "and such lyke" who have fled to London and other port cities pretending to be fleeing religious oppression. If her officials did not act expeditiously, "the Churche of God in this Realme shall sustaine great daunger of corruption," leading to sectarian divisions. Any unwilling to be reconciled with the teaching of the Church of England will be expelled.[32] While Puritans who themselves had been liable to arrest and execution tended to emphasize persuasion over judicial action, Elizabeth and many Anglican bishops were convinced that lay dissent in theological matters and practice

---

[30] John Aylmer, *An harborowe for faithfull and trewe subiectes agaynst the late blowne blaste, concerninge the gouernme[n]t of wemen. wherin be confuted all such reasons as a straunger of late made in that behalfe, with a breife exhortation to obedience* (London: John Day 1559), fols. A3^v, H2^r.

[31] Waite, *Eradicating the Devil's Minions*, and "Sixteenth Century Religious Reform and the Witch-Hunts."

[32] Single page broadsheet: England and Wales, Sovereign (Elizabeth I), *By the quene the quenes maiestie vnderstandyng that of late tyme sundrye persons beyng infected with certayne dangerous and pernicious opinions in matters of religion, contrary to the faith of the church of christe, as anabaptistes ...* (London: Rycharde Jugge and John Cawood, 1560).

was a disease that needed to be cut out of the body politic before it could infect her entire populace.³³

The Translation of Johannes Sleidanus' Chronicle, 1560

Anxiety regarding Anabaptism increased significantly with the publication in 1560 of an English translation of the chronicle by the Luxembourg Protestant historian Johannes Sleidanus (1506-1556) who spent most of his career in Strasbourg. This work was frequently cited by English writers because it included the most detailed account of Anabaptist Münster available to the English.³⁴ Here are all the leading characters: Jan van Leiden as king, his mayor Bernhard Knipperdolling, his preacher and propagandist Bernhard Rothmann, and others. Here is displayed Satan's spectacular efforts to deceive simple folk to overthrow church and state, to pretend piety, to abhor matrimony and civic office, and to allow polygamy.

Sleidanus concludes that "surely when God's wrath is kindled, there is no error so absurd or unsavoury, which the Devil cannot persuade, as we see happened in the doctrine of Mahomet."³⁵ In polemical works the comparison between the polygamy of Münster and polygamy in Islam was commonplace, in large measure because many Christian writers viewed Islam as originally a variant of a Christian

---

³³ Elizabeth I, *By the quene the quenes maiestie*.
³⁴ Johannes Sleidanus, *A Famouse Cronicle of Oure Time, Called Sleidanes Commentaries Concerning the State of Religion and Common Wealth, during the Raigne of the Emperour Charles the Fift, with the Argumentes Set before Euery Booke, Conteyninge the Summe Or Effecte of the Booke Following. Translated Out of Latin into Englishe, by Ihon Daus. here Vnto is Added also an Apology of the Authoure* (London: John Daie, 1560), "The tenth Booke of Sleidanes Commentaries, concerning the state of Religion," esp. fols. Cxxvij^r-Cxxxvj^r, a total of some 20 pages.
³⁵ Sleidanus, *A Famouse Cronicle*, fol. Cxxxiiij^v.

heresy – also known as Nestorianism – which was supposedly concocted by the Prophet Muhammad and a disgraced Nestorian monk named Sergius.[36] This view is clear, for example, in the extremely popular *Abomination of the Foremost Head Heretics* produced first in Dutch in 1607 by the Leiden bookseller Hendrik van Haestens and illustrated with woodcut drawings by Christoffel van Sichem. This first edition had eight heretics – Müntzer, Matthijs, Van Leiden, Knipperdolling, Diederick Sartor (the prophet of the naaktloopers), Herman van 't Sant (Harmen Schoenmaker, the self-acclaimed "God the Father" at the Anabaptist gathering in 't Zand, Groningen, in 1535), Joris, and Servetus. Many subsequent editions added the ancient denier of the divinity of Christ, Arius, and the Prophet Muhammad, along with Hendrik Niclaes and six other Anabaptist leaders.[37] It was this latter version that was translated for an English audience in 1655, in the hope of dissuading English readers from Turning Turke or Anabaptist. We will examine this edition later in Chapter 6. By associating Islam with Anabaptism, authors could discredit both at the same time. Such polemical strategies developed by English writers in the three decades after the rise of Dutch Anabaptism in 1530 provided the essential building blocks for more elaborate treatments to come. Over

---

[36] On this, see Gary K. Waite, *Jews and Muslims in Seventeenth-Century Discourse: From Religious Enemies to Allies and Friends* (London, 2019), 81-105; and Mehmet Karabela, *Islamic Thought Through Protestant Eyes* (London, 2021).

[37] *Grouwelen der voornaemster hooft-ketteren die haer in dese laeste tijden soo in Duytslandt, als oock in dese Nederlanden opgheworpen hebben, haer leven, leere, begin ende eynde, enz. Mits-gaders haere af-beeldingen* (Leiden: Henrick Lodewijcxsoon van Haestens, 1607); the larger edition was produced first in German in 1608 as *Greuwel der vornehmsten Haupt-Ketzeren, so wohl Wiedertauffer als auch andern]* (Leiden, 1608), and in Dutch in 1623. See Schroeder, "Heretics and Martyrs," 235-40.

the following century, writers moved the description of Anabaptism even further away from its historical roots, to shape it into an all-encompassing threat to civic and religious order led explicitly by the devil. This threat took on added urgency with the rise of an indigenous English Baptist movement by 1612, followed by the incredible surge in other new religious groups during the English Civil War in the 1640s. Now polemicists believed they possessed plenty of evidence that these later developments were caused by the Anabaptist movement about which they had been warning for some time. They feared that these new developments would be a replay of the Münster Anabaptist atrocities, and worse. In the next chapter we will trace these developments up to the start of the Civil War, focusing especially on reactions to the self-baptism of John Smyth in 1609. We will also begin to see several intriguing examples of unintended consequences of the polemics, which included possibly inspiring Smyth to commit his controversial act.

Chapter 3
Anti-Anabaptist Polemics, 1562-1640

Anabaptists, "an vnquyetouse kynde of men"

In 1570 the London printer Henrie Denham printed a translation of a long (just under 100 folio pages) German poem composed by the controversial Lutheran preacher and playwright Thomas Naogeorgus, or Kirchmeyer (1511-1563) and translated by Barnabe Googe.[1] Regarded as a Renaissance poet of some repute, Naogeorgus got into a number of conflicts with his colleagues and Lutheran princes over his crypto-Calvinist opinions and was forced to move frequently. When he wrote this work in February 1553, he was residing in the tolerant Swiss city of Basel, where his Reformed sympathies would not be out of place. This was also where the arch-heretic David Joris was living in refuge, under a pseudonym, Johann van Brugge, but we have no idea if Naogeorgus was aware of this coincidence.[2] In any event, in this poem against the "popish kingdome," Naogeorgus follows the Lutheran line of attacking the Catholic Church as a satanic kingdom ruled by the Antichrist. He also writes against the Anabaptists, whom he calls "franticke," who, being widely dispersed, despise books, "learned artes," and

---

[1] Thomas Naogeorgus, *The popish kingdome, or reigne of antichrist, written in latine verse by thomas naogeorgus, and englyshed by barnabe googe* (London: Henrie Denham, for Richarde Watkins, 1570).
[2] Dieter Fauth, "Kirchmeyer, Thomas," in *The Oxford Encyclopedia of the Reformation*, Hans J. Hillerbrand, ed., 4 vols. (Oxford, 1996) 2: 378. Fauth writes that Naogeorgus was called to a post in Stuttgart in 1551, but the dedicatory foreword by Naogeorgus in this work is dated February 20, 1553.

languages apart from their own "Countrie tongue" and who, common artisans, are not ashamed

> ... the Preachers place with greasie handes to touch
> Still boasting of the holy ghost,
> and so with passing pride,
> They hedlong throwe themselues to hell, and
> numbers great beside.³

None of this is particularly harsh for the time, and certainly not in comparison with his demonizing rhetoric against the Catholic Church, and in this we can see some of his Reformed sympathy, for German and Dutch Reformed writers tended not to demonize the Anabaptists nearly as much as strict Lutherans did. That said, Naogeorgus' last controversy, the one that got him fired from his post as Superintendent of the Lutheran Church in Esslingen, Württemberg in 1563, was his preaching of fiery sermons supporting the calls for witch trials following a large and destructive hailstorm in the region. These calls were taken up not by Naogeorgus' prince, but by a neighbour, Count Ulrich of Helfenstein, who then burned over sixty accused witches in Wiesensteig, Reformation Germany's first major witch panic.⁴

It is difficult to tell if Googe's translation found many readers in England. According to EEBO this work survives in only the one printing and only a of handful of English authors refer to Naogeorgus, and most of these are second hand references – but the point here is that such association of one's religious enemies with Satan could have profound and unexpected consequences. While Naogeorgus aimed his most profoundly demonizing language at his Catholic opponents, he soon expanded his target to include a sect of

---

³ Naogeorgus, *The popish kingdome*, fol. 72ᵛ.
⁴ See Waite, *Eradicating the Devil's Minions*, 138-51.

demonic witches, even though many of his fellow Protestants, including the Duke of Württemberg, did not follow him in this, seeing witch hunting as a Catholic activity. We will return to this real-world impact of anti-Anabaptist rhetoric and anxiety over witchcraft in the 1640s in Chapter 5 below.

The use of the epithet "Anabaptist" carried enormous negative baggage and was used with great abandon over the late sixteenth and seventeenth centuries in thousands of pamphlets, treatises, and books, to critique any opponent who dared to diverge from officially approved teaching on faith or society. Many writers had to publish works to prove that they were not in fact Anabaptists.[5] In 1548 Edward Hall pleaded from a fraternal, Christian spirit that his fellows would stop labelling opponents as heretics, papists, and Anabaptists.[6] Based on the surviving works, it appears his pleas went unheeded. In 1549 the antiquarian John Leland bemoaned the pillaging of monastic libraries after the suppression of the monasteries by Henry VIII. He had in fact been tasked with cataloguing the books for the king, and in his printed complaint, he turned to the example of the Anabaptists who "in our tyme, an vnquyetouse kynde of men, arrogaunt without measure, capcyose and vnlerned, do leaue non olde workes vnbrent, that they maye easely come

---

[5] See, for example, I. B., *A bryefe and plaine declaracion of certayne sente[n]ces in this litle boke folowing to satisfie the consciences of them that haue iudged me therby to be a fauourer of the anabaptistes* (London: J. Day, 1547), fol. Aii^r.

[6] Edward Hall, *The vnion of the two noble and illustre famelies of lancastre [and] yorke, beeyng long in continual discension for the croune of this noble realme with all the actes done in bothe the tymes of the princes, bothe of the one linage and of the other, beginnyng at the tyme of kyng henry the fowerth, the first aucthor of this deuision, and so successiuely proceadyng to the reigne of the high and prudent prince kyng henry the eight, the vndubitate flower and very heire of both the sayd linages* (London: Richard Grafton, 1548), fol. XXXiiij^r.

by, as apered by the lybraryes at Mynster in the lande of Westphaly, whom they most furyously destroyed."[7]

Why resort to this obscure cross-Channel incident of 15 years earlier if it had no rhetorical power to inspire an emotional response? Thanks to such polemics, by mid-century the term "Anabaptist" had become so loaded that it could be used for a variety of rhetorical purposes, even though the Anabaptist movement in England was a very small and underground affair. Some English writers, such as the Anglican bishop John Jewel, in fact believed that such heterodoxy was entirely foreign; in 1562 he listed the various enemies of the faith – Anabaptists, Libertines, Mennonites (Mennonions), Schwenckfeldians – while asserting that "the world seeth now wel inough that we nother haue bred, nor taught, nor fostered these monsters."[8] He spoke too soon.

Until the second decade of the seventeenth century, Anabaptism was regarded as a foreign import in England, for it was not until c. 1612 that there was an actual congregation of Separatists practising believer's baptism in England. By this time the English Baptists were struggling against the Anabaptist stereotype of sectarian extremism, sedition, prophetic and millenarian enthusiasm, sexual immorality, and the abandonment of civic matrimony and of the concept of a Christian magistracy, despite none of these applying to them. There were, however, important connections between Baptists and continental Anabaptists, and with spiritualistic Familists and Seekers before 1640. As we shall see, the set of relationships become even more complex with the rise of

---

[7] John Leland, *The laboryouse iourney [and] serche of iohan leylande, for englandes antiquitees geuen of hym as a newe yeares gyfte to kynge henry the viij. in the. xxxvij. yeare of his reygne, with declaracyons enlarged: By iohan bale* (London: S. Mierdman, 1549), fol. Eviij^v.

[8] John Jewel, *An apologie, or aunswer in defence of the Church of England concerning the state of religion vsed in the same. Newly set forth in Latin, and nowe translated into Englishe* (London: Reginald Wolf, 1562), fol. 19^v.

new religious groups during the Civil War, and various Separatists interacted with leaders of the Seekers, Ranters, Fifth Monarchy Men, and Quakers, to mention only the most prominent of these. Such interrelations were the stuff of propaganda, such as Turner's and Featley's, but they were also true, to a certain extent. There were several networks of cross-Channel nonconformists, such as the intriguing circle around the philosopher Samuel Hartlib (c.1600-1662) which included Anglicans like the Cambridge philosopher Henry More, the Scottish irenicist John Dury, and the English Baptist Henry Jessey (1602-1663), along with a number of Dutch Collegiants and the fascinating Walloon nonconformist Peter Serrarius (1600-1669). These even assisted the Amsterdam rabbi Menasseh ben Israel in his 1655 mission to convince Parliament to allow the Jews to return to England.[9] These nonconformists looked positively at the level of religious diversity of the Dutch Republic which, after 1600, included Jews who had discovered they could remove their Catholic identity as New Christians once in the Republic.[10] Polemicists fought hard to demonize such laxity in matters of confession, but as they condemned in detail Anabaptist ideas, they helped to raise interest in them.

From 1600 to 1660, and especially between 1640 and 1660, the rhetorical attacks on Anabaptism increased dramatically. In the remainder of this chapter I will look most closely at the period around the establishment of an English Baptist community, c.1609 to 1620 and, in the

---

[9] See David S. Katz, *The Jews in the History of England, 1485-1850* (Oxford, 1994); and Gary K. Waite, "Seventeenth-Century English Writers on Dutch Nonconformists: the Cases of David Joris (George) and Menasseh ben Israel in Sjoerd Levelt, Esther van Raamsdonk, and Michael Rose, eds, *Anglo-Dutch Connections in the Early Modern World* (Abingdon, 2023), 225-234. See also the other essays in that volume.
[10] Daniel M. Swetschinski, *Reluctant Cosmopolitans: The Portuguese Jews of Seventeenth-Century Amsterdam* (Oxford, 2000); and Waite, *Jews and Muslims*, 28-30.

subsequent chapter, I will examine the era of the Civil War and Interregnum when Featley and other Puritans, Anglicans, and Presbyterians sought vainly to put the stopper back into the religious diversity bottle. What is clear is that well before 1609, the term Anabaptist had become so loaded with images of wild visionaries stripping naked and promoting community of goods, polygamy, and denying the devil, that no one could imagine using it positively.

"Howling Anabaptists" & "Hell-maisters:" A Catholic Attack by Edmund Thomas Hill, 1600

This is certainly true in the controversial works produced in reaction to John Smyth's self-baptism in 1609. Many writers simply attacked his action by using the label "Anabaptist" without providing any of the salacious details which were obviously already familiar to readers. Smyth's opponents had plenty of rhetorical weaponry at their disposal already, as writers had become quite creative in their descriptions. For example, in 1600 the Catholic Edmund Thomas Hill was already listing no fewer than 56 continental sectarians that he argued had descended from Luther, including the typical Muntzerans, Anabaptists, Davidgeorgians, and Adamites. Most were fictional creations, but who wouldn't be interested to hear about Daemonians, Commonholders, Howling Anabaptists, Polygamistes, Metamorphists, Hell-maisters, Hell-tormentors, Antidaemonians, Hand-impositors, or Inuisibilists, whatever these were, "all which haue sucked their errors out of the dregges of *Luthers* Doctrine, and yet forsooth, will be sound Protestantes all."[11] Apart from revealing a great level of creativity on Hill's part, this list of names – even without any detail – associated any

---

[11] Edmund Hill, *A quartron of reasons of catholike religion, with as many briefe reasons of refusall* (n.p.: English Secret Press], 1600), 13-14.

form of religious dissent with sexual deviance, diabolical plotting, and madness. Of course, however, Protestant writers disassociated Luther from this list of demonic agents, instead portraying him as an opponent of Thomas Müntzer and the Anabaptists; such was the case for Thomas Edwards' famed *Gangraena* of 1646, to which we shall return in chapter 4 below.[12]

"Certaine rash-pates and giddy-headed preachers," Oliver Ormerod vs the Puritans, 1605

As noted above, in 1605 the learned Anglican Oliver Ormerod (1580-1626) published a dialogue between an Englishman and a German which "firmly proved" that Puritans "doe resemble the anabaptists" in over eighty distinct ways.[13] The German tells his fellow that about six years after Luther began preaching, "The Deuil (to disturbe this worke) stirred vp certaine rash-pates and giddy-headed preachers," who critiqued both Luther and the Pope, eventually leading to the peasants' rebellion. How did these ideas arise, the Englishman inquires? Through private conventicles which linked themselves together, the German replies. To this the Englishman notes that "so holde our Sectaries also their conuenticles in priuate houses, and in secret corners." The implication could hardly be clearer, especially as he gives several recent examples of English meetings of unlearned ministers who "meddle with matters too high for them" and whose following is said to exceed 10,000 and growing.[14] Ormerod turns of course to Anabaptist Münster where Jan van Leiden and his preachers "raised vp factions, and bred discord," which The Englishman affirms, "so haue our Sectaries likewise

---

[12] Edwards, *The first and second part of gangræna*, fol., Ci^r.
[13] Ormerod, *The picture of a puritane*, titlepage.
[14] Ormerod, *The picture of a puritane*, 3, 7-8.

insinuated themselues" where the gospel was not firmly planted and "haue disquieted the Church, and sowne the seede of contention euen in our chiefe Cities."[15] Every example of unusual dissenter activity that the author could find to link with the continental Anabaptists he did, including the Puritan prophet William Hacket who was executed in London in 1591 for his messianic claims and treasonous sermons, and Ormerod naturally compared him with Van Leiden.[16]

Error on the Right and Left: Henoch Clapham's Dialogues, 1608

Similarly the Anglican pastor of the English Church in Amsterdam, Henoch Clapham, produced two dialogues against schism the year before Smyth's self-baptism.[17] In one of these, the main character, Flyer, a Separatist Puritan, is travelling to Middelburg, in Zeeland, and meets with a Malcontent, a Dutch Anabaptist from Norwich, a Legatinearrian – another name for the Seekers – , a Familist, and finally a Mediocritie, Clapham's voice.[18] It is important to

---

[15] Ormerod, *The picture of a puritane*, 67-68.
[16] Ormerod, *The picture of a puritane*, 75-79. On Hackett, see A. Walsham, "'Frantick Hacket': Prophecy, Sorcery, Insanity, and the Elizabethan Puritan Movement," *Historical Journal*, 41 (1998), 27-66.
[17] Henoch Clapham, *Errour on the right hand, through a preposterous zeale acted by way of dialogue. betweene 1 mal-content and flyer. 2 flyer and anabaptist. 3 anabaptist, & legatine-arrian. 4 flyer and legatine-arrian. 5 flier, legaine-arria[n] & familist. 6 flyer and familist. 7 flyer and mediocritie. whereto is also added, certaine positions touching church and antichrist: As without the true holding thereof, it is impossible for a zelous soule, to auoyde either schisme or faction* (London: W. White, 1608).
[18] Clapham, *Errour on the right hand*, 17-20. The Anabaptist was a member of the Dutch Church in Norwich whose eyes were opened to join the purely Christian congregation that had split from the Brownists, and which is commonly termed Anabaptism. Clapham relies

note here that Legatine-arrian would become an alternative term for the Seekers, a movement which became visible around 1620. At the time of Clapham's dialogue, there was an informal following of the Legate brothers, especially Bartholomew, who was executed for heresy in 1612. This was a diffuse spiritualistic group who taught the importance of the invisible church and the quest for inner spirituality. Clapham is therefore writing before the Seekers movement had coalesced around Legate's martyrdom. It seems quite possible then, that Clapham's Legatine-arrian was actually an amalgam of Dutch and English spiritualistic groups intended to give more coherence to the informal group of supporters of Legate. For example, as Flyer converses, he becomes persuaded to join each group in turn, descending from Anabaptist sectarians into the Spiritualism of Legatine-arrian – who argues for an entirely invisible church – and the Familist who internalizes the supernatural world, including Christ himself, to the human mind.[19] Legatine-arrian notes that "some of our late Brownistes are entered into that Familie," thereby associating Separatist Puritans with the scandal of Niclaes's Family of Love.[20] In the end, Flyer becomes thoroughly confused, and is persuaded by Mediocritie that he should return to unity "with our Church," for if he does not do so, "I must turne Turke" out of shame for his inconstancy in faith.[21]

Clapham's characters were thus shaped not only by English sectarians, but perhaps even more directly by his knowledge of real Dutch dissenters, for the Legatine-arrian

---

on the chronicle of Sleidanus for his treatment of Dutch Anabaptism; ibid., 31. On Legate, see Ian Atherton and David Como, "The Burning of Edward Wightman: Puritanism, Prelacy and the Politics of Heresy in Early Modern England," *English Historical Review*, 120 (2005), 1215–1250.

[19] Clapham, *Errour on the right hand*, 46.
[20] Clapham, *Errour on the right hand*, 46-47.
[21] Clapham, *Errour on the right hand*, 61.

is reminiscent of the contemporary Dutch Spiritualist and former Mennonite Robbert Robbertsz le Canu, who at that very moment was causing a stir in the Republic for his satires on all churches and for arguing that they were merely doors through which individuals could enter into the true, invisible church.[22] In turn, Clapham's transposition of Dutch Spiritualism onto the English scene may have helped give the actual Legatine-arrians a clearer sense of purpose and spiritualistic ecclesiology.

John Smyth's Self-Baptism in 1609: Reaction and Inspiration, 1609-1620

Even though they despised the label of Anabaptist, the Brownists used it against each other, as the Separatist pastor in Amsterdam Francis Johnson complained. Opposing Smyth's adoption of believer's baptism and association with the Doopsgezinden, Johnson sought to free his group from "the imputation of Anabaptistry, which hath most vniustly been laid vpon vs."[23] In a 1618 sermon, the Amsterdam Brownist Henry Ainsworth (1571-1622) also fretted about Smyth's "marching us among the Anabaptists, for our more disgrace," and accused Smyth of calling Ainsworth, "miserable and Anabaptisticall."[24] In one critique of Smyth's

---

[22] On Robbertsz, see Gary K. Waite "The Drama of the Two Word Debate among Liberal Dutch Mennonites, c. 1620-1660: Preparing the Way for Baruch Spinoza?" in Heal and Kremers, *Radicalism and Dissent*, 118-36, esp. 129-31.

[23] Francis Johnson, *A brief treatise conteyning some grounds and reasons, against two errours of the anabaptists 1. the one, concerning baptisme of infants. 2. the other, concerning anabaptisme of elder people* (Amsterdam: G. Thorp, 1609), 3-4. See also
https://gameo.org/index.php?title=Johnson,_Francis_(1562-1618)

[24] Henry Ainsworth, *A reply to a pretended christian plea for the antichistian [sic] church of rome: Published by mr. francis iohnson a°. 1617*

self-baptism, Richard Clifton (d.1616) defended infant baptism against Smyth's innovation, observing that Smyth had objected to his views being called Anabaptisticall, to which Clifton responded, more or less, that if the shoe fits, he should wear it.[25] Another opponent of Smyth, John Etherington, explicitly called the Dutch Anabaptists (not Mennonites, however) as Smyth's fellows.[26] Other writers claimed that Anabaptists taught that the soul is not immortal, linking them to Sadducees and Atheists as "limmes of sathan."[27] The Puritan preacher Richard Bernard condemned not only Smyth's action, but also that he did so in a "strange Country, among a people of a strange language,

---

wherin the weakness of the sayd plea is manifested, and arguments alleaged for the church of rome, and baptisme therein, are refuted (Amsterdam: Giles Thorp 1620), fol. A2ʳ, 76. On the polemics among English Separatists in Amsterdam, see also Sprunger and Sprunger, "The Church in the Bakehouse," esp. 244-51.

[25] Richard Clyfton, *The plea for infants and elder people, concerning their baptisme, or, A processe of the passages between M. iohn smyth and richard clyfton wherein, first is proved, that the baptising of infants of beleevers, is an ordinance of god, secondly, that the rebaptising of such, as have been formerly baptised in the apostate churches of christians, is utterly unlawful, also, the reasons and objects to the contrarie, answered : Divided into two principal heads, I. of the first position, concerning the baptising of infants, II. of the second position, concerning the rebaptising of elder people* (Amsterdam: Gyles Thorp, 1610).

[26] John Etherington, *A description of the church of christ, with her peculiar priuiledges, and also of her commons, and entercommoners with some oppositions and answers of defence, for the maintenance of the truth which shee professeth: Against certaine anabaptisticall and erronious opinions, verie hurtfull and dangerous to weake christians. maintained and practised by one master iohn smith, sometimes a preacher in lincolneshire, and a companie of english people with him now at amsterdam in holland. whome he hath there with himselfe rebaptised* (London: W. Stansby, 1610), 9.

[27] John Jackson, *The soule is immortall, or, certaine discourses defending the immortalitie of the soule against the limmes of sathan to wit, saducees, anabaptists, atheists and such like of the hellish crue of aduersaries* (London: W.W., 1611), titlepage.

where they spend all, are pinched with pouertie, and liue among Schismatickes, Heretiques, Papists, Turkes, Iewes, Arians, Anabaptists, and among people of an ill disposition, onely to auoide some corruptions here."[28] Following a well-worn path of English bemusement over the Dutch religious scene, Bernard asserts that Smyth's arguments "proue himself a Jew, a Turke, a Papist, a Brownist, an Hereticke: for in some things hee agreeth with them all, and with Arrians and Familists his next neighbours in his Anabaptisme."[29] The Dutch environment was thus leading English dissenters into a labyrinth through which they move from "Brownisme to Anabaptisme, from this to Familisme," and eventually to becoming "an Antichristian Papist."[30]

Such slippery-slope polemical characterizations may have in fact inspired the very rebaptizing activity that they condemned. In a 1600 work, Clapham had referred to a fellow who "baptizeth himselfe … and then he baptizeth other."[31] He expands on this alleged incident in his second

---

[28] Richard Bernard, *Plaine euidences the church of england is apostolicall, the separation schismaticall. directed against mr. ainsworth the separatist, and mr. smith the se-baptist: Both of them seuerally opposing the booke called the separatists schisme. by richard bernard, preacher of the word of god at worsop* (London: T. Snodham, 1610), 5.

[29] Bernard, *Plaine euidences*, 55. On English views of the Dutch, see Andrew Taber, "'You May Be What Devil You Will': Depictions of Dutch Religious Plurality in English Print, 1609-1699" (MA Thesis, University of New Brunswick, 2018); and Benjamin J. Kaplan, *Muslims in the Dutch Golden Age: Representations and Realities of Religious Toleration* (Amsterdam, 2007).

[30] Bernard, *Plaine euidences*, 56, 169, 184.

[31] Henoch Clapham, *Antidoton or a soueraigne remedie against schisme and heresie: Gathered to analogie and proportion of faith, from that parable of tares. matth.13. aug.ep.3.nullorum disput.&c. we ought to haue no men their disputations (although men catholike and praise worthie) in that count as we haue the canonicall scriptures: So that it should be vnlawfull for vs to improue and refuse some things in their writings, if happily we finde that they thought otherwise then the truth hath. such a one*

dialogue from 1608, in which he has "Libertine" defend religious diversity by saying,

> And therefore [it is] lawfull for me to heare Papist, Protestant, Anabaptist or any that so professe. This point I learned of a William, that sometimes liued in Netherland; who running from the English Church here, to the Brownist; from the Brownist to a particular faction of his owne, wherto he did baptize himself; from that to one sect of the Anabaptists, where they baptized him againe, from that to another sect of the Anabaptists etc, finding no rest in any, till he settled ... to heare all, to walke with all, and to hold all true Christians confessed Christ as afore.[32]

If this story is true, then Smyth was not the first to self-baptize and then join a Mennonite community. Or, perhaps Clapham was, despite himself, a prophet? Or, it is entirely possible that Clapham's polemical account of how believer's baptism had to begin gave Smyth the idea to take this step. This work was composed, after all, by an English pastor in Holland and published a mere year before Smyth's action, and would have been available to Smyth, who in fact mentions Clapham by name in his 1609 defence of his act of self-baptism.[33]

---

am I in other mens writings, and so would I haue others to vnderstand of my writings (London: Felix Kingston, 1600), 30.

[32] Henoch Clapham, *Errour on the left hand, through a frozen securitie howsoeuer hot in opposition, when satan so hears them. acted by way of dialogue. betw. 1 malcontent and romanista. 2 mal-content romanista & libertinus. 3 malcontent and libertinus. 4 malcontent and atheos. 5 malcontent and atheoi. 6 malcontent & the good & bad spirit. 7 malcontent and mediocrity* (London: N. Okes, 1608), 22-23.

[33] John Smyth, *Paralleles, censures, observations aperteyning: To three several writings ...* (Middelburg, 1609), 5.

Leonard Busher's *Religions Peace*, 1614

Several other English Baptists wrote against the Anabaptist label. In 1615 an anonymous writer published in the Dutch Republic a dialogue against persecuting those "falsely called Annabaptists" and against any coercion in matters of faith.[34] This dialogue was likely shaped by the works of Dutch Mennonites, such as the 1609 tract *Religions Freedom* by the conservative Mennonite Pieter Jansz Twisck, in which he trumpeted the value of the Dutch approach to religious diversity. One of the English Baptists living in Holland and who was in fact financially supported by the Doopsgezinden, Leonard Busher, produced his own version in the year 1614, *Religion's Peace: or a plea for liberty of conscience* encouraging King James I to follow a Dutch-style freedom of conscience for all peaceable Christians, Jews, Turks, and even pagans.[35] In this work, Busher argues that compulsion in religion leads only to forcing people to "dissemble their religion, as for example the Iewes in Spaine and Portugale, and the Papists, Reformists, and others in England."[36] He concludes that "perseqution for difference in religion is a monstrous and cruel beast, that destroyeth both Prince and people,

---

[34] *Obiections: Answered by way of dialogue wherein is proved by the law of god: By the law of our land: And by his maties many testimonies that no man ought to be persecuted for his religion, so he testifie his allegeance by the oath, appointed by law* (n.p.: n.p., 1615).

[35] Leonard Busher, *Religions peace or A reconciliation, between princes & peoples, & nations* (by leonard busher: Of the county of gloucester, of the towne of wotton, and a citticen, of the famous and most honorable city london, and of the second right worshipfull company) supplicated (vnto the hygh and mighty king of great brittayne: Etc: And to the princely and right honorable parliament) with all loyalty, humility and carefull fidelity (Amsterdam: n.p., 1614). See Rodolphe Peter, Martin Rothkegel und William H. Brackney, *Clemens Ziegler. Christoph Freisleben, Leonhard Freisleben. Leonard Busher* [Bibliotheca Dissidentium 30] (Baden-Baden/Bouxwiller, 2016), 197-223.

[36] Busher, *Religions peace or A reconciliation*, 8.

hindereth the gospell of Christ, and scattereth his Disciples that professe and witnes his name," while "permission of conscience in difference of Religion saveth both Prince and people, for it is a meeke and gentle lamb, which not onely furthereth and advanceth the gospel, but also fostereth and cherisheth these that professe it, as may bee seene by the permission of the Princesse *Elizabeth*: and others that were permitted and fostered in Dutchland at that time."[37]

In crafting his arguments and citing examples, Busher borrowed heavily from Twisck's *Religions Freedom*, although Busher was certainly more millenarian-inclined than the Mennonite.[38] It is interesting to note that a London printer produced another edition of this work in 1646, during the Civil War, with a slightly different title and with a foreword that emphasized Busher's critique of the state church over his gentler pleas for toleration, arguing that had Busher's critique of the bishops been taken seriously by King James I, the Civil War could have been avoided. The writer of the foreword, an H. B., also uses Busher's work to criticize those who oppose complete freedom of religion, such as "you my Brethren in the Presbyterian way," telling them that peace will come to England only when the persecution of dissent ends. He hopes that they "will abate much of your misguided eagernesse in prosecuting your conscientious Brethren," following St Paul who before his conversion followed his zeal to persecute the saints, thinking "hee did God good service

---

[37] Busher, *Religions peace or A reconciliation*, 14.
[38] Gary K. Waite, "'Turning Turke the Anabaptist Way': Muslims, Jews, Christian Spiritualists, and Polemical Discourse in the Dutch Republic, c. 1570 to c. 1630," in *Global Reformations: Transforming Early Modern Religions, Societies, and Cultures*, Nicholas Terpstra, ed. (London, 2019), 73-94; on Busher's eschatological perspective, see Brackney, *Leonard Busher*, 198-99.

in the suppression of a rising Sect" that opposed the religious establishment at the time.[39]

While Busher led a fellowship distinct from Smyth's and seems not to have joined the Doopsgezinden as Smyth sought to do, Busher's inner world was clearly shaped by living in the context of Dutch culture, never mind a Doopsgezind community. So, even though Smyth and his fellow English Baptists fought vigorously against being associated with Anabaptism, they were deeply enmeshed in its contemporary variants, while adopting and adapting the practice of believers' baptism and absorbing Dutch Doopsgezind attitudes toward religious freedom and tolerance. Returning to our anonymous 1615 dialogue, we note that its author concludes with a plea to stop using such polemical terms against those who disagree with them, including labels like "schismatique, Brownist, Annabaptist and what not," for they do not allow for important differences of opinions; he, for one, does not hold to the Anabaptist "Celestial Flesh doctrine" and approves of Christians holding civic office, yet is still called Anabaptist.[40] And, the author realizes that the blurring of such important distinctions is the polemicist's goal of deterring people from heterodoxy.

However, his pleas went unheeded. In a work two years later, a John Terry asserted that "the Anabaptists, as all other heretikes are after a sort mad men, and haue lost a sound mind."[41] This was, like so many other aspersions, one

---

[39] Leonard Busher, *Religions peace: Or, A plea for liberty of conscience. long since presented to king james, and the high court of parliament then sitting, / by leonard busher citizen of london, and printed in the year 1614. wherein is contained certain reasons against persecution for religion, also a designe for a peaceable reconciling of those that differ in opinion* (London: for John Sweeting, 1646), fols. A3^v-A4^v.

[40] *Obiections: Answered by way of dialogue*, 53, 79-80.

[41] John Terry, *The reasonablenesse of wise and holy truth: And the absurditie of foolish and wicked errour* (Oxford: John Lichfield and William Wrench, 1617), 25.

that had been attached to the Anabaptists from the early days of the movement, thanks to the ecstatic behaviour of a few of their number, such as the naaktloopers, whom judicial officials pondered must be possessed or mad.[42]

Polemics in the lead up to the Civil War, 1620-1640

Such polemical exaggerations against Anabaptists continued apace through the next two decades (1620-1640), during which 431 works mentioning "Anabaptist" were published in England. Overall, these continued the kind of distortions of Anabaptist beliefs and activities that writers were on the search for to fit them into the English scene, and to attack Puritans believed to be extremists. For example, in 1630 the learned Oxford Anglican preacher Giles Widdowes – who tutored William Prynne, and later engaged in disputes with him – published a sermon on the "schysmatical puritan" as a means of defending High Church policies and rites.[43] In it he identified ten types of these problematical Protestants: Perfectists, factious Sermonists, Separatists, Anabaptists, Brownists, Lovesfamilists, Precisians, Sabbatarians, Antedisciplinarians, and Presuming Predestinatists. The Anabaptists he identifies are those "whose purenes is a supposed birth without originall sinne." His argument against this stance is rather obtuse, but boils down to a

---

[42] Gary K. Waite, "Naked Harlots or Devout Maidens? Images of Anabaptist Women in the Context of the Iconography of Witches in Europe, 1525-1650," in *Sisters: Myth and Reality of Anabaptist, Mennonite, and Doopsgezind Women ca 1525-1900*, Mirjam van Veen et al., eds. (Leiden, 2014), 17-51, esp. 27-33.

[43] Giles Widdowes, *The schysmatical puritan A sermon preached at witney concerning the lawfulnesse of church-authority, for ordaining, and commanding of rites, and ceremonies, to beautifie the church* (Oxford: John Lichfield, 1630). On Widdowes see https://en.wikisource.org/wiki/Dictionary_of_National_Biography,_1885-1900/Widdowes,_Giles

defence of infant baptism as a necessary counter to Original Sin and as the continuation of circumcision in the New Covenant. In other words, Widdowes has boiled down Anabaptism to its rejection of the doctrine of Original Sin, a doctrine that was absolutely required for all Protestants who believed the Church of England was the New Israel, the chosen people of God. Interestingly, Widdowes also suggested that the Brownists sought to tear down churches in their iconoclastic frenzy "to serue God in woods and fields," while Love Familists taught community of goods, since even labourers were taught only to "meditate on the word" rather than work for their bread.[44]

In an earlier work from 1623 composed by our above-mentioned opponent of Anabaptists, John Etherington, ghostwriting for Edmund Jessop – whose name is on the titlepage – the author lists the many errors of the English Anabaptists. Claiming to have formerly "walked in the said errors" as the Anabaptists, Jessop deeply regrets that he had allowed himself to be "strangely deluded" by them, for their goal was to overturn "the foundation of all Christian religion" and eventually to "destroy the faith of Iesus Christ." He warns that he was extremely close to the ultimate "poysonable" heresy of the Familists, which leads only to blaspheming the word of God and dishonouring Christian life. He was freed finally from these delusions to return to the Church of England and its doctrine, especially justification by faith, original sin, and predestination.[45] The

---

[44] Widdowes, *The schysmatical puritan*, fols. B3^v-B4^v.

[45] [John Etherington], *A discouery of the errors of the english anabaptists as also an admonition to all such as are led by the like spirit of error. wherein is set downe all their seuerall and maine points of error, which they hold. with a full answer to euery one of them seuerally, wherein the truth is manifested. by edmond iessop who sometime walked in the said errors with them* (London: W. Iones for Robert Bird, 1623), "To the Reader," fols. [3^r-3^v]. On the authorship by Etherington, which is accepted by EEBO,

Anabaptist attacks on the state church as the agent of the Antichrist and on a Christian magistracy also merit critique, but Etherington/Jessop is most concerned about the promotion of free will and rejection of Original Sin by these dissidents.[46] And, like so many others, Etherington implies that Anabaptists work with "popish priests and Iesuites" to "sow heresies among the people."[47]

Such examples could be multiplied dozens of times to show how churchmen who opposed sectarism focused on Anabaptism's renunciation of infant baptism and Original Sin to dissuade readers and hearers from following that dangerous path. Some resorted to more extreme rhetoric, such as the London preacher Stephen Denison who in February 1627 preached a sermon at St. Paul's Cross – an open air pulpit located on the grounds of Old St. Paul's Cathedral – which he later printed and dedicated to King Charles I.[48] Denison had earlier argued that Anabaptists were like witches in renouncing their infant baptism (see Chapter 5 below), and here he emphasizes the delusions of "*occaecated* [blinded]" Anabaptist leaders who pretend to speak "from the Oracle of Gods word by an especial insight as they suppose," and who, like the devil did to Christ, come as wolves in sheep's clothing to deceive the faithful; the Familists were "diabolized."[49] Throughout he associates the

---

see Champlin Burrage, "The Antecedents of Quakerism," *The English Historical Review* 30 (1915), 78-90, here 78.

[46] [Etherington], *A discouery of the errors*, 67-68 (Anglican Church as the agent of the Antichrist), and 94 (magistracy).

[47] [Etherington], *A discouery of the errors*, 97-98.

[48] Stephen Denison, *The white wolfe, or, A sermon preached at pauls crosse, feb. 11 being the last sonday in hillarie tearme, anno 1627, and printed somewhat more largely then the time would permit at that present to deliuer wherein faction is vnmasked, and iustly taxed without malice, for the safetie of weake christians: Especially, the hetheringtonian faction growne very impudent in this citie of late yeeres, is here confuted* (London: George Miller, 1627).

[49] Denison, *the white wolfe*, 6, 23.

Anabaptists with the Familists, describing both as "very idiots" who "brabbling against Learned Ministers" shut their eyes to the truth of "sound Diuinitie."[50]

Despite these statements against ignorant Anabaptists, Denison's polemic was actually aimed at John Etherington's aforementioned work against John Smyth, as Denison argues that Etherington was merely using his anti-Smyth tract of 1610 to "very cunningly" insert "his owne familisticall errors," including his plea for "the liberty of Conuenticles." Denison asserts that Etherington was as much a Separatist as Smyth, just subtler in his approach.[51]

Some writers continued to refer to Anabaptist Münster, such as the preacher Samuel Torshell in 1632 who warned that the Anabaptists "reject all law," and were thus mad from "a disease begun in the distempered heads of *Iohn of Leiden*, and the mad men of Munster*," which Luther had zealously opposed.[52] Among those beliefs Torshell focused on was the

---

[50] Denison, *the white wolfe*, 28.

[51] Denison, *the white wolfe*, 43-46. Denison here also notes that Etherington was the author of *A discouery of the errors* (p.45).

[52] Samuel Torshell, *The three questions of free iustification. christian liberty. the use of the law explicated in a briefe comment on st. paul to the galatians, from the 16. ver. of the second chapter, to the 26. of the third* (London: I. Beale, for H. Overton, 1632), 67-68. A search for works citing both Anabaptist and Münster (Munster) produced 58 results, but many of these refer to the author Sebastian Munster, rather than the Anabaptist city, while others are historical accounts. Another exception is Sebastian Benefield, *A commentary or exposition vpon the first chapter of the prophecie of amos deliuered in xxi. sermons in the parish church of meysey-hampton in the diocese of glocester* (London: Iohn Hauiland, 1629), 88, who refers to some of the infamous events of the kingdom, including that of the woman who, inspired by the biblical account of Judith who beheaded Holofernes and thus ended the siege of Jerusalem, attempted to sneak into the camp of the Archbishop of Münster to deliver the Anabaptists. Although Benefield does not identify her, she was Hille Feicken who was caught and executed before entering the camp. Waite, "Naked Harlots," 37-38. Other referrals to

alleged perfectionism of the Anabaptists, which he called "Pure Sinlesse Anabaptists." Yet this use of Anabaptist Münster seems to have been relatively rare in the two decades leading up to the Civil War, and the tone of these polemics much less extreme than those centred around Smyth's baptism, and certainly so than those which would appear in the 1640s, as we now shall see.

Anabaptist Münster include Joseph Hall *The works of ioseph hall doctor in diuinitie, and deane of worcester with a table newly added to the whole worke* (London: John Haviland, Miles Flesher, and John Beale, for Nath. Butter, Thomas Pavier, Miles Flesher, John Haviland, George Winder, and Hanna Barret, 1625), which, for example, mentions "those phanaticall Anabaptists of Munster" who burned all books apart from the bible (p. 413).

Chapter 4
Anabaptism and Interregnum Polemics, 1640-1650: The Era of the Heresiographers

With the end to royal oversight over religion in England in 1642, concern over Anabaptism increased dramatically in English publications, as Puritan, Anglican, and Catholic writers saw Anabaptism bubbling back to the surface in a dizzying array of new sects that were replicating the very ideas and practices they had been condemning for decades. As noted above, between 1620 and 1640, these writers had produced over 400 publications referencing the term "Anabaptist." In the two decades of the Civil War and Interregnum, they published no fewer than 2,000 such works. Featley's *The Dippers dipt* was one of the most prominent of these, and that it went through several editions until the Restoration in 1660 indicates its popularity. It was part of a very large body of heresiographical works attacking the contemporary new religious movements by association with heresies both ancient and modern, especially those on the continent.

Thomas Edwards' *Gangraena*, 1646

The London Presbyterian Thomas Edwards' *Gangraena*, published in three parts in 1646, was the most comprehensive of these; in his justification for his very large project, Edwards noted that in the work of his predecessors, such as Ephraim Pagitt's *Heresiography* of 1645 (to which we will return), the author "relates more then any late Authors, but many of them are of the old Anabaptists, and old

Sectaries of other Countries rather then of the new, and of this Kingdom," while other writers focused on the Familists in New England.[1]

Edwards therefore does not utilize the continental examples of Anabaptists to quite the same extent as other polemicists. It has been suggested that Edwards may have been influenced in his project by the earlier treatise by the Dutch Calvinist Johannes Cloppenburg (1592-1652), titled *Gangraena theologiae Anabaptisticae* of 1625, especially since this Latin work was cited by two major polemicists, the Scots Presbyterian Robert Baillie and English Puritan William Prynne.[2] Yet, apart from the title, the two works are decidedly different. Cloppenburg's is a long critique of virtually every theological point held by contemporary

---

[1] Edwards, *The first and second part of gangræna*, 3. See also Thomas Edwards, *The third part of gangræna. or, A new and higher discovery of the errors, heresies, blasphemies, and insolent proceedings of the sectaries of these times; with some animadversions by way of confutation upon many of the errors and heresies named. ... briefe animadversions on many of the sectaries late pamphlets, as lilburnes and overtons books against the house of peeres, M. peters his last report of the english warres, the lord mayors farewell from his office of maioralty, M. goodwins thirty eight queres upon the ordinance against heresies and blasphemies, M. burtons conformities deformity, M. dells sermon before the house of commons; ... as also some few hints and briefe observations on divers pamphlets written lately against me and some of my books* (London: for Ralph Smith, 1646), fol. *3ᵛ; and Ephraim Pagitt, *Heresiography, or, A discription of the hereticks and sectaries of these latter times* (London: W. Wilson for John Marshall and Robert Trot, 1645), fol. A2ᵛ, which cites Sleidanus, Lambertus Hortensius, and other continental authors.

[2] Ann Hughes, "Thomas Edwards's *Gangraena* and heresiological traditions," in Marshall and Loewenstein, *Heresy, Literature and Politics*, 137-59, here 156 n.6. There was a Dutch translation, which I have used here: *Gangraena Theologiae Anabaptisticae, Dat is: Cancker van de leere der Weder-dooperen: Ontdeckt uyt hare eygene Schriften: [tot bewijs dat hare Bekentenisse A° 1624. Uytgegeven/ enckel bedecking der schande is.] Met een Teghen-gift, der ghesonde Woorden Godes* (Amsterdam: for Hans Walschaert, 1625).

Mennonites, with occasional references to early Anabaptism. As with the disputations held between Calvinists and Mennonites in the sixteenth century, this is a detailed theological work. Furthermore, Cloppenburg relies heavily upon the publications of the Mennonites themselves, including Menno, and later writers. And finally, our Dutch Calvinist's tone is extremely critical of Mennonites, but he does not stoop to the same level of scandal-mongering as would Edwards in his attacks on English nonconformists. If Edwards had read *Gangraena Theologiae Anabaptisticae*, he mined it mostly for its title.

That said, in the third volume of *Gangraena* Edwards takes issue with the "Sectaries" of his day denying the validity of the "stories of the old Anabaptists in Germany *written by* Sleydan, Bullinger, Lambertus Hortens ... and other worthy men," for these provided extremely useful warnings for his own day. Like so many other writers of heresiography, Edwards seeks to blur the distinctions among the many various religious groups, past and present, as a means of dissuading readers from sampling any form of religious diversity. For him, the only sane path was the one that followed the Church of England, despite the fact that for Catholics, Protestantism in general was itself heresy. And, as we shall see, some polemicists, such as William Prynne, were not averse to utilizing those very same Catholic sources in their fevered efforts to demonize religious dissent. Here we will sample from only a few of the more prominent heresiographical works to get a sense of their approach as it related to Anabaptism, beginning with Ephraim Pagitt's 1645 work that essentially created the name for this genre of anti-dissent propaganda, *Heresiography*. It needs first to be noted that these Presbyterian and Congregationalist writers, who opposed the high church Anglican episcopacy but who sought a national church, condemned Anabaptism so strongly as a means of distinguishing their ecclesiastical positions from those of even more extreme dissenters who were also critiquing the state church. We will see again and again their efforts, as Andrew Crome puts it, "to differentiate themselves clearly from the 'radicals', and to profess loyalty to both the English authorities and to established reformed tradition."[3] This was a fine tightrope to walk, and while they may have succeeded by 1660, at least in ensuring that they would not be prosecuted as dangerous heretics, the rhetoric that they used also took on a life of its own, with harmful, real world impacts, some of it clearly unanticipated.

Ephraim Pagitt's *Heresiography*, 1645

For the royalist minister Pagitt, opposition to Independency pushed him to align with the Presbyterians. So great was his fear of uncontrolled religious diversity, despite his natural affinity for the Anglican Church and its hierarchical order.[4] Among the many accusations that Pagitt makes of his "Anabaptists" and Brownists is they focus their recruitment efforts on "silly women" who seek to know more than they should and who are deceived by the "counterfeit holinesse" of the Independents who model their behaviour on the devil who "turneth himself into an Angell of Light."[5] On this point he also sarcastically turns the Family of Love's slogan of being "godded with god" on its head, so that they are instead "divelified like their Father the Divell."[6] The continental Anabaptists offer a warning for England's dissenters who gathered together in their secret meetings, for "the Anabaptists meeting first in Conventicles, surprized

---

[3] Crome, "The Münster Rising," 951.
[4] https://en.wikisource.org/wiki/Dictionary_of_National_Biography,_1885-1900/Pagit,_Ephraim
[5] Pagitt, *Heresiography*, fol. A4^r.
[6] Pagitt, *Heresiography*, fol. B2^r.

Munster: and how hardly Amsterdam escaped them," as Pagitt's source, Lambertus Hortensius, had described, for such heresy spreads even faster than a plague and is more destructive than fire, unless the authorities act to separate the infected from the healthy.[7] Pagitt's language here reveals how the terror of plague outbreaks continued to haunt the imagination of English writers and offered them language to frighten their readers.

Pagitt's history of the rise of Anabaptism is by now familiar to the reader. Luther is a heroic figure against whom the devil instigated a new sect of "certain fanaticall people, who boasted that they talked with God, and God with them, who commanded them to kill all the wicked, … and make a new world" filled exclusively with their own people.[8] With his dreams of slaying the godless, Thomas Müntzer became the major instigator, not only of the peasants' uprising, but of Anabaptism.[9] The apex of this catastrophe was of course the Anabaptist kingdom of Münster, and Pagitt does not hold back in retelling some of Hortensius' stories to make the actors appear as mad as possible, including, of course, Jan van Leiden's beheading of one of his wives, and the sad recourse to cannibalism among the besieged.[10] He then provides extensive if distorted stories of the militant Anabaptists after Münster, the Batenburgers and the followers of Johan Willemsz, who was indeed executed in 1580 for attempting to revive the Münsterite plot of slaying all false preachers and governmental agents on the eve of the

---

[7] Pagitt, *Heresiography*, fol. A2ᵛ. Hortensius wrote his account of Münster in Latin: Lambertus Hortensius, *Tumultuum anabaptistarum liber unus* (Basel: Johann Oporinus, 1548). It was later translated into Dutch, with a number of widely used engravings: *Het Boeck van den Oproeren der Weder-dooperen* (Enkhuizen: Jacob Lenaertsz Meyn, 1614). On the images, see Schroeder, "Heretics and Martyrs."
[8] Pagitt, *Heresiography*, 2.
[9] Pagitt, *Heresiography*, 3-4.
[10] Pagitt, *Heresiography*, 5-9.

establishment of the New Jerusalem.[11] All of Pagitt's detail is to make clear that, even though the Anabaptists began with a show of great holiness and assertions that they would never take up arms or serve in government, their actions at Münster, Amsterdam, and elsewhere, gave the lie to those claims.[12] He of course ignores the fact that Anabaptists took up arms only reluctantly and in the face of serious governmental repression. Anxiety over displeasing God in the Last Days was, I have noted elsewhere, a motivating factor behind the violent actions not only of the Melchiorite Anabaptists, but also of their state persecutors, whose violence far outweighed that of the dissenters, in terms of scale.[13]

After this historical review, Pagitt turns to the errors of the Anabaptists, as recorded by continental writers like Osiander, Bullinger, and the Danish resident of Amsterdam Johan Isaksson Pontanus (1571-1639), whose history of the city of Amsterdam was printed in Latin in 1611, followed by a Dutch edition in 1614 but not an English one.[14] Pagitt tars Anabaptists with a broad brush, implicating all of them in the Melchiorite Incarnation doctrine, the denial of Christ's divinity, the promotion of works for salvation, and their "dream" that prior to the Last Judgement "their Church shall destroy all the wicked, and obtaine a Monarchy, in which the godly shall reigne alone."[15] Their rejection of a Christian

---

[11] For more on these, see Gary K. Waite, "Apocalyptical Terrorists or a Figment of Governmental Paranoia? Re-evaluating the Religious Terrorism of Sixteenth-Century Anabaptists in the Netherlands and Holy Roman Empire, 1535-1570," in *Grenzen des Täufertums / Boundaries of Anabaptism: Neue Forschungen*, Anselm Schubert, Astrid von Schlachta, and Michael Driedger, eds. (Gütersloh, 2009), 105-25.

[12] Pagitt, *Heresiography*, 11.

[13] Waite, "Apocalyptical Terrorists," 122-25.

[14] Johan Isaksson Pontanus, *Rerum et Urbis Amstelodamensium Historia* (Amsterdam: Judocus Hondius, 1611), and *Historische Beschrijvinghe der seer wijt beroemde Coop-stadt Amsterdam* (Amsterdam: Judocus Hondius, 1614). See Waite, *Jews and Muslims*, 151-53.

[15] Pagitt, *Heresiography*, 12.

magistracy and of the taking of oaths was a danger to the survival of a commonwealth, and their alleged polygamy and easy divorce a threat to the family.[16] He then sets about to confute these "Blasphemous and detestable Errors" in detail.[17] In the process of his attacks, he uses language strongly implying that his English contemporaries who are drawn to Independency were following the Anabaptists in believing they were "all Preachers," without learning, meeting "in woods and secret places, and this rather in the night then in the day, darknesse being fittest for their devotions," pleasing "the common people" in "preaching community of goods, every man to bee alike, exemption from paying of Rent, Tribute, and Tythes; putting down of Magistrates; and commonly they raile as if they were mad against the Reformed Preachers."[18] While miracles should be required for such a new religious movement, they cannot do any, "except it be a miracle ... to make halfe-witted men starke mad."[19] Pagitt then turns to how governments have suppressed the movement, focusing on English examples, concluding his section on Anabaptists with a summary of *The Confession of Faith of those Churches which are commonly called Anabaptists* (London, 1644), a document with 52 articles that Pagitt declares "in which you shall finde some Rats bane covered with a great deale of honey."[20] Pagitt's goal is to support a state-mandated, single church that was Protestant in theology, and to suppress alternatives.

Pagitt's reference to community of goods was, as seen already above, a commonplace in anti-Anabaptist polemics by 1645. These attacks on the economic practices of some of

---

[16] Pagitt, *Heresiography*, 13.
[17] Pagitt, *Heresiography*, 13-27. This he follows with an explication of the 39 Articles of the Church of England.
[18] Pagitt, *Heresiography*, 38-39.
[19] Pagitt, *Heresiography*, 39.
[20] Pagitt, *Heresiography*, 43-47.

the Anabaptists – especially the Münsterites and Hutterites – thus predated the rise of the English Levellers which became a public affair with Gerald Winstanley's Diggers movement in 1649/1650. In a recent essay on this controversial group, Ariel Hessayon searched for antecedents and influences, referring to ancient Christian heresies and more contemporary variants, including the Family of Love, which was often accused of practising community of goods, especially the alleged "Family of the mount" sect accused of it in 1638.

There is, however, very little evidence that there was a formal adoption of the practice by any of these English groups.[21] Noting the biblical passages advocating the practice, especially Acts 2 and 4, Hessayon suggests that indigenous Baptists, Familists, and other Separatists emphasized communal support in their gatherings. He also affirms that community of goods was formally attacked as an Anabaptist thing, as in the 38th of the 39 Articles of the Church of England of 1563 which condemned the practice as a "false boast of certain Anabaptists."[22] Winstanley himself had, like so many of his fellow dissenters, moved from Puritanism to Separatism, to fellowshipping with the General Baptists, before abandoning outward religious observance altogether, like a Seeker. A visionary experience in late 1648 or early 1649 convinced him to make "a common treasury through righteous communal labor."[23] One possibly important if neglected source of influence on Winstanley and his fellows could very well have been the decades of polemical attacks on Anabaptism as the fountain of community of goods (as well as of community of wives). In

---

[21] Ariel Hessayon, "Early Modern Communism: The Diggers and Community of Goods," *Journal for the Study of Radicalism* 3 (2009), 1-50, esp. 12-15.
[22] Hessayon, "Early Modern Communism," 10.
[23] Hessayon, "Early Modern Communism," 22.

this case, again, the constant warnings that Anabaptist innovations would lead to economic and political change (which polemicists clearly intended to mean chaos and anarchy) might instead have led some readers to consider them more closely as useful for transforming the social life of the realm. The fact that by the middle of the 1640s the dangers of Anabaptist Münster were long past, and groups of Hutterites had been following the biblical mandate of communal living and support quite successfully, meant that the negative stereotyping of community of goods by writers like Pagitt could be readily stripped away, and readers could consider, once again, the biblical references to communal support as a serious matter for the Christian state.

Daniel Featley's 1645 *The Dippers Dipt*

Such broad, comparative treatments of various forms of religious dissent can be dizzying to read and confusing in the mashing together of so many different groups and ideas. So here we will turn to Daniel Featley's more narrowly confined attack on Baptists. Featley was a committed Anglican and royalist who opposed both Catholicism and any form of Protestant dissent, seeing them as linked in a diabolical assault on the true faith. To him, Anabaptists were the most dangerous threat to the English realm, for "they flock in great multitudes to their *Jordans,* and both Sexes enter into the River, and are dipt after their manner with a kind of *spell* containing the heads of their erroneous tenets," ultimately engaging in separatism. "As they defile our Rivers with their impure washings, and our Pulpits with their false prophecies and phanaticall enthusiasmes, so the Presses sweat and groane under the load of their blasphemies." For they not only print "*Anabaptisme,*" but many other most damnable doctrines, tending to carnall liberty, Familisme, and a *medley* and *hodg-podge* of all Religions."²⁴ Not only Featley, but many such writers had already implied that immersive baptism had a sexual component since it required men physically to dip women, as well as men, into the water.

Featley's sentiment is obvious from his illustrated titlepage (see figure1); the images, at the very least, exude sarcasm and extremism. Here he has identified fourteen continental Anabaptist sects, the same listed by the Jesuit Leonardus Lessius (1554-1623) whose 1618 treatise offered that "The Anabaptists differ among themselues in very many things, so as of them there be numbred 14 diuers Sects, distinct both in names, and in points of doctrine."²⁵ It is not just the number of Anabaptist groups that Featley shared with his Catholic opponents, for he, like them, believed that Anabaptism needed to be exterminated, in real terms. He writes: "Now of all Heretiques and Schismatiques the Anabaptist in three regards ought to be most carefully looked unto, and severely punished, if not utterly exterminated and banished out of the Church and Kingdome."²⁶ "Why so serious?" one might ask. His reasons include that they follow the ancient, medieval, and modern heresies in proclaiming the establishment of Christ's kingdom on earth, deny "the substance of Christs humane body made of a woman," and follow the Donatists in rebaptizing.

---

[24] Daniel Featley, *Kataباptistai kataptustoi the dippers dipt, or, the anabaptists duck'd and plung'd over head and eares, at a disputation in southwark: Together with a large and full discourse of their 1. original. 2. severall sorts. 3. peculiar errours. 4. high attempts against the state. 5. capitall punishments, with an application to these times* (London: for Nicholas Bourne, 1645), fols. B2ᵛ-3ʳ. On Edwards and Featley's polemics, see also Crome, "The Münster Rising," 952-54.
[25] Leonardus Lessius, *A consultation what faith and religion is best to be imbraced ... and translated into english by W.I* (Saint-Omer: English College Press, 1618), 180.
[26] Featley, *The dippers dipt*, fol. B1ᵛ.

In sum, in "one Anabaptist you have many Heretiques, and in this one Sect as it were one stock, many erroneous and schismatically positions." Those "Anabaptists" currently in Parliament's army are pushing for full religious toleration, and the right to preach and practice their "Hereticall impieties openly." They prophesy in their conventicles and flock to their Jordan Rivers. Featley seethes at recent publications pleading for an end to interference in matters of conscience and religion. Anabaptism's rejection of the magistracy will, he fears, lead to the undermining of all authority, of the "powers that are ordained of God," and ultimately to anarchy.[27] Such heresy is vermin, a venomous serpent infecting paradise, an obvious allusion to the devil/snake in the Garden of Eden.

Like so many of his fellow Puritans who were fighting to maintain the purity of a national church, Featley knitted together a variety of dissenter groups and ideas into one diabolical threat.[28] Most of Featley's groups were gross exaggerations or even fictional. For example, Thomas Müntzer's following dissipated quickly with the crushing of the Peasants' War. Featley, however, claims that Müntzer had inspired the apostolic community of goods of the "Apostolians," a largely fictional sect.[29] He mentions some real groups, such as the English Separatists; the Hutterite Anabaptists who practiced community of goods; the Mennonites and their predecessors the Melchiorites; and the Münsterites, whom Featley labels the Bucheldians, after Jan Beukelszoon van Leiden. The Georgians were the followers of David Joris whose significant movement was pretty much a spent force by 1550, although his promotion of an end to religious intolerance, his spiritualistic treatment of religious identity, and his internalizing of demons to the human

---

[27] Featley, *The dippers dipt*, fols. B2^v-3^r.
[28] Featley, *The dippers dipt*, 1-18.
[29] Featley, *The dippers dipt*, 31.

conscience, had a profound, long-term influence, hence the demon on Featley's image of Joris. Other sects, like the Hemerobaptists, who supposedly baptized themselves daily, and the Silents, were merely imagined. Most other labels are generic ones used against opponents, such as the Libertines whose major crime was their desire to avoid persecution and to soften the harder edges of Calvinist theology.[30]

Figure 5: Anabaptists walk naked through the Dam at Amsterdam, 1535, by Jan Lucas van der Beek, after a drawing by Bernard Picart, 1723-1818. Courtesy The Rijksmuseum, Amsterdam, RP-P-1911-2920.

---

[30] See Kaplan, *Reformation and the Practice of Toleration*, 46-83.

Figure 6: Anonymous engraver, after lost original 1536 painting by Barend Dircksz, in Lambertus Hortensius, *Van den oproer der weder-dooperen* (Enkhuizen: J.L. Meyn, 1614), 18. Courtesy of the Rijksmuseum, Amsterdam, RP-P-AO-28-5-1(R).

One of the groups that merits closer attention here are the Adamites, who may have included real practitioners in England at the start of the Civil War. Believed to have rejected clothing as a symbol of their restoration to pre-lapsarian innocence, the Adamites were modelled, according to David Cressy, on a few ancient and medieval sects which had practised some form of nudity, most prominently a fifteenth-century sect of the Bohemian Taborites.[31] The story of this small group of Hussites, suppressed in 1421, was, according to Cressy, told in the 1563 edition of John Foxe's *Acts and Monuments*, which was to be found in many parish churches. Yet, since later editions did not include this account, one is left wondering from whence the alleged English Adamites of the 1640s might have gotten the idea. Cressy suggests that public interest in Charles I's sister who was the Queen of Bohemia might have revived the story; yet a more obvious source is hinted at by Cressy when he notes that "naked sectarians were also known to have emerged in the course of the radical reformation in the Low Countries in the sixteenth century." These were, of course, the notorious naaktloopers of 1535. Even though a story of a small group of Anabaptists active on one day in 1535, the naaktlooper incident was told over and over again by our anti-Anabaptist polemicists, who enlarged it into a separate sect, feeding into it elements drawn from the medieval antecedents.

This development is clear from the images above (figures 5 and 6). Figure 5 is an eighteenth-century Dutch print based on an engraving included in the multivolume *The Religious Ceremonies and Customs of All the Peoples of the World* by the engraver Bernard Picart and the author and

---

[31] David Cressy, *Travesties and Transgressions in Tudor and Stuart England: Tales of Discord and Dissension* (Oxford, 1999), 257-58.

publisher Jean Frederic Bernard.[32] Picart's original French caption simply identified the scene as "Adamites of Amsterdam." The version we have here is by the Dutch engraver Jan Lucas van der Beek (1753-1818) whose caption added "the Naaktloopers." The other image (figure 6) was an early seventeenth-century engraving based on a painting by Barend Dircksz which was commissioned in 1536 by Amsterdam's city council for their city hall. While that painting is now lost, it was faithfully engraved in Lambertus Hortensius's 1614 edition *Of the Uproar of the Anabaptists*. By comparing these two images, we can see that Picart has used considerable artistic license in depicting the naaktloopers as a sect of Adamites, moving the scene from an Amsterdam canal street to the city centre, the Dam. For Picart, the specific historical incident of the Anabaptist naaktloopers is obscure, and the image now portrays an organized sect of Adamites. The modern scholars who in 2010 analyzed *The Religious Ceremonies and Customs* seemed unaware of the naaktlooper event, commenting about the picture, "In the case of the enthusiastic Adamites -- of whose existence there is little to no evidence -- their ranting naked in the streets of Amsterdam offered the engraver ... a golden opportunity to depict naked men and women for the delectation of his audience."[33] It seems clear, then, that the Adamites of seventeenth-century English and continental writers were a polemical creation based on a single, infamous event. The idea of the Adamites was so useful, these writers believed, because public nudism implied also sexual perversion. So too, many of them alleged, did adult baptism. Thomas Edwards, for example, sneeringly commented that

---

[32] See Lynn Hunt, Margaret C. Jacob, and Wijnand Mijnhardt, *The Book that Changed Europe: Picart & Bernard's Religious Ceremonies of the World* (Cambridge, MA, 2010), 277.

[33] Hunt, Jacob, and Mijnhardt, *The Book that Changed Europe*, 276.

many such turned Dippers to dip young maids and young women naked, for it was the fittest trade to serve their turns that could be, and no question but it was found out and propagated with so much industry as being fed by lust, that a company of uncleane men under the pretence of Religion, might have thereby faire opportunities to feed their eyes full of adultery in beholding young women naked, and in handling young women naked, being about them in dressing and undressing them.[34]

We can see this propensity to associate believers' baptism with licentiousness in the leering baptiser of the Virgins of Sion on Featley's titlepage (see figure 7).[35]

Figure 7: Featley, *The Dippers Dipt*, closeup of titlepage (see Figure 1). Courtesy of the Cambridge University Library, F.3.117.

---

[34] Edwards, *The third part of gangræna*, 189; see also Hessayon, "Early Modern Communism," 13-14; and Hughes, Gangraena, 91.
[35] On such images, see Waite, "Naked Harlots," and Schroeder, "Heretics and Martyrs." Featley's image certainly implies that rebaptism made virgins more susceptible to sexual abuse.

Featley wrote his treatise while in prison for his royalist sentiments. Here he disputed with his fellow prisoner, the Baptist Henry Denne (1606-1660), and he attacked an anonymous work printed in 1644 defending Baptists from accusations of Anabaptism.[36] Their claims to not clinging to the Celestial Flesh of Christ doctrine or the Anabaptist renunciation of a Christian magistracy notwithstanding, Baptists, Featley asserted, were secretly Anabaptists who would bring the same chaos to England as they had in Germany. Towards the end of his diatribe, he claimed that "for the Anabaptists, all their often washing will neither cleanse their conscience from the guilt, nor their reputation from the staine of carnall impurity. For though they tolerate not Stewes as the Pope doth, yet they allow of plurality of wives, and most uncleane practices under the name of spirituall marriages; nay some of them have not blushed to affirme that none of their Sect can commit adultery."

He then cites the example of two young women at "Sanctogall" (St Gall, Switzerland) who immediately after their "second Baptisme, made ship-wrack of their virginity" because they were told that baptism had "so knit one to the other, that they are all one body." Then Featley turns to Van Leiden their King and Prophet, "though he pretended to never so much holinesse, yet was observed by a souldier in the night to steale from his wives bed, and truckle with the maid," justifying this immoral act with a vision to proclaim polygamy for all of Münster. And then Featley turns to an English case, that of "two false Prophets," the weavers Richard Farnham and John Bull, whom he claims were discovered in London in 1642, although it was six years

---

[36] *The confession of faith, of those churches which are commonly (though falsly) called anabaptists; presented to the view of all that feare god, to examine by the touchstone of the word of truth: As likewise for the taking off those aspersions which are frequently both in pulpit and print, (although unjustly) cast upon them* (London: n.p., 1644).

earlier that Farnham had been arrested for heresy and for bigamous marriage; Farnham died in 1642, and his group seems to have dissipated.[37]

What we have here then is another blatant attempt to blur any distinction among various dissenter groups separated geographically and chronologically by over a century as a means of tarring all Baptists with the brush of Münster's alleged sexual license. It did not matter that Van Leiden's polygamy mandate was inspired by a combination of the need to produce the 144,000 pure children of God in record time and his fear of women acting independently.[38]

The Baptist Samuel Richardson (fl. 1643-58) responded to such libel, condemning Featley's frontispiece and arguing that continental Anabaptism had nothing to do with English groups. It would have been better, Richardson fumes, if Featley "had written his book in their language (if he be not illiterate in it) and sent it into those parts of the world as a means to reforme them." Just because Baptists were siding with Parliament against the crown did not mean they were involved in sedition; it was, in fact, the royalists who were going "about to destroy the Kingdome."[39]

---

[37] Featley, *The dippers dipt*, 209-10; see also Jerome Friedman, *The Battle of the Frogs and Fairford's Flies: Miracles and the Pulp Press during the English Revolution* (London, 1993), 118-20.

[38] Klötzer, "The Melchiorites and Münster," 240-42.

[39] Samuel Richardson, *Some briefe considerations on doctor featley his book, intituled, the dipper dipt, wherein in some measure is discovered his many great and false accusations of divers persons, commonly called anabaptists, with an answer to them, and some brief reasons of their practice* (London: n.p., 1645), 3, 16-18. See also Henry Denne, *Antichrist unmasked in two treatises. the first, an answer unto two pædobaptists, dan. featly, D.D. and stephen marshall, B.D. the arguments for childrens baptisme opened, and answered. the second, the man of sinne discovered in doctrine; the root and foundation of antichrist laid open* (London: n.p., 1645). Denne wrote this rebuttal while in prison, noting that Featley was a fellow prisoner, but "though not for the like Cause," ibid., 3. See also Coffey, "'The Last and Greatest Triumph'," 215-16.

Yet, some of these polemical images proved attractive to those English discontented with the religious, political, and economic status quo. Seekers, Ranters, Adamites(?), Diggers, Levellers, Fifth Monarchy Men, Muggletonians, and Quakers may not have been influenced by contact with continental Mennonites, communitarian Hutterites, or Spiritualists (but they may have), but they didn't need to be to pick up new ideas about religious dissent, sharing of property, levelling of social distinctions, new approaches to secular and religious authority, or the idea that the true church was not the Church of England, but an invisible one that required no external manifestations.[40] These were, as we have seen, extremely prominent features of English polemics against Anabaptism that were hammered again and again into the minds of readers and parishioners. The constant warnings about the dangers of prophetic and visionary enthusiasm sparked interest in the same, as many of the leaders of these new English groups were led by ecstatic prophets. New religious movements of course could arise in ways similar to predecessors without direct influence, thanks to humans behaving in similar ways under similar socio-economic circumstances.[41] But, the story of Dutch Anabaptism told by polemical writers offered plenty of new ideas for the discontented.

I have made this point about Joris's restricting the devil to the inner conscience and the sudden appearance around 1650 of this very idea in the writings of new religious leaders like Lodowick Muggleton just as English polemicists were

---

[40] Como, "The Family of Love and the Making of English Revolutionary Religion"; also Como, *Blown by the Spirit*; Lake, *The Boxmaker's Revenge*; Hessayon, "Early Modern Communism;" and, of course, Hill, *The World Turned Upside Down*.

[41] On the historical analysis of new religious movements, see Michael Driedger and Johannes C. Wolfart, "Reframing the History of New Religious Movements," *Nova Religio* 21 (2018), 5–12, and the other essays in that special issue.

attacking Joris's demonology.⁴² The same could therefore be said about the impact of polemical attacks on Anabaptist community of goods and resistance to godless authority inspiring imitation by the Levellers and Diggers, or the descriptions of Anabaptism's exhilarating eschatological expectations of a new world order inspiring the Fifth Monarchy Men, or Anabaptism's alleged new approaches to marital and sexual relations giving ideas to the Ranters.⁴³

Featley concludes his angry treatise with a section on "the untimely deaths, and fearfull ends of the Ring-leaders of this Sect" in which he joyfully recounts stories from medieval Catholic heresiologies how "*Arius* …came to a most shamefull end … voyding his bowells at his easement"; all such arch-heretics now "suck the very dregs in Hell." He then turns to the Anabaptists "who defiled their first Baptisme by their second, were baptized the third time with their own blood, yet suffered death." Incorrectly identifying Michael Servetus as an Anabaptist, Featley gloats that he was deservedly executed in Calvin's Geneva. The theologian of Anabaptist Münster, Bernhard Rothmann, Featley describes as "that sacrilegious Anabaptist [who] was slaine in Saint Lamberts Church-yard," although Rothmann's body was not found among the slain and he seems to have escaped the slaughter and found refuge in Oldenburg.⁴⁴ Featley observes that "three hundred Anabaptists that fell upon the

---

⁴² Waite, "The Devil of Delft," 472-74. See especially [John Reeve], *A Transcendent Spiritual Treatise* (London: for the authors, [1651]), 24; and also Christopher Hill, "John Reeve and the Origins of Muggletonianism," in *The World of the Muggletonians*, Christopher Hill, Barry Reay, and William Lamont, eds. (London, 1983), 64-110.
⁴³ See Christopher Hill, *Milton and the English Revolution* (New York, 1977). On the Ranters, see esp. Nigel Smith, ed., *A Collection of Ranter Writings: Spiritual Liberty and Sexual Freedom in the English Revolution* (London, 2014), *Perfection Proclaimed*, and "To Network or Not to Network."
⁴⁴ De Bakker, Driedger, and Stayer, *Bernhard Rothmann*, 207.

Monastery of *Bilsward* [Oldeklooster] in *Frizland*, and rifled it, were all of them (save 62 that fled) either killed in the ruines of the Monasterie, or put to death by the hangman." King John of Leiden and his consul Knipperdolling "were tyed to a stake, had their flesh torne from them with hot pinchers, in the end they were stabbed to the hearts, and after they were dead, their bodies were put in iron cages, and hanged on the Steeple of Saint Lambert."[45] And so on.

These are not lessons against religious persecution, but the reverse. The author is revelling in the horrible demise of these heretics, hoping that this would deter anyone from following their lead. Featley himself died in prison in 1645 before he could witness the wild fluorescence of religious diversity to follow. As already mentioned, there were printed responses to Featley's fulminations; that by Richardson associated his anti-Anabaptist rhetoric with Catholic and treasonous attacks on Parliament.[46]

Robert Baillie, Scots Presbyterian and Reader of Continental Works, 1647

Scottish Presbyterians also led the charge in the battle against religious dissidence. We will use one example here, that of the minister and professor at the University of Glasgow, Robert Baillie (1602-1662), who published a learned treatise in 1647 against "Independency, Brownisme, Antinomy, Familisme" troubling the Church of England, all of which he lumped together under the category of Anabaptism.[47] As I have noted elsewhere, Baillie relied

---

[45] Featley, *The dippers dipt*, 218-19.
[46] Richardson, *Some briefe considerations on doctor featley his book*.
[47] Robert Baillie, *Anabaptism, the true fountaine of Independency, Brownisme, Antinomy, Familisme, and the most of the other errours, which for the time doe trouble the Church of England, unsealed. Also the*

heavily on continental works to build his case, and it was his work, rather than Edwards', that was closer in approach to Cloppenburg's. His knowledge of the history of the Reformation in the Netherlands is far more detailed than most of his English and Scottish contemporaries, especially that of the Anabaptists. He read the critical biography of David Joris written by Nicolaas Meyndertsz van Blesdijk, who had married one of the prophet's daughters and become Joris's right-hand man, only leaving the movement a few years before his father-in-law's death in 1556. He became a Reformed minister, and wrote his critical, yet accurate, Latin biography of Joris, but it was only printed post mortem in 1642.[48] Within a few years English and Scottish polemicists like Baillie became more aware of Joris's unusual teachings, especially his demonology, and these become a major focus of their anti-heresy diatribes, culminating in Henry More's fascinating diagnosis of Joris in his 1656 *Enthusiasmus triumphatus*.[49] For his part, Baillie cites the anti-Anabaptist works of continental authors Georgius Cassander, a sixteenth-century Flemish Catholic who sought compromise between Catholicism and Protestantism; the Walloon Calvinist pastor Guy de Bres (1522-67) who also wrote the Belgic Confession of the French Reformed (1561); Bullinger; Blesdijk; Sleidanus; Hortensius; Cloppenburg; and a work he calls *Apocalypsis Haeresiarcharum* but which was the Latin edition of Haestens' illustrated *Abomination of the*

---

questions of paedobaptisme and dipping handled from Scripture (London: for Samuel Gellibrand, 1647).

[48] On Baillie and Blesdijk, see Waite, "The Devil of Delft," 451-55. The best work on Blesdijk remains Samme Zijlstra, *Nicolaas Meyndertsz van Blesdijk. Een bijdrage tot de Geschiedenis van het Davidjorisme* (Assen, 1983).

[49] Henry More, *Enthusiasmus triumphatus, or, A discourse of the nature, causes, kinds, and cure, of enthusiasm ...* (London: J. Flesher, 1656); Waite, "The Devil of Delft," 456-63.

Foremost Head Heretics.[50] He also lists thirty-nine English works, admitting that he relied heavily on Edwards' *Gangrena*.[51]

For Baillie, Anabaptism was a magnet for all unorthodox beliefs, as "the men whom I deal with in this part are Anabaptists, albeit they bring in with themselves both Antinomians, Socinians, Familists, and the most of all the Heretiques of the time."[52] Like many other Protestants he identified the origin of Anabaptism in the radicals around Thomas Müntzer, whom he thinks Luther's lieutenant Phillip Melanchthon treated too mildly. The devil, he notes, worked particularly through the Holy Roman Emperor Charles V in opposing Luther's reform. Even though the Anabaptists made up by far the largest portion of victims of the Emperor's anti-heresy actions, Baillie essentially blames the victims for the chaos that afflicted the German lands, commenting that the "spirit of Mahomet was no more hellish in setting afoot most grosse errors, and countenancing abominable lusts; nor was it any thing so much hellish in making an open trade of bloodshed, robbery, confusion and Catholick oppression through the whole earth, as the spirit of Anabaptisme." Even so, he observes that they began with good intentions, as in the beginning the Anabaptists displayed

---

[50] Baillie, *Anabaptism*, unpaginated [191]. The last is entitled *Apocalypsis insignium aliquot haeresiarcharum: qua visiones & insomnia ipsis per somnia patefactae, blasphemias puta inauditas, ac deliramenta enthysiastica revelantur, unaque opera vitae ac mortes coelo latino donantur : superadditae septendecim eorum, qui insigni supra reliquos temeritate ac depudendi audacia eminere visi, icones aereis expressae* (Leiden: Henrick Lodewijcxsoon van Haestens, 1608).

[51] Baillie, *Anabaptism*, [191]. He cites also Richardson's work against Featley.

[52] Baillie, *Anabaptism*, fol. b4ʳ.

> a great deal more then ordinary piety, zeal, and honesty: in prayer and meditation they were very frequent and long, their discourses were only of matters Divine, the errours and superstitions of the time were to them abominations; for life and conversation, they seemed to be composed of all vertue; in their apparell poor and base; in their behaviour and speech exceeding humble and grave; for charity towards all in want, singularly liberall.[53]

They wanted a new church freed from papacy, and yet their reliance on new revelations, their insistence that believers renounce their first baptism, their opposition to a civic magistracy and promotion of nonviolence and of the equality of all "the sons of *Adam*" and their community of goods began to show their true colours. While as long as they "keeped themselves within these bounds," the orthodox preachers dealt with them through loving disputations. The massive disturbance of the social order that was the Peasants' War (which Baillie, like so many writers, blames on Müntzer and the Anabaptists), changed everything. Even though the rebellion was put down, soon the Anabaptists found a new centre in Münster.

His telling of the reformation in that city is certainly better informed than most of his English fellows, for he observes that the reform of the city was in progress already in 1533 before the Anabaptists arrived, led by "the labours of *Bernard Rotman*" who "cast out the Popish corruptions." It was only then that "the Anabaptists came in and immixed themselves according to their custome," a horror for Baillie, confirming that such "Schismaticks, like drones and wasps" took advantage of the "labours of others," only to spoil the good work that had begun.[54] He then describes the

---

[53] Baillie, *Anabaptism*, 3-4.
[54] Baillie, *Anabaptism*, 5.

developments in the city as relayed in the works of Hortensius and Sleidanus, which of course emphasized the "Anabaptistick ravery." At least in Baillie's treatment, there is a measure of historical basis to his polemic, although his descriptions of the visionary excesses and the "ambition and lust" of Jan van Leiden (Becold) returns his story telling to the polemical extremes of the other works consulted here.[55] He is so well informed that he knows of the activities of the Anabaptist militant Jan van Batenburg, and the several meetings and disagreements among the various leaders in the post-Münster movement, including Batenburg, Menno Simons, and David Joris.[56] He is, however, amazed at the "incredible increase" of Anabaptism, despite its "grievous absurdities" in both doctrine and practice, an increase he says was stopped only by their divisions amongst themselves, a parallel he sees to God confounding sinners at Babel.[57] And even though Menno Simons and his followers renounced the violence and polygamy of the Münsterites and Batenburgers, as well as the revelations of the Melchiorites and "most of the blasphemies of *David George*," against all of whom Menno "did write with passion," yet his "separation from all other reformed Churches to independency" deserved Baillie's scorn, who called it a "wickednesse of that spirit which reigned in *Menno*, and yet rages in his followers, notwithstanding of all their profession of great piety."[58] Baillie, relying on Cloppenburg, then turns to the divisions among the early seventeenth-century Mennonites and their various confessions of faith. These separatists had not been a problem in England, he concludes, and until recently their numbers were small, consisting mainly of "*Dutch* strangers." Now that has changed, because English Independents have

---

[55] Baillie, *Anabaptism*, 10.
[56] Baillie, *Anabaptism*, 12-16.
[57] Baillie, *Anabaptism*, 11-12.
[58] Baillie, *Anabaptism*, 16.

"corrupted and made worse the principles of the old Separatists, proclaiming for errours a liberty both in Church and State; under this shelter the Anabaptists have lift up their head, and increased their numbers, much above all other sects of the Land."[59] Hence Baillie's critique was now necessary, to show the continental roots of the current rise in sectarianism in Britain.

The Rabid Puritan, William Prynne

While Baillie sought to be very careful in his use of Catholic anti-heresy works – for example, correcting Cassander's accusation that Anabaptism was the heir of the Albigensians, whom he thought the "Popish Writers" had unfairly treated,[60] – this was not the case with the Puritan lawyer William Prynne (1600-1669, see figure 8) who in the 1640s and 1650s proved an irascible opponent of religious diversity, targeting Catholicism, new Christian sects, and Judaism.[61] Prynne is a complex and often contradictory figure, author of over 200 publications, ranging from his infamous and massive *Histriomastix* of 1632 attacking drama, to treatises against drinking and the fashion of long hair for men, and of course his many polemical works against episcopacy, Arminian theology (i.e., those who taught freedom of the will in opposition to Calvinism's predestination), Catholicism, and religious diversity in general. Being a strong advocate of governmental control over religion, he yet criticized the crown when it appeared to

---

[59] Baillie, *Anabaptism*, 16-18.
[60] Baillie, *Anabaptism*, 2.
[61] On him see Lamont, *Puritanism and Historical Controversy*, 15-25. Like Como and Lake, Lamont's lively book also reminds readers of the wide range of approaches that the term "puritan" encompasses, since it is a study of three "representative Puritans" in Prynne, Richard Baxter, and Lodowicke Muggleton.

be lax on prosecuting Catholicism. He wanted a Presbyterian-style church structure but with full state oversight and support. Elected to Parliament in 1648, he was an opponent of Cromwell's New Model Army, which had many Independent soldiers. He was quickly imprisoned again, remaining so until February 1653 because he refused to pledge that he would stop opposing the government. He returned to pamphleteering. Here we are of course most interested in what he wrote about Anabaptism. A few years into the Civil War, in 1645, for example, he reminded readers of "the Tragicall Wars and Commotions of the Anabaptists in Germany; whose Opinions where-ever they predominate, are fatall to the Government," a statement to which we shall return.[62]

Prynne's often noxious writings deserve a closer look here, as they were so numerous and diverse they allow us to arrive at a better understanding of the complexity of thinking when it came to polemics against religious diversity, particularly how continental Anabaptism fit into them. A lawyer of Lincolns Inn, Prynne's theology was thoroughly Calvinist – despite his propensity to support the crown – writing works condemning nonconformists whom he linked

---

[62] William Prynne *A fresh discovery of some prodigious new wandring-blasing-stars, & firebrands, stiling themselves new-lights, firing our church and state into new combustions. divided into ten sections, comprising severall most libellous, scandalous, seditious, insolent, uncharitable, (and some blasphemous) passages; published in late unlicensed printed pamphlets, against the ecclesiasticall jurisdiction and power of parliaments, councels, synods, christian kings and magistrates, in generall; the ordinances and proceedings of this present parliament, in speciall: The nationall covenant, assembly, directory, our brethren of scotland, presbyterian government; the church of england, with her ministers, worship; the opposers of independent novelties; ... whereunto some letters and papers lately sent from the sommer-islands, are subjoyned, relating the schismaticall, illegal, tyrannicall proceedings of some independents there* (London: John Macock, for Michael Spark Sr., 1645). [fol. A2^{r-v}], 14.

to what he perceived as the arm of the Antichrist, the Jesuits.[63]

Anabaptists as Secret Jesuit Agents

This strategy of associating Jesuits with various Protestant sects was a popular one, as seen in a contemporary broadsheet image from 1647 which portrays ten separate sects: Jesuits; a Welsh blasphemer named Evins who called himself Christ (presumably the Welsh visionary Arise Evans); Arminians; Arians; Adamites; Libertines taking a pick axe to the Ten Commandments; Antescripturians; Soul sleepers, having a nice doze; Anabaptists in the process of baptizing; Familists; Seekers; and a new one, Divorcers (see Figure 9).

---

[63] Walsham comments on this tactic of spreading "bizarre rumours" during the decades leading up to the Civil War "that Baptists, Brownists, Levellers, Ranters and other sectarians were Jesuits and papists in disguise. The tendency to jumble all deviants into a single category of evil was rooted in an outlook that viewed history in terms of an unending duel between Satan and Christ. It was a time-honoured polemical tactic to discredit a sect by alleging that it was actually in secret league with its own mortal enemies. In the 1540s, Anabaptist refugees were reported to have been sent from Rome as agents of the Pope and Cardinal Pole to disrupt the unity of the Protestant Church in England and the charge of being papist spies was also sometimes levelled at the French and Walloon Calvinist communities." Walsham, *Charitable Hatred*, 204. She further notes that in 1659 William Prynne and others believed that the Jesuits had been responsible for the deposition of Richard Cromwell, who had replaced his father as Lord Protector the year before, and were "in the guise of the Quakers," seeking to buy Whitehall for a seminary. Walsham, *Charitable Hatred*, 204-206.

Mr: William Prynne, for writing a booke
against Stage-players called Histrio-mastix
was first censured in the Starr-Chamber to loo
se both his Eares in the pillorie, fined 5000ᵗ & p
petuall imprisonment in the Towre of Londo
After this, on a meer suspition of writing oth
bookes, but nothing at all proved against him,
hee was again censured in the Starr-chamber
loose the small remainder of both his eares
the pillorie, to be Stigmatized on both his Cheek
with a firey-iron, was fined again 5000ᵗ and ba
nished into yᵉ Isle of Iersey, there to suffer perp
tuall Close-imprisonmᵗ. no freinds being pe
mitted to see him, on pain of imprisonment

Figure 8: Wenceslaus Hollar, portrait of William Prynne, The Wenceslaus Hollar Collection, Hollar-k-1216, courtesy of the Thomas Fischer Rare Book Room, University of Toronto.

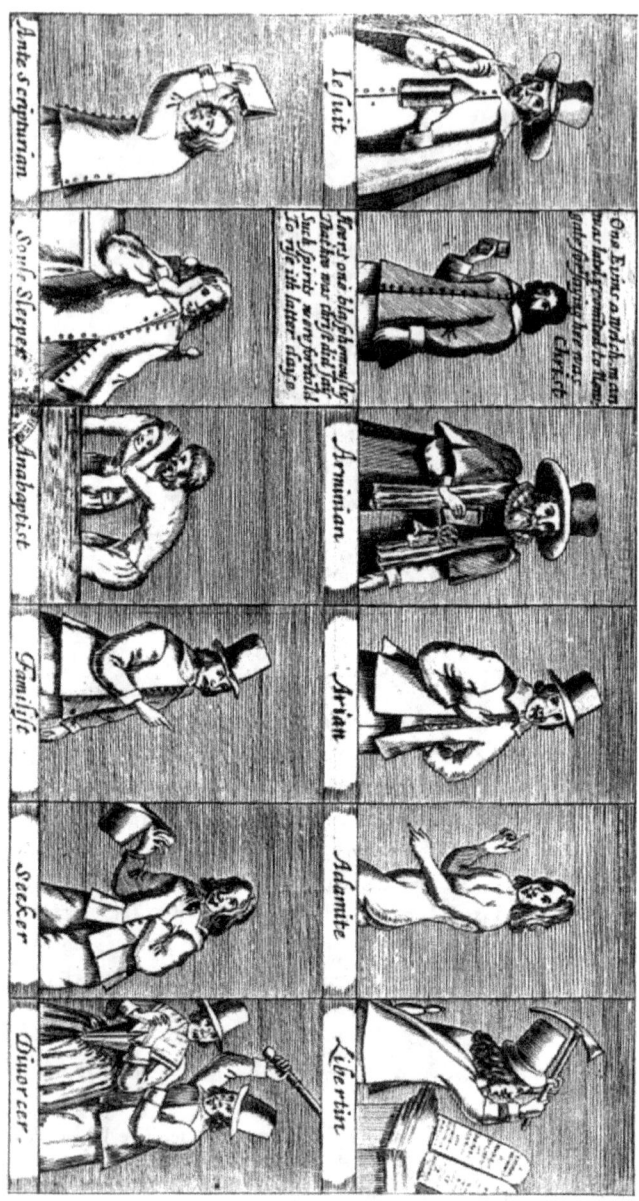

Figure 9: A Catalogue of the Severall Sects and Opinions in England and other Nations: With a briefe Rehearsall of their false and dangerous Tenents, broadsheet, 1647; public domain, https://commons.wikimedia.org/wiki/File:Catalogue_of_Sects.GIF

The text itself also satirizes Socinians, Pelagians, Separatists or Independents, Anti-Sabbatarians, Anti-Trinitarians, Apostolicks (who expect a new revealed way outside of scripture), Thraskites (a Christian group which followed Jewish law), Hetheringtonians (who called the English Church false), and a couple ancient sects apparently revived in the Tatians and Marchionites.[64] As for the Anabaptists, the author waxed poetical in writing that

> Poore men contrive strange fancies in the braine,
> To cleanse that guilt which is a Leopard staine:
> 'Tis but a fain'd conceit, contended for,
> Since water can but act its outward matter:
> Regenerate, new-born; these babes indeed
> of watry Elements have little need.

The Jesuits are worse, for their aim "by hellish wiles the States to ruine bring, My Tenents are to murder Prince or King." Since, the writer notes, the "Roman Papall State doth totter," he is framing his "sly-conceits" to work better, presumably through the other sects listed. These included the Anabaptists, whose responsibility it seems was to encourage people to abandon morality and ecclesiastical order:

> Be in Christ and sin if thou canst; meaning, that regenerate men cannot sinne; this is the Doctrine of the Anabaptists: also that to receive the Communion with a prophane person, is to partake of his sinne; that the Lords Prayer was never taught to be said; that the Gospell was never purely taught since the Apostles times; that a liberty of Prophecying must

---

[64] *A catalogue of the several sects and opinions in england and other nations with a briefe rehearsall of their false and dangerous tenents* (London: R.A., 1647).

be allowed; that all humane Lawes must be abolished; that Ministers of Gods Word should rule both the Spirituall and the Temporall; that distinction of Parishes is Antichristian.

The writer concludes with a plea to Parliament to create an ordinance to prevent the spread of such heresy.

Prynne: Punishment and Polemics

Returning to Prynne, one is left wondering how his personal experience with state censorship and punishment for his opinions affected his thinking about other persecuted groups. It seems in fact to have had a rather contradictory effect on him. In 1634 he was punished by the Star Chamber for publishing *Histriomatrix*, a work that condemned contemporary drama and playhouses; according to the author of the 1660 catalogue of Prynne's works, this censure was "afterwards Repealed as Causelesse" by both houses of Parliament, "and Playes and Playhouses suppressed."[65] This catalogue of titles reveals Prynne's shifting interests nicely. In 1637 he, John Bastwick and Henry Burton were punished (having their ears clipped, the second time for Prynne) for

---

[65] *An Exact Catalogue of all Printed Books and Papers of Various Subjects, Written upon sundry Occasions by William Prynne Esq; a Bencher of the Honourable Society of Lincolns-Inne. Before, During, Since, His Imprisonments* (London: for Michael Sparke, 1643, reprinted for Edward Thomas, by T. Childe and L. Parry, 1660). In 1649 Prynne was still engaged in a polemic against drama in the realm, publishing *A vindication of Wiliam prynne esquire from some scandalous papers and imputations, newly printed and published, to traduce and defame him in his reputation* (London: n.p., 1649). Further on Prynne and his associates, see Lamont, *Puritanism*, and Hughes, *Gangraena*.

attacking Laudian bishops.[66] The catalogue lists Prynne's compositions while in the Tower of London (works printed between 1635 and 1641), which included several attacks on Anglican episcopacy, including one in which he accused prelacy in general as treasonous, as well as diatribes against pastimes on the Lord's Day. While in prison in Jersey in 1641, he wrote *A pleasant Purge for a Roman Catholick to evacuate his euil Humors* (London, 1642), indicating that he was becoming concerned not just about episcopacy, but also shared the Protestant anxiety about the remnants of Catholicism in the realm.

Upon his release, he published a tract blaming the Civil War on King Charles I, yet he also published works defending the rights of kings to control religion, and in 1649 he published a plea to Parliament to spare the king's life.[67] His critique of Charles was not, however, a contradiction of his defence of royal prerogatives over ecclesiastical matters, for in 1643 he clarified that it was Charles I's refusal to apply the laws against the Jesuits that had led to the unnecessary Civil War.[68] Despite the fact that many leaders in the New

---

[66] Lamont, *Puritanism*, 18-20; Walsham, *Charitable Hatred*, 82; Christopher Hill, "Censorship and English Literature," *The Collected Essays of Christopher Hill*, vol. 1, *Writing and Revolution in Seventeenth-Century England* (Amherst, MA, 1985), 32-71, here 37.

[67] William Prynne, *A Soveraigne Antidote to Prevent, Appease, and Determine our Unnaturall and Destructive Civill Wars and Dissentions* (London: A.N., for Richard Lowads, 1642), and *A brief memento to the present unparliamentary juncto touching their present intentions and proceedings to depose and execute, charles stuart, their lawful king* (London: n.p., 1649).

[68] William Prynne, *The popish royall favourite: Or, A full discovery of his majesties extraordinary favours to, and protections of notorious papists, priests, jesuits, against all prosecutions and penalties of the laws enacted against them; notwithstanding his many royall proclamations, declarations, and protestations to the contrary. as likewise of a most desperate long prosecuted designe to set up popery, and extirpate the protestant religion by*

Model Army of Parliament were members of nonconformist groups, including Baptists, Seekers, and Ranters, Prynne continued to attack Independency, beginning seriously in 1644 with his *Independency Examined, Vnmasked, Refuted* (London, 1644), written in response to the proposals of some Independents to establish a new form of church government freed from explicit governmental control. Why, he complains, this would mean

> that every Christian hath a free liberty, by the Law of God, to unite himselfe to what Independent Congregation hee pleaseth; the husband to one Congregation, the wife to another, the children to a third, the servants to a fourth; nay, every distinct person in a family to a severall Church, (and that not onely without, but against the consents of their owne Magistrates, Ministers, Husbands, Parents, Masters, who have no jurisdiction (as some say) over their consciences herein; so as one great family shall be divided into members of twenty or thirty severall Independent Churches, if they please, and those perchance different one from another in their government, opinions, discipline, ceremonies?[69]

---

degrees, in this our realme of england, and all his majesties dominions. manifested by sundry letters of grace, warrants, and other writings under the kings owne signe-manuall, privy-signet, his privy-councels, and secretary windebanks hands and seals, by divers orders and proceedings in open sessions at newgate, in the kings bench, and elsewhere ... / collected and published by authority of parliament (London: for Michael Spark Senior, 1643).

[69] William Prynne, *Independency examined, vnmasked, refuted, by twelve new particular interrogatories: Detecting both the manifold absurdities, inconveniences that must necessarily attend it, to the great disturbance of church, state, the diminution, subversion of the lawfull undoubted power of all christian magistrates, parliaments, synods: And shaking the chiefe pillars, wherwith its patrons would support it* (London: F.L., for Michael

Deeply concerned about the surge in new religious groups in the wake of Parliament's informal ending of censorship, Prynne went on the offensive to make very clear the major implications of such slackness in control over religious affairs; he explained that

> every man will *heap to himselfe Teachers*, and erect Churches after his own lusts: meer Papists and Popishly affected persons, will set up Popish Churches and Priests; Arminians, Arminian Churches and Preachers; Anabaptists, Anabaptisticall Ministers and Assemblies; Arrians, Anti-Trinitarians, such conventicles and Pastors; Libertines, a licentious Church and Ministry; yea, every Heretick, Sectary, or guidy-pated Enthusiast, upon pretext of new Revelations and discoveries of concealed Evangelicall truths, (though when exactly scanned they may oft times prove old errors or meer diabolicall delusions) will erect new Independent Churches of their own (and that for succession and perpetuity to the perverting of infinit soules), uncontroulable, unsuppressible by any Ecclesiasticall or Civill authority: And thus in few moneths, or yeares space at least, through Satans instigations, our owne depraved judgments, (a verse to unity, piety, purity, but *prone to Errour, Heresie, Schismes, lyes yea lying phantasies*) and through defect of a severe coercive power, in Ecclesiasticall Synods-Parliaments, temporall Magistrates, (who as some new Independent Lights informe us, have no coercive power to suppresse these springing heresies, but onely by a non-communion with or refuting them by the word to which they will

---

Sparke Senior, 1644), 4-5. The orphaned round bracket is original with Prynne.

> obstinately refuse to hearken, as deeming their own opinions most divine:) we shall have almost as many severall heresies, sects, Churches, as there are families, persons; ... Yea, if they thus admit every Minister, or secular person, to have a divine right, freedom, to set up such an independent Church and government as he pleaseth; then by the self-same reason, they must have a like liberty to elect erect, what civill forme of government they please; to set up a new Independent Republike, Corporation Kingdome, Magistracy, in every family, parish, city, county, and to cast off all former civill Governours, Governments, Lawes at pleasure, as well as Ecclesiasticall; there being the selfe-same grounds both of obligation, obedience to, and exemption from the one as other.[70]

Here, then, we see Prynne trying desperately to push back the rising tide of religious variety by arguing that such diversity in religious affairs will lead necessarily to the undoing of civil governance and its replacement with anarchy.

He thus became an even more trenchant defender of governmental authority over ecclesiastical affairs, in 1645 producing *Truth triumphing over Falshood, Antiquity over Novelty; Or, A Seasonable Vindication of the Vndoubted Ecclesiastical Jurisdiction, Right, Legislative and Coercive power of Christian Emperors, Kings, Magistrates, parliaments, in matter of Religion, Church Government, Discipline, Ceremonies, Manners* (London 1645). The following year he wrote his appeal to Parliament to oppose "some *Anabaptisticall Independent Sectaries,* and *New-lighted FIRE-BRANDS*" who were plotting against Parliament and whose

---

[70] Prynne, *Independency examined,* 5-6.

efforts would lead the realm inexorably into chaos.[71] He begins this treatise proper with quotations drawn from a letter that he had received from one of the Independent ringleaders, John Lilburne, who had criticized the lawyer for spending "a great deale of paines in citing old rusty Authors" to prove that kings, councils and magistrates had authority over religious affairs (as we shall see, this would not be the only time that Prynne would be accused of using old, musty tomes to support his arguments).[72] It is in this work where we first quoted Prynne's warnings about the "Tragicall Wars and Commotions of the Anabaptists in Germany," and it is worth citing the entirety of this passage:

> but these *New furious Sectaries:* who to engage all sorts of people in their *Quarrell,* proclaim a free *Toleration* and *Liberty of Conscience,* to all *Sects,* all *Religions* whatsoever, be it *Judaisme, Paganisme, Turcisme, Arianisme, Popery;* (as all their Pamphlets manifest) And to interest the female Sex, and draw them to their party, they *(contrary to the Apostles precept)* allow them not only *decisive Votes,* but Liberty of *Preaching Prophesying, speaking* in their Congregations; yea, power to meet in their *Nocturnall Conventicles,* without their *Husbands, Parents, Ministers Privitie,* the better to propagate Christs Kingdome, and multiply the *Godly party:* Which, what confusion and Ataxy it will soon produce in Church and State, if not prevented by your Honours extraordinary speedy *Diligence, Wisdome, Power,* I humbly submit to your deepest Judgements.

At this point he turns to the continental Anabaptists:

---

[71] Prynne, *A fresh discovery.*
[72] Prynne, *A fresh discovery,* 3.

> I am certain your Honours have read the Histories of the Tragicall Wars and Commotions of the Anabaptists in *Germany;* whose Opinions where-ever they predominate, are fatall to the Government, Magistracy, Ministery of all States, Churches, and bring in *popular Tyranny*, and licentiousnesse, the worst of evils. O then let not your *Honours* Patience or Indulgence to such Anabaptisticall Libellers involve both you, us, our Realm, in like *German popular Sedicions, Devastations, and bloody Massacres,* which they threaten: but if these New seditious Lights and Fire-brands, will needs set up New Churches, Heresies, Church-governments, and vent their new errors or opinions against your Power and Authority, let them doe it onely in *NEW-ENGLAND*, or other *NEW-FOVNDLANDS*, since *OLD ENGLAND* needes them not, unlesse it be to set her all on fire.[73]

There is so much here to untangle. Prynne is worried not just about the potential for anarchy and sedition should the sectarians be allowed to propagate, but he is enraged that these groups allow women to have a voice in their assemblies. They do so under the inspiration of Satan, for, he explains, Independents, many of whom are Anabaptists, fit the bill of Paul's warning of II Tim. 3 about the decline in morality in the Last Days when supposed Christians would instead be lovers of themselves rather than God, forsaking "publike assemblies" in order to "creep into private houses, working principally (as the Devill did at first) upon the weakest Sex."[74] His final sentence in the long quotation above seems to suggest, however, that Prynne would be happy to ship all

---

[73] Prynne, *A fresh discovery*, fols. A2$^{r\text{-}v}$.
[74] Prynne, *A fresh discovery*, 1.

of these Independents to New England and Newfoundland to purge the realm of such noxious poison. Independency is becoming an epidemic, as English "Anabaptistical sectaries" will, he fears, "sodainly involve us in the Germane, Anabaptisticall distractions, insolencies, warres and disolations, recorded by Sleidan and others."[75] Prynne sought to persuade Cromwell to fight against both *Seditious Sectaries*, as against *Rebellious Cavaleers*," to maintain governmental control over a single church, thereby pushing back Catholicism and sectarian chaos both.

Prynne is trying desperately in his works to maintain a church polity that excluded Laudian episcopacy, but which didn't quite get to full Presbyterianism, instead allowing the crown jurisdiction over ecclesiastical matters, as long as this supported a single Protestant (Calvinist) faith and excluded Catholicism. He was walking a very narrow tightrope; in 1647 he published a tract criticizing the actions of Independents within the Army who were seeking to force Parliament to disband the New Militia of London and hand London's munitions over to them; he described these efforts in typical terms as "a *Jesuitical* device of some swaying *Sectaries* and *Independents*; partly for to alienate and divide the City from the Parliament."[76]

---

[75] Prynne, *A fresh discovery*, 14. He also cites Bullinger, Guy de Bres, Daniel Featly's *Dippers Dipt*, among other works.

[76] William Prynne, *New presbyterian light springing out of independent darkness. or VI. important new queries proposed to the army, and their friends and party of the houses; concerning the late ordinance for repeal of the new militia of london, setled by an ordinance of both houses, when full and free, for an whole year, (not yet one quarter expired;) and other late repeals of ordinances and votes; and the high declaration against the intended petition and engagement of the londoners and others, for the speedy settlement of the kingdomes peace: Occasioned by the debates thereof in the common councel in the guildhal on saturday last, the 24 of this instant iuly. discovering the dangerous consequences of repealing ordinances and votes, and the independents, sectaries, and armies plots, to blast the*

The following year (1648) he produced an attack on the Levellers, who sought to eradicate royal governance in favour of a "levelled" House of Commons. In response, Prynne reviewed the long history of England's royal government and why having both houses and the crown remained a bulwark against lawlessness.[77] He followed this work with another one defending the right of Christian magistrates to punish idolatry, blasphemy, heresy, and schism, even to the extreme of capital punishment, a work he directed against "*Donatists, Anabaptists, &c.*"[78] Why? he asks his reader. His answer is that despite the preaching and disputations directed at such heretics, they continue to refuse to be "reformed by the Word," and this risks drawing "down Gods Judgments not only on the persons who are guilty of them, but likewise on the Christian Rulers States and places which permit, tolerate, or not severely punish and suppresse them."[79]

This was the same rationale for the prosecution of Anabaptists in the sixteenth century, and reads like the justification for the witch-trials as described by the great

---

honour, justice, and reputation of this parliament, thereby to dissolve it and all others in it; their false pretences of peace, when they intend nought lesse; and their strange injustice and malice against presbyterians, which will end in their own dishonour and downfal (London: n.p., 1647), 5.

[77] William Prynne, *The levellers levelled to the very ground. wherein this dangerous seditious opinion and design of some of them; that it is necessary, decent, and expedient, now to reduce the house of peeres, and bring down the lords into the commons house, to sit and vote together with them, as one house. and the false absurd, grounds whereon they build this paradox, are briefly examined, refuted, and laid in the dust* (London: T.B. for Michael Spark, 1648).

[78] William Prynne, *The sword of christian magistracy supported, or, A vindication of the christian magistrates authority under the gospell, to punish idolatry, apostacy, heresie, blasphemy, and obstinate schism, with corporall, and in some cases with capitall punishments* (London: R.I. for John Bellamy, 1653; first edition London: John Macock for John Bellamie, 1647).

[79] Prynne, *The sword of christian magistracy*, 1-2.

French legal theorist Jean Bodin in 1580 who asserted that it was an absolute requirement of magistrates to attack such demonic heresy with the utmost zeal, as a means of diverting or appeasing divine anger.[80] And it is furthermore puzzling for the contemporary reader in the light of the fact that Prynne himself had twice been victim of such corporeal punishment and imprisonment for his own expression of dissident views. Obviously, his experiences did the opposite of what might be expected, convincing him that his punishment was a sign that he was on the side of the persecuted godly and/or that such harsh punishment for the expression of dissenting ideas was a good thing. His torture and imprisonment in fact became something of a cause célèbre for the Puritans in their struggle against royal power.[81] His painful experiences clearly did not make him more sympathetic to the plight of the accused. Regardless, Prynne wrote at virtually every turn in the history of Parliament's struggle to maintain civic order, as he advocated for a single Church of England with a Presbyterian format that would be free of prelacy while still maintained by tithing. We need not pursue these works further, as the catalogue's list of titles are revealing enough.[82]

Demonizing Diversity: Prynne and the Quakers

In 1655, Prynne interrupted his political writings to return to attacking religious dissent with a second, enlarged edition of *The Quakers unmasked* in 1655, followed in 1656 by *A new Discovery of some Romish Emissaries, Quakers, and Popish Errors, unadvisedly embraced, pursued by Anti-Communion Ministers* (London, 1656) and his two-part attack on the efforts of the Amsterdam rabbi Menasseh ben

---

[80] Bodin, *On the Demon-Mania of Witches*.
[81] Lamont, *Puritanism*, 21.
[82] *An exact catalogue.*

Israel to convince Parliament and Cromwell to allow the Jews back into the realm (we will return to this last work after chapter 5's discussion of demonizing rhetoric). It seems likely that it was the efforts of some English writers to replicate some measure of Dutch religious diversity that inspired Prynne's new attacks on Quakers and other Independents. In the *Quakers unmasked*, Prynne elaborates on his thesis that the papacy was behind the plot to infect England with religious diversity:

> That by this their New *Stratagem* and *Liberty,* they have (under the Disguises of being *Quakers, Seekers, Anabaptists, Independents, Ranters, Dippers, Anti-Trinitarians, Anti-Scripturists* and the like) gained more *Proselytes, Disciples,* and done more harme in eight or nine yeares space to the *Church* and *Realm* of *England,* more prejudice, dishonour, scandall to our *Religion* and *Ministers,* then ever they did by *saying Masse,* or preaching, printing *any points of grossest Popery* in 80 yeares time heretofore. And if not speedily, diligently, restrained, repressed, will soon utterly overturne both our *Church, Religion, Ministry,* and *State* too in conclusion, having already brought them to sad confusions and distractions.[83]

Prynne was not alone in seeing the Catholic papacy behind the rise of sects in England; as John Marshall has observed, "[t]here was, moreover, a huge literature holding Quakers and Baptists to be Catholics in disguise," based on the

---

[83] William Prynne, *The quakers unmasked, and clearly detected to be but the spawn of romish frogs, jesuites, and franciscan fryers; sent from rome to seduce the intoxicated giddy-headed english nation. by an information newly taken upon oath in the city of bristol, jan. 22. 1654. and some evident demonstrations.* ... (London: for Edward Thomas, 1655), 5. There were later editions of this work, including ones in 1664 and 1691.

reasoning that by dividing the Protestant community, the sectarians were paving the way for a return of papal authority.[84] Of course, Prynne and his likeminded polemicists had no real evidence that the Catholic Church was behind the rise of these sects, except that the results – religious confusion and apathy toward the Church of England and the state – were what the papacy surely was hoping for. And, he continues, is the suspicious similarity between the Quakers and the Franciscans, both of which travel in pairs to proselytize, wear the simplest of outfits, advocate that people abandon their "lawful Callings" in favour of *"idle Monkish lasy life,* and *ramble about* from place to place to vent their pretended Visions" and *"New Lights"* and follow St. Francis in their *"rude and uncivill behaviour* in refusing to *salute, or shew any reverential respect, honor, or humble deportment* towards Magistrates or other persons of what quality so ever."[85]

Similarly, Prynne suggests that the moral perfectionism of the Quakers was the same as taught by St. Francis, and he cites Franciscan hagiographies as proof.[86] But, his central argument is that the ecstatic experiences of the Quakers, their *"extraordinary sudden extravagant Agonies, Trances, Quakings, Shaking, Raptures, Visions, Apparitions, Conflicts with Satan, Revelations, Illuminations, instructions in new divine Mysteries and Seraphicall Divinity,"* gave illiterate folk the assurance they were experiencing *"intimate familiarity and immediate communion with God & Jesus Christ."* They then engaged in missions as a result of these divine communications and suddenly comprehend languages in which they had no training. These experiences are all "the very same in form and substance with *those ridiculous*

---

[84] Marshall, *John Locke,* 74, 463-4, the latter where he cites Prynne on the Quakers.
[85] Prynne, *The quakers unmasked,* 5-6.
[86] Prynne, *The quakers unmasked,* 6.

lying Enthusiasms, Impostures, Cheats, Agonies, Revelations, Visions, Raptures, Illuminations, Inspirations, Apparitions &c. of Popish Saints, Fryers, Priests, Jesuites, Nunnes," as recorded in Catholic lives of the saints, some of which Prynne has obviously read. These similarities are proof enough for him to assert that in a Quaker "we may as visibly discover *a Jesuit, a Popish Priest* or *Fryer* in them, as we may *a Lion by his paw.*"[87] Like the Catholics, Prynne claims, Quakers use magic to win adepts, in the form of enchanted potions, bracelets, ribbons, and witchcraft, intoxicating their novices, just as "*Enchantments, Sorceries, Charmes, Fascinations* and *Exorcismes* are very frequent amongst *Popes,* and *Popish Priests, Monkes, Fryers, Jesuites,*" citing as evidence Johan Wier's *De praestigiis daemonum* (*On the Illusion of Demons*) of 1563 (Prynne cites the 1568 edition), as well as the infamous stories of medieval popes who had recourse to sorcery.

The devil, working with the permission of God, Prynne continues, caused the physical quakings and fits of the Quakers.[88] Such people are *possessed by the Devill himselfe,* or *bewitched by his Instruments*"; and in this he also implies that they are ultimately witches or sorcerers, a subject to which we will return in the next chapter.

Prynne's Sources: Inquisitors and Witch-Hunting Sceptics

Prynne's use of his sources needs some discussion and analysis. He cites widely, including works by his fellow Protestant anti-heresy polemicists, but he is also widely read in Catholic material. Of particular note here are two sources, the first by the sixteenth-century Catholic Inquisitor

---

[87] Prynne, *The quakers unmasked*, 7-8.
[88] Prynne, *The quakers unmasked*, 9.

William Lindanus, who described how "some of the Ringleaders and Captaines of the Anabaptists, and some of their new Converts, have not only communion and familiarity with the Devil, but in all probability, are likewise actually possessed by him," as seen by the "raptures, Agonies, Fits and Quakings as persons actually possessed by the Devil use to have." Prynne then recounts Lindanus' story of how when some Catholics converted to Anabaptism, they were given a 'potion' providing them with magical literacy, which they lost the moment they returned to Catholicism.[89] Prynne's reliance on Catholic polemics, which were firmly targeted at Protestants like himself as well as Anabaptists, is a clear contradiction of Prynne's distaste for "Popish Monkes, Friers, Priests, Nunnes, Papists, specially Females," whom he claims "Have likewise been actually possessed, seduced, cast into strange, reall, or feigned Extasies, Agonies, Shakings, … and inspired with strang Revelations, Visions, … Prophecies and Enthusiasms by the very Devil himself." As we will see below, it is not just the modern reader who has difficulty squaring the lawyer's hatred for such Catholic writers with his naïve adoption of the irrational stories that they tell.

Prynne will cite anyone for such stories, including those told by the second notable source, Wier's famous *De praestigiis daemonum*. In the way that he cites this treatise, Prynne seems unaware that this work was written from a skeptical posture toward magic, one that aimed to defend women from charges of witchcraft by arguing that the devil hardly needed old women suffering from the hallucinations

---

[89] Prynne, *The quakers unmasked*, 12; on Lindanus's anti-Anabaptist polemics, see Waite, *Eradicating the Devil's Minions*, 45-49. This was a story that was also in the Jesuit Leonard Lessius's 1618 treatise against Anabaptism, "Some counterfeited miracles, and some sodainely could read, which knew no letter in the booke before; who comming againe to be Catholikes, lost their skil in reading." Lessius, *A consultation what faith and religion is best*, fol. Diiij^r.

caused by melancholia (for Wier the medical explanation behind witch confessions) to perform his evil in the world. As is apparent mostly in the forewords to his German editions, Wier also wrote this work as a critique of the religious prejudice and superstitious beliefs that led to persecution of heretics, promoting a level of toleration in accord with the attitude of his Erasmian-minded employer, Duke Wilhelm of Cleves, Jülich and Berg, in whose court Wier worked as chief surgeon of Cleves. Instead, Prynne cites Wier as a source for the reality of demonic magic, quoting him as if he believed that demons caused pagans to be "cast into strang reall or feigned Extasies, Trances and Quaking fits" that were for Prynne obvious parallels to the Quakers, as were those stories being told by writers about the Indigenous Peoples of the Americas.[90] Wier did not believe any of these stories, as he intended them as examples showing how easily people could be tricked by the devil. At a deeper level, he seems also to have been critiquing naïve belief in the devil itself, who, as the title of Wier's work implies, was also an illusion.[91]

Prynne might, however, be forgiven for not knowing Wier's actual demonology or religious beliefs, as he kept them well covered, a wise approach for someone wishing to maintain his livelihood and who knew that expressing his real views would alienate many readers. Hans de Waardt has recently argued in fact that Wier's real position was a Spiritualists' belief, like Joris's, that the devil did not in fact exist external to the human conscience, and that a true

---

[90] Prynne, *The quakers unmasked*, 9-10.
[91] See esp. De Waardt, "Inflating the Prestige of Demons"; also Michaela Valente, "'Against the devil, the subtle and cunning enemy': Johann Wier's *De praestigiis daemonum*, in *The Science of Demons: Early Modern Authors Facing Witchcraft and the Devil*, Jan Machielsen, ed. (London, 2020), 103-18, and *Johann Wier: Debating the Devil and Witches in Early Modern Europe* (Amsterdam, 2022). I am grateful to Dr. Valente for sending me copies of her works.

believer could easily defeat this "impotent" devil; Reginald Scot made Wier's implicit skepticism toward diabolical activity explicit in his *The Discoverie of Witchcraft* of 1584.[92] Prynne instead asserts that Anabaptists were literally possessed by the devil, so when their impressive quoting of scripture confounded the inquisitors, this was not from their own knowledge, "but that the devils speake in the Anabaptists," just as when demoniacs spoke in languages that they did not know. Prynne then applies this canard to "all our Quakers, Shakers, and other Anabaptisticall Enthusiasts" who were in the thrall of the "Delusions and Inspirations of the Devil himself" and his ministers, "sent over from Jesuiticall and Popish Seminaries," to "seduce them by such Sorceries."[93] He concludes that the Quakers were a creation of the Jesuits "by Diabolicall delusions, sorceries, enchantments" to extirpate the Anglican Church.[94]

So, while Prynne read widely, he either did not fully comprehend his sources or, as was very common in the era, simply mined them for bits that would support his own arguments, twisting the original meaning to push his agenda regardless of the author's intent. His goal was to discredit both Catholicism and new religious groups by associating them with each other and with diabolical plotting. Before turning to Prynne's final polemical target, the Jews, we need

---

[92] See De Waardt, "Inflating the Prestige of Demons," and Waite, "Knowing the Spirit(s)." This demonology became influential within the liberal Mennonite (*Doopsgezind*) fellowships. Prynne cites both Lindanus and Wier from a collection by the Jesuit Petrus Thyareus, *Daemoniaci: hoc est, De obsessis a Spiritibus Demoniorum Hominibus* (Cologne, 1598), and in Edwin Sandys, *Europe Speculum* of 1629, 169; on Sandys' intriguing work, see Theodore K. Rabb, "The Editions of Sir Edwin Sandys's 'Relation of the State of Religion,'" *Huntington Library Quarterly* 26 (1963), 323–36.
[93] Prynne, *The quakers unmasked*, 12-13.
[94] Prynne, *The quakers unmasked*, 20-24.

to look more carefully at the impact of the demonizing language used by Prynne and his fellows, especially as how these related to the contemporaneous rise of large-scale witch-hunting in 1644 in East Anglia, a panic that included, for the first time in England, significant elements of the diabolical witch stereotype common on the continent.

Chapter 5
Anti-Anabaptist Polemics and English Witch-hunting, 1600-1660

It is now necessary to point out the key role played by the demonizing rhetoric of anti-heresy preachers in inspiring the European witch hunts, both in their first iteration in the 1420s, and then in their revival in the second half of the sixteenth century.[1] In an earlier study I had observed the convergence of the demonizing of Anabaptists in Southwest Germany leading up to the first major witch panic of the Reformation era in 1562 in Wiesensteig, and we have already mentioned the work of one of the most important agents in inspiring the Wiesensteig witch-hunts, Thomas Naogeorgus.[2]

Many Catholic and Lutheran churchmen had tried to persuade their parishioners that Anabaptists and witches were separate wings of Satan's two-prong strategy to destroy Christendom. Hoping to inspire their congregants to become suspicious, even frightened, of their Anabaptist neighbours and to cooperate in the government's efforts to suppress the movement, many preachers used extreme demonizing language to characterize the Anabaptists.

---

[1] See Ronald Hutton, *The Witch: A History of Fear, from Ancient Times to the Present* (New Haven, CT, 2017), especially for the fifteenth century, and Rita Voltmer, "Debating the Devil's Clergy. Demonology and the Media," *Religions* 10 (2019), 648, https://doi.org/10.3390/rel10120648, for the sixteenth. See also A. Karim Baccouche, "Speak of the Devil and he Shall Appear: Preaching Against Heresy and Witchcraft in the Fifteenth and Sixteenth Centuries in France," PhD Dissertation, University of New Brunswick (2022).

[2] Waite, *Eradicating the Devil's Minions*, 138-51; and chapter 3 above.

It appears that in this they failed, for most people came to regard the Anabaptists as sincere, if rather too pious. Instead, this preaching and writing campaign against Anabaptism coincided with the rise in popular pressure to prosecute witches, and I have suggested that parishioners merely took the demonizing rhetoric of their preachers to apply to those they already had associated with the devil.

Here I wish to apply that comparative approach to England, focusing in particular on references to the devil and witchcraft in published attacks on Anabaptism. While on the continent, Reformed ministers tended to shy away from the same kind of demonizing language against Anabaptists used by their Catholic and Lutheran fellows, this seems not to have been the case in England. Part of this might be due to the fact that continental Reformed, including Calvin, saw the Spiritualists or Libertines as the greatest threat to the survival of the Reformed faith, since they were seen as fifth-column subversives, pretending to be orthodox while undermining faith from within.[3] Since anti-Anabaptist polemics had for decades blurred the distinctions between Anabaptism and Spiritualism, it seems that by the 1640s Puritan writers were less reluctant to demonize both groups.

Matthew Hopkins and the East Anglia Witch Hunts, 1644-1647

The associating of heretics with the devil and evil magic was a powerful factor in the European witch panics, and we need to examine if this tendency played a role in the development of England's sole mass trials in 1644-1647 in East Anglia conducted by the Puritan Matthew Hopkins, who styled himself the Witchfinder General, and his colleague John Stearne. Hopkins's book, *The Discovery of Witches*, was

---

[3] Apart from my own work, see Kaplan, *Calvinists and Libertines*.

printed in 1647, the year of his retirement and early death. Hopkins's fame and writing inspired imitation in both England and New England.[4] It must be said, however, that neither he nor most other witch hunters made any explicit link between polemics against Anabaptism and their witch-hunting activity.

Hopkins's *Discovery of Witches* is, moreover, a brief response to questions of procedure relating to Hopkins's use of the prick test for the devil's mark, rather than a demonological work per se. He does include two theological points relevant to our discussion here: first, he cites King James VI of Scotland's *Daemonologie* in explaining why the water or dunking test was valid: "Witches deny their baptisme when they Covenant with the Devill," hence the water will refuse to receive such witches.[5] Many continental anti-Anabaptist polemicists had tried to portray Anabaptists as members of a demonic sect with their renunciation of infant baptism – an action which had been associated with the witch sabbath since the fifteenth century – and especially with their adoption of adult baptism, portrayed by their opponents as a second, diabolical baptism, and which became a hallmark of the demonic witch sabbath after the rise of Anabaptism in 1525.[6]

As noted above, most of these sixteenth-century continental polemicists were Catholics or Lutherans, because Calvinists, like the Anabaptists and the Spiritualists they opposed, strongly rejected the "realism" inherent in the more traditional theologies of the Catholics and Lutherans,

---

[4] Matthew Hopkins, *The Discovery of Witches: in Answer to several Queries, lately delivered to the Judges of Assize for the County of Norfolk* (London: for R. Royston, 1647). See Malcolm Gaskill, *Witchfinders: A Seventeenth-Century English Tragedy* (Cambridge, MA, 2005); and James Sharpe, *Witchcraft in Early Modern England* (Harlow, 2001), 70-73.
[5] Hopkins, *The Discovery of Witches*, 6.
[6] Waite, *Eradicating the Devil's Minions*, esp. 58, 75, 83, 100, and 152.

especially with respect to the doctrine of the Real Presence in the Eucharist. Like the Mennonites, the Reformed were inspired by this anti-materialism to renounced even artistic representations of the divine in churches. And, like the Mennonites with whom they debated, Dutch Calvinists strongly emphasized disciplinary measures to maintain the purity of the Christian fellowship. In general terms, Reformed theology, including that of English Puritans and Scottish Presbyterians, contained within it a strong internalizing dynamic that emphasized the spiritual struggle as occurring within each individual, and this at times came close to a spiritualistic position on the devil, whose attacks came primarily within one's mind. Yet Calvinists never went so far as to argue, as Joris did, that the devil had no external reality.[7] In contrast to their English brethren, moreover, continental Reformed writers tended to treat their Mennonite neighbours as erring brethren rather than as diabolical agents. English Puritans, on the other hand, had little to no personal experience with Mennonites, thus they were not preoccupied with trying to convince such dissenters that their theology was mistaken; instead, they could simply demonize them, as we have seen already.

For his part, Luther had distinguished between material and spiritual witchcraft, the latter defined as the devil blinding the ignorant to the truth of the gospel, as preached by Luther. The Anabaptists he described as bewitched or possessed by the devil for their divergence from Lutheran orthodoxy, and as mad for their willingness to become martyrs for their dissident beliefs. Their bewitchment was thus more dangerous to the soul that mere physical witchcraft. Luther made this explicit in a newssheet on Anabaptist Münster when he declared that "the devil

---

[7] Michelle D. Brock, "Internalizing the Demonic: Satan and the Self in Early Modern Scottish Piety," *Journal of British Studies* 54 (2015), 23-43.

himself lived" in the city. The reform-minded Archbishop of Cologne, Herman von Wied, had similarly declared that the Münster Anabaptists "had cast a spell on the ignorant people" in the region.[8] Not all of Luther's hearers and readers made such a clear distinction between the two types of witchcraft, transposing what Luther and his fellow preachers said about Anabaptists onto neighbours they actually feared to be practicing witchcraft, in the process emphasizing the demonic aspects of the witch stereotype. As observed above, continental Calvinists instead regarded their Anabaptist opponents as erring and regularly disputed with them to persuade them to return to the Reformed faith. This seems not to have been the case for England's Puritans.

The second of Hopkins' theological points is his general Reformed perspective on the diabolical, for when he answers the question as to whether or not witches are granted real magical powers to harm their neighbours, his answer falls in line with Puritan theology: the devil, working under God's permission, deludes "these Witches" to believe they had caused the intended harm, when in fact Satan, with his extensive knowledge of the natural world, merely identifies those neighbours who are suffering from mortal ailments and tells his adepts to curse them, so that when the victim dies, the witch is convinced that she had done the deed. Reformed and Puritan theologians, with their emphasis on the Providence of God, tended not to believe in the reality of magic or of the various preternatural events at the witches' sabbath, for this is what superstitious Catholics believed.[9] Instead, they focused on the pact that witches made with the devil, who constantly queried his followers with "a *What will you have me doe for you, my deare and nearest children, covenanted and compacted with me in my hellish league, and sealed with your blood, my delicate firebrand-darlings.*" They

---

[8] Cited in Waite, *Eradicating the Devil's Minions*, 52.
[9] See Clark, *Thinking with Demons*, 526-45.

respond, of course, that they wish harm to their enemies, and the devil uses his vast knowledge to select those identified who were already close to death, thereby gaining "a world of reverence, credence and respect for his power and activeness, when and indeed the disease kills the party, not the Witch, nor the Devill."[10]

This is a demonology fully in accord with Protestant principles of the sovereignty of God and the relative powerlessness of humans, even aided by the devil. God, Puritans and Presbyterians argued, was angered by the blasphemy of humans who turned to Satan rather than him in times of crisis, and it was necessary for the state to suppress such apostasy. Such thinking played a significant role in the Hopkins' trials, and in the major witch panics of neighbouring Presbyterian Scotland.[11] On this model, all blasphemy needed to be eradicated, whether of the sort of Anabaptist heresy or apostate witches. All of this to say that William Prynne's demonizing rhetoric had potentially explosive force, yet he threw it about with great abandon.

Demonizing Rhetoric and Witchcraft in England

As Peter Elmer has shown in his excellent study of the intersection of politics, religion, and witchcraft in early-modern England, this demonizing of confessional opponents crossed over into witch fears in real ways. Observing that Puritanism "almost certainly provided the early inspiration" for witch-hunting in Essex and Suffolk and that local Puritan ministers and lay leaders "were often the driving force

---

[10] Hopkins, *The Discovery of Witches*, 8-9.
[11] See in particular Brian P. Levack, *Witch-Hunting in Scotland: Law, Politics and Religion* (New York, 2008), 30-32 and 84-85. I have discussed this in Waite, *Heresy, Magic, and Witchcraft* and more recently in "Sixteenth Century Religious Reform and the Witch-Hunts."

behind local prosecution," he comments that in both counties "the campaign to eradicate witches often became conflated with the war against two other sets of apostates – royalists and religious radicals." Supporters of the royalist side were frequently accused of witchcraft as Puritan preachers purged their communities of "spiritual pollutants." On the other side, Elmer suggests that the fear of "resurgent religious unorthodoxy" was "primarily responsible for generating a climate of fear and spiritual anxiety among Presbyterians" that gave credence to talk of a "diabolical conspiracy of witches and sectaries." Such a connection between religious apostasy and witchcraft was well established prior to the Civil War but received extra impetus thanks to Puritan preachers linking the beliefs of the new religious groups with those of demonic witches.[12]

Richard Byfield on Witches, Libertines, and Anabaptists, 1645

Peter Elmer provides a fascinating case study: in February 1645 the Presbyterian Richard Byfield preached a sermon in Surrey comparing "the activities of witches with those of libertines and Anabaptists."[13] Composed under a cloud of perceived persecution of his fellow Presbyterians who in the preceding years had had to flee to the corners of the earth to maintain the true faith against the proto-Catholic Episcopalians – Byfield calls them "Luciferian Vsurpers" – who had infected England's ruling elite, Byfield now worries that the current support for "glorious Gospel liberty" was also encouraging the breeding of a new satanic "Vermine" to swarm over the church and which needed a thorough

---

[12] Peter Elmer, *Witchcraft, Witch-Hunting, and Politics in Early Modern England* (Oxford, 2016), 127-28; see also Walsham, "'Frantick Hackett'."
[13] Elmer, *Witchcraft*, 128.

purging.¹⁴ Like friars and monks, these pests seek to "inchant the people through a mournfull behaviour" and to "bewitch with fascinations; that is, to delude simple mindes" like "witches do to the eyes of the body, that they thinke verily, they see that which they do not see." Such "be witchings are most dangerous," for the conjurers pretend to reveal Christ and grace to their victims, while in truth they cast a mist over the soul. They also convince their hearers to focus on the "conceit of the great power of God in them, and some inspirations of the Holy Ghost," thereby corrupting their minds from the purity of the gospel and turning divine grace into "wantonnesse."¹⁵

He rails against the religious sorcery of those who claim to have "a great light," which Byfield asserts was nothing but "some old errour raised from Hell again and new painted." Like other Presbyterians he believed that there were in fact no new truths to reveal, although believers can certainly hope to receive "shining knowledge of received truths." He then attacks the tendency of his enemies to avoid the plain sense of scripture in their presentations. These include those who "utterly deny the Baptizing of Infants of Professors of the Faith of Iesus Christ," for they cannot present a single, straightforward scripture passage to justify their claim, and Byfield provides the traditional defence of infant baptism as a covenantal relationship between God and his people.¹⁶

---

[14] Richard Byfield, *Temple Defilers Defiled, Wherein a True Visible Church of Christ is Described ... Delivered in two Sermons Preached at the Lecture in Kingston Upon Thames* (London: John Field, for Ralph Smith, 1645), fol. A2ᵛ. This work was reprinted in 1653: Richard Byfield, *A short treatise describing the true church of christ, and the evills of schisme, anabaptism and libertinism ... delivered in two sermons* (London: for Ralph Smith, 1653).

[15] Byfield, *Temple Defilers*, fol. A3ʳ. Also cited by Elmer, *Witchcraft*, 128.

[16] Byfield, *Temple Defilers*, fols. A3ᵛ-A4ʳ.

Byfield's "Temple-defilers" are of course those setting up "so many Independant Churches, as there be Christian Congregations in the world," all claiming to be the mystical body of Christ, leading to the ridiculous image of the single head of Christ upon a multitude of bodies.[17] There could be only one true temple or church, and that for Byfield was of course a national Presbyterian Church with a stringent disciplinary process that would suppress "all that *make Schismes and divisions* in the Church" and especially heretics, for heresy is "a cunning serpentine invasion of Christ" that will destroy the foundation of the church.[18] His list of major heresies that the authorities needed to attack included Antinomians possessed of "the spirit of Libertinisme"; the Anti-Sabbatarians who ignore the stringent regulations regarding the Lord's Day; the "Germane Anabaptists" who teach that Christians cannot be magistrates or take up the sword; the Arminians who teach universal grace; the Socinians who deny the divinity of Christ and the salvific nature of his death; and "*Antichrist*, and the *Spirit of Popery*" who crafted the "Popish Apostaticall Synagogue" which in truth is the "Whore of Babylon."[19]

Once again we see a Protestant linking sectarians and the Papacy in a demonic plot against the true church. As for the German Anabaptists, Byfield notes that over the last century there have developed "divers Sects of them," some of which have begun to "spread in England," as "these ghosts can passe the Seas." They need to be seriously examined, "for who knows unto what destructive Principles and Practices such giddy self-willed spirits may run?" While the Catholic Jesuit polemicist Robert Bellarmine (1542-1621) had blamed Luther for these heretics, Byfield knows better that they are "the off spring of hell," that "Satan ... sent these Furies out

---

[17] Byfield, *Temple Defilers*, 3.
[18] Byfield, *Temple Defilers*, 17-19.
[19] Byfield, *Temple Defilers*, 19-20.

to defame the work of Reformation" at the time of Luther, and Satan continues to send "these furies among us for the very same end."[20]

Renunciation of Infant Baptism and Demonic Witches

Such language was not uncommon, and it was certainly no mere rhetorical flourish. Elmer cites other such examples by Byfield's coreligionists.[21] The first of these was a 1651 treatise defending infant baptism by the Presbyterian minister Nathaniel Stephens (d.1678). Here he responds to what was becoming a standard polemical ploy of comparing the Baptist rejection of paedobaptism with witches who, when they made their pact with Satan, were compelled to renounce their Christian baptism. Writing against a pamphlet by a Robert Everard who had jeered at a Mr. Angel of Leicester for saying that *"witches after conviction say that the Devil perswaded them to deny their first Baptisme,"* Stephens suggests that while Everard admitted that it was evil to "deny Christ, and to turne Turk, to deny Christ and enter into confederacy with the Devil," his pamphlet implied that it was no breach of the covenant with God to refuse baptism to infants.[22]

Why make such a convoluted argument? The obvious reason is that Stephens and Angel were arguing with Baptists in the immediate wake of the infamous Hopkins'

---

[20] Byfield, *Temple Defilers*, 20. Byfield is clearly also deeply concerned about the Socinians.
[21] Elmer, *Witchcraft*, 128, esp. n. 179.
[22] Nathaniel Stephens, *A precept for the baptisme of infants out of the new testament. where the matter is first proved from three severall scriptures, that there is such a word of command. secondly it is vindicated, as from the exceptions of the separation, so in special from the cavils of mr. robert everard in a late treatise of his intituled baby-baptisme routed* (London: T.R. and E.M. for Edmund Paxton, Nathanaell Webb and William Grantham, 1651), 38.

witch-hunts, and witches and Satan were at the forefront of their parishioners' minds. Also, the Anabaptist denial of infant baptism was widely feared to make those unbaptized more susceptible to the devil's interference, whether in demonic possession or witchcraft.[23] Stephens comes close to saying this when he defends Angel's position that "the first Baptisme is of great moment; and that a man cannot well make a compact with the Devil, but he must renounce the Christ to which he hath obliged himself in Infant-Baptisme."[24]

Mr. Angel furthermore had countered the Baptists by making what he thought was a brilliant argument in defence of infant baptism, by saying *"that Witches after their conviction, say the Devill perswaded them to deny their first Baptisme: Ergo it was good, otherwise he [the devil] would not perswade them from it."*[25] Using the confession of witches as evidence in a philosophical or theological argument was a commonplace in the mid-seventeenth century, one that was developed in particular by the Cambridge Platonists Henry More and Joseph Glanvill (1636-1680) as they sought to counteract the rise of atheism.[26] Of course such efforts

---

[23] This is a point I make in Waite, *Eradicating the Devil's Minions*, 39 and passim.

[24] Stephens, *A precept for the baptisme of infants*, 61.

[25] Stephens, *A precept for the baptisme of infants*, 64.

[26] Henry More, *An antidote against atheisme, or, An appeal to the natural faculties of the minde of man, whether there be not a God* (London: Roger Daniel, 1653), esp. 112-15; Glanvill was particularly obsessed with using witch confessions to prove the existence of God in *Saducismus triumphatus, or, Full and plain evidence concerning witches and apparitions in two parts … With a letter of Dr. Henry More on the same subject and an authentick but wonderful story of certain Swedish witches done into English by Anth. Horneck* (London: for J. Collins and S. Lownds, 1681). See Sharpe, *Instruments of Darkness: Witchcraft in England, 1550-1750* (London, 1996), 236-50; Brian P. Levack, *The Witch-Hunt in Early Modern Europe*, 4th ed. (London, 2016), 242; and

collapsed under the weight of the essential contradiction of using confessions of witches to having made a pact with the father of lies as a means to establish truth.

Thomas Hall on Pacts with the Devil, 1652

The second of Elmer's examples is another defence of paedobaptism by Thomas Hall (1610-1665) and printed in 1652. This tract was, the titlepage tells us, occasioned in part by a disputation with a number of Baptists whose artisanal status Hall identifies, satirizing their relative unlearned status by composing his dedicatory foreword in Latin in which he cites several continental Reformed polemicists, such as Bullinger, to critique all such Arians, Arminians, Socinians, Georgists (followers of Joris), Schwenckfeldians, Bucoldians, "as well as many other fanatics and madmen of the same mania, whom we commonly call Anabaptists."[27] To his friends in Birmingham, Hall describes Anabaptism as an immoral "Gangrene" that is fast spreading, supporting his point by quoting Dr. Featley's *The Dippers Dipt*.[28] To leave children unbaptized, he warns, inflames the wrath of God and leaves them open to the devil, drawing "them on to other

---

Euan Cameron, *Enchanted Europe: Superstition, Reason, & Religion, 1250-1750* (Oxford, 2010), 275-82.

[27] Thomas Hall, *The font guarded with XX arguments. containing a compendium of that great controversie of infant-baptism, proving the lawfulness thereof; as being grounded on the word of god, agreeable to the practice of all reformed churches; together with the concurrent consent of a whole jury of judicious and pious divines. occasioned partly by a dispute at bely in worcestershire, aug. 13. 1651. against joseph paget, dyer. walter rose, and john rose. butchers of bromesgrove. john evans a scribe, yet antiscripturist. francis loxly, sho-maker. here you have the question fully stated, ... with a word to one collier, and another to mr. tombs in the end of the book* (London: R.W. for Thomas Simmons, 1652), fol. A2^v.

[28] Hall, *The font guarded*, fol. A5^r.

dangerous Errors."²⁹ He then makes the implication explicit, arguing that Anabaptism

> 'Tis little better then *Witchcraft*: for Witches, before they can make a league with the Devil, must renounce their *Infant-Baptism* either implicitely or explicitly; they differ only in degree; the one renounceth it totally and for ever, the *Anabaptist* in part, as a nullity and of no effect, etc.³⁰

And, of course, Catholicism comes in for its share of condemnation:

> Thus the Devil drives men into Extremes: in time of Popery they made an Idol of Baptism, and did attribute too much to it in respect of Necessity and Efficacy; and now the *Anabaptists* and *Libertines* make an idle Ceremony of it, and contemn it: the one deny Baptism to Infants bodies; the other deny

---

[29] Hall, *The font guarded*, fol. A5ᵛ.
[30] Hall, *The font guarded*, fol. a2ᵛ. Elmer notes that this comparison between Anabaptist rejection of infant baptism and the apostasy of witches denying their baptism to the devil was made earlier in a 1621 work, Stephen Denison, *The doctrine of both the sacraments to witte, baptisme, and the supper of the lord. or A commentary vpon the 16. verse of the 22. of the acts of the apostles: And vpon a great part of the 11. chapter of the former epistle to the corinthyans: To wit, from the beginning of the 23. verse vnto the ende of the chapter. deliuered in sundry sermons by stephen denison preacher of gods word at kree-church, london* (London: Augustine Mathewes for Robert Mylbourne, 1621), 22-23. Denison writes of Anabaptists: "These differ but in degree from such as giuing themselues to the Diuell, renounce their baptisme; they differ I say in the degree of renoncing, but they agree in this, that both of them renounce and reiect their holy baptisme, which they receiued from the Church. And therefore woe wil be vnto them, vnless the Lord vouchsafe to giue them repentance for this their wicked and dispightfull practise."

Salvation to their souls for want of it: The *Papists* shut Infants out of the Church-Triumphant, and the *Anabaptists* out of the Church-Militant.[31]

Hall follows the long tradition of identifying Anabaptism as a disease: "a loathsom Leprosie" spreading across the nation. He has clearly read some of the heresiographies we have noted and at one point he lists the "Bastard brood" of the Anabaptists, including mention of 24 separate groups, "Hofniannians, Georgians, Serverians, Silentiarians, Eucheldians [Bucheldians?], Swenkfeldians, Hamanarians or Dung-wagons, Euchites, Huttites, Adamites, Gabrielites, Mennonites, Melchiorites, Apostolists, Adiaphorists, Spiritualists, Enthusiasts, Catharists, Separatists, Hemerobaptists, Se-baptists, Libertines," along with a "*Squadron*" of Arians, Arminians, Socinians, Familists, "Atheists, Millenaries," and so on.[32] Should their views prevail, Hall concludes, all of the British Isles would become unchurched, and all its residents heathens.[33]

John Eachard on the Devil and Baptism, 1646

Another minister, John Eachard of Darsham, where witch trials were common, "conflated the practices of witches with those of Baptists" since both denied their baptism.[34] In his work on the subject, he argued that

---

[31] Hall, *The font guarded*, fol. a2ᵛ. The main part of Hall's treatise is a detailed argument defending infant baptism, without the demonizing rhetoric of the prologues.
[32] Hall, *The font guarded*, 74.
[33] Hall, *The font guarded*, 85.
[34] Elmer, *Witchcraft*, 128-29. John Eachard, *The axe, against sin and error; and the truth conquering. A sermon on matthew 3. 10. now also the ax is laid to the root of the trees, therefore every tree, that bringeth not forth good fruit, is hewn down, and cast into the fire. at which, a christian*

First, When a man forsakes his baptisme, and turnes Turke, and will be circumcised, or turnes Witch, that will make a Covenant with the Devill to deny her baptisme, and deny God and Christ; or turne Anabaptist, to be rebaptized, he doth not abide in his baptisme into Christ; these will have a new baptisme, which is not of God, for he hath but one, the second must be of the Devill; these are gathered in the judgement of all Churches, and justly excommunicated, and cast into the fire of Gods wrath. Such as turne Turkes, Witches, or Anabaptists, have denied their first baptisme, because *they have trod underfoot the bloud wherewith they were sanctified, and done despight to the Spirit of Grace, and withdrawne themselves to perdition,* ... I heare the Anabaptists brag they have a Church, but I would know of them, whether the witches of *England* can make a Church? No; why, because they have denied their Baptisme; no more can Anabaptists, because they have denied their baptisme, that made them of the Church.[35]

Eachard's argument that renouncing one's baptism as an infant in order to be baptized as an adult is the equivalent of "turning Turke" and making a covenant with Satan is a truly nasty polemic with potentially far-reaching xenophobic effects. He further lumps together all the opponents of Reformed Protestantism as excluded from the true church,

---

confessed, she was converted; and because it did good to her, desired it might be preached again at her funerall, that it might do good to others, ... *wherein are shewed the causes of the sword upon england, and on the lutherans, and the remedies that must be used, before the judgements cease* (London: Matthew Simmons, 1646).

[35] Eachard, *The Axe*, 16-17.

as subject to "the judgement of God," to be gathered and "cast into the fire of Gods wrath, and they burn; as they that turn *Jews, Turks, Heathens, Papists, Witches*, and *Anabaptists*, all these are justly excommunicated out of the true Church of God, and judged to be under wrath, because they have denied or forsaken, or forgotten their Baptisme into Christ."[36] He treats witches as another damned sect, suggesting that he supported the concept of the demonic witch stereotype prevalent on the continent (especially in Catholic lands) and in the Hopkins' trials. Eachard's is an extraordinary statement, composed at the height of the Hopkin's witch-trials, as were Byfield's sermons.

Elmer's examples are undoubtedly the tip of the iceberg. An EEBO search for works that mention both "Anabaptist" and "witch" printed up to 1660 produced just over 800 hits, most of which were published during the Civil War and Interregnum period. I have examined only a few dozen of those deemed the most relevant by EEBO's algorithms, and these reveal that there were a few different approaches to the association between Anabaptism (and Quakerism) and the devil and witchcraft. For example, many writers followed Luther in arguing that Anabaptist leaders spiritually bewitched their followers with their false teachings, leading them into the devil's clutches and hell.[37] This claim was then

---

[36] Eachard, *The Axe*, 27.
[37] For example, in 1579 W. Wilkinson (d.1613) argued that Hendrik Niclaes, founder of the Family of Love, was bewitched: *A confutation of certaine articles deliuered vnto the familye of loue with the exposition of theophilus, a supposed elder in the sayd familye vpon the same articles. by william wilkinson maister of artes and student of diuinitye. hereunto are prefixed by the right reuerend father in god I.Y. byshop of rochester, certaine notes collected out of their gospell, and aunswered by the fam. by the author, a description of the tyme, places, authors, and manner of spreading the same: Of their liues, and wrestyng of scriptures: With notes in the end how to know an heretique* (London: Iohn Daye, 1579), fol.

applied to subsequent nonconformists, so that Baptists, Independents, and especially Quakers, were accused of bewitching the ignorant and weak, especially women. In 1610, for example, Richard Clyfton had attacked John Smyth for his promotion of believers' baptism by suggesting that such a position "geveth vs to mynd how Satan hath bewitched his soule to beleeve that such can be the effects of his heritical opinions."[38] The potential impact of such strong language in inspiring witch trials needs further research, for when we look carefully at the very difficult experiences of Baptists and other Independents, as well as the rise of demonic witch-trials at the exact time when these polemics were being disseminated, we must acknowledge the deep motivational power of such words.

Devilish Dreams, Anabaptist Enthusiasm, and Witchcraft

Other writers focused on the ecstatic excesses of the early Anabaptist movement, especially that of Hoffman and Van Leiden, as a parallel to the radical enthusiasm of modern Seekers, Ranters, and Quakers, arguing further that this behaviour was demonic. The Elizabethan Puritan and Cambridge scholar William Perkins (1558-1602) was doing this decades before the Civil War when in his *discourse of the damned art of witchcraft* (printed in 1608) he identified the visions of "the first authors of the sect of the Anabaptists" and the Familists to be merely evidence of the "deuill

---

Pii[v]. In 1597 J. Payne asked of the Anabaptists, "who hathe bewitched you?" for denying core Christian doctrines: *Royall exchange to suche worshipfull citezins, marchants, gentlemen and other occupiers of the contrey as resorte therevnto. try to retaine, or send back agayne. the contents ys after the preface. sene and allowed here* (Haarlem: Gilis Romaen, 1597), 25.

[38] Clyfton, *The plea for infants*, fol. 4[r].

preuailing so strongly, that many haue fallen away by this meanes, beeing corrupted by a doctrin meerely carnall, howsoeuer maintained with pretense of great holynes." Good "Angels may cause diuine dreames from God," to reveal his will, "so no doubt the euill spirits may cause in men diabolicall dreames, and therein reueile vnto them many strange things, which they by meanes vnknowne to men, may foresee and knowe. By all which it is euident, that there are and may be as well diabolicall, as diuine dreames."[39]

Like their continental Reformed coreligionists, English Puritans were deeply distrustful of any claims to new revelations, believing that the age of such miracles had passed and that all divine truth was established in the scriptures. Associating any such claims of new inspiration with the devil, therefore, remained a polemical tool throughout the seventeenth century.

Other writers on witchcraft followed suit, such as in the Anglican Vicar Thomas Cooper's 1617 *The Mystery of Witchcraft* which sought to counteract the growing atheism of his day. In the course of his discussion he attacks Separatism, suggesting "May not this be an occasion to despise the holy Ordinances of God, the Word, Baptisme, &c. seeing they are thus prophaned by these cursed miscreants, and so in seeking to runne from God, or rather from the deuill abusing these things, euen to runne to him, with the Anabaptist and Familist, for Reuelations and Enthusiasmes," which he noted was a parallel to Satan's demand that a witch similarly "Renounce her Baptisme: as

---

[39] William Perkins, *A discourse of the damned art of witchcraft so farre forth as it is reuealed in the scriptures, and manifest by true experience. framed and deliuered by M. william perkins, in his ordinarie course of preaching, and now published by tho. pickering batchelour of diuinitie, and minister of finchingfield in essex. whereunto is adioyned a twofold table; one of the order and heades of the treatise; another of the texts of scripture explaned, or vindicated from the corrupt interpretation of the aduersarie* (Cambridge: Cantrel Legge, 1610), 98-99.

heerein he entends to harden her heart the more, by this blasphemous disclaiming of the Seale of her saluation, and so to bind her more firme vnto him." Thus, he concludes, "doth Satan deceiue by this Ceremonie of Renouncing Baptisme."[40] Other of his tools are the "Diuellish Dreames framed in the braine by Satan," as seen in the "practise of Heretikes, as the Maniches, Anabaptists, Familists," and so on, "who haue been confirmed in their diuellish errours by Reuelations and Dreames."[41]

An obvious question springs to mind from these diatribes against believers' baptism: how did they shape the thinking of their readers? Did they contribute to increased hostility toward those regarded as Anabaptists or, alternatively, to neighbours suspected of practising witchcraft? Did they lead to a convergence of beliefs about these two types of heresy, and thus to the rise of the witch-hunts in Civil War England in the 1640s?

While we must, as Marion Gibson has warned, be very careful in using pamphlet literature as historical records, they can certainly help us comprehend ways of thinking and argumentation that helped incite popular suspicion and

---

[40] Thomas Cooper, *The mystery of witch-craft discouering, the truth, nature, occasions, growth and power thereof. together with the detection and punishment of the same. as also, the seuerall stratagems of sathan, ensnaring the poore soule by this desperate practize of annoying the bodie: With the seuerall vses therof to the church of christ. very necessary for the redeeming of these atheisticall and secure times* (London: Nicholas Okes, 1617), 114-15. I discuss this work in Waite, *Heresy*, 186, but without reference to Anabaptism.

[41] Cooper, *The mystery of witch-craft*, 146. This work was more or less reproduced under a different title in 1622: *Sathan transformed into an angell of light expressing his dangerous impostures vnder glorious shewes. emplified [sic] specially in the doctrine of witchcraft, and such sleights of satan, as are incident thereunto. very necessary to discerne the speciplague raging in these dayes, and so to hide our selues from the snare thereof* (London: Barnard Alsop, 1622).

motivate lawmakers to enact decrees and conduct trials.[42] Peter Elmer has included a number of such examples of ministers preaching sermons and publishing works that clearly intended to stimulate distrust of the devil's alleged agents and to increase support for trials. Yet, the unintended effects of the demonizing language utilized against religious heretics in escalating anxiety about diabolical witches requires further study.[43] Examining the demonizing rhetoric in anti-Anabaptist tracts provides us with further clues to this query.

Diabolical Sedition, Spiritual Sorcery, and Atheism

With the start of the Civil War, some preachers focused on the alleged seditiousness of the Anabaptists to warn against the rebellion; such was the case with a print version of a sermon that the learned Puritan Rector of Remenham (on the Thames West of London), Nathaniel Bernard, had preached in Oxford to members of both Houses of Parliament on June 16, 1644. Taking as his theme the phrase in I Samuel 15:23 "rebellion is as the sin of witchcraft," Bernard makes a number of comparisons for the assembled gentlemen to deter them from rebellion against the crown, one of which was the violent iconoclasm of the Anabaptists. Citing the *Malleus Maleficarum* of 1486, Bernard notes how witches profaned the Lord's Day and sacred church buildings, shot arrows at sacred images of Christ, distorted the meaning of scripture, and abused unbaptized infants, all

---

[42] Marion Gibson, *Reading Witchcraft: Stories of Early English Witches* (London, 1999).

[43] Elmer, *Witchcraft*. I make this point in more general terms in "Demonizing Rhetoric, Reformation Heretics and the Witch Sabbaths: Anabaptists and Witches in Elite Discourse," in *The Devil in Society in the Premodern World*, Richard Raiswell and Peter Dendle, eds. (Toronto, 2012), 195-219.

to commit their mischief. These actions, Bernard reminds his audience, found parallels in the Anabaptists and the current iconoclastic rebels.[44] And, he continues, most of "your primitive Schismatiques, and Heresiarchs" were "malefici Wizards, or Witches."[45] While he does not explicitly tie the dissenters of his own day to witchcraft, the implication is obvious.

Such implicit warnings against diabolical enchantment are everywhere in the anti-Anabaptist polemics. We can, for example, turn to Pagitt's comment in his *Heresiography* cited above about the Anabaptists, Brownists, and other sectarians seducing "not drunkards, Adulterers, Swearers, and pro-phane persons whom the Devill hath ensnared already," but those who "are desirous of heaven," focusing their efforts on "silly women" who wish to know too much. These deceivers come "in sheeps cloathing" with an appearance of holiness, as Pagitt warns finally that the devil can perform no greater mischief "then to make a schisme in the Church," and thereby cast millions out of the communion of the church; "let us take heed that we do not renounce that holy Covenant, as Witches doe when they compact with the Devill."[46]

Over and over polemicists critiquing the Baptists make parallels with demonic witches, and (one suspects) this is thanks largely to the infamy of the Hopkins' witch-trials, not to mention those recently transpired on the continent (although these had peaked in the first decades of the

---

[44] Nathaniel Bernard, *Esoptron tes antimachias, or, A looking-glasse for rebellion being a sermon preached upon sunday the 16 of iune 1644, in saint maries oxford, before the members of the two houses of parliament* (Oxford: Leonard Lichfield, 1644), 12.

[45] Bernard, *Esoptron tes antimachias*, 20. Certainly the fusion of Waldensian heresy and witchcraft in the minds of churchmen was a major feature behind the rise of the witch-hunts in the 1420s. See Hutton, *The Witch*.

[46] Pagitt, *Heresiography*, fol. A4^r, 20.

century in western polities) and still the rage in Presbyterian Scotland. We will cite just a few more examples here.

In 1646, a Thomas Bakewell (b. 1618 or 1619) wrote against some of the dissenters, asking "will they dispise the Baptism of the Holy Ghost, because it was done upon Infants, or because they were sprinkled and not plunged into the water? And so like Witches renounce the Covenant of Grace, … when they enter into Covenant with the Divel; so these people, it is to be feared, many of them do commit that unpardonable sin, when they turn *Anabaptists*, despising and trampling under feet the Spirit of God, whereby they *should be Sealed to the day of Redemption*." He concludes that many of these present-day dissenters "are ran so far from God, that they do not beleeve that there is either God or Devil, Heaven or Hell, Church of Grace or Glory; Thus they are now faln to notorious Atheism, calling themselves *Seckers* of the forementioned things, which for the present they have lost."[47] As noted above, the Seekers or Legatine-Arians, were a post-Familist Spiritualist group that loosely formed in the 1620s around the ideas of the Legate brothers – Walter, Thomas, and Bartholomew.

Like so many other Spiritualists, Seekers condemned all denominations as corrupt and emphasized the importance of inner religious experience over the outer. For this they, like

---

[47] Thomas Bakewell, *A iustification of two points now in controversie with the anabaptists concerning baptisme: The first is, that infants of christians ought to be baptized, with grounds to prove it, and their objections answered. with a briefe answer to master tombes twelve doubtfull arguments against it in his exercitation about infants baptisme. also a briefe answer to captaine hobsons five arguments in his falacy of infants baptisme, being (as he saith) that which should have beene disputed by him, and mr. knowles, and some others; against mr. calamy and mr. cranford. the second point is, that the sprinckling the baptized more agreeth with the minde of christ then dipping or plunging in or under the water: With grounds to prove it, and a briefe auswer [sic] to what they have to say against it* (London: for Henry Shepard and William Ley, 1646), 30.

the Familists before them and the Quakers after them, were condemned as atheists. The parallel with alleged witches in the demonological literature was clear, for women witches were believed to be the devil's ultimate tool of apostasy to spread disbelief and atheism, and women were prominent in Spiritualist groups like the Quakers.

In 1653 Prynne too made the point, a commonplace in Protestant demonologies, that spiritual witchcraft was worse than physical, and that governments must not tolerate any "spiritual Sorcerers, Witches, Murtherers, Adulterers (such as all Idolaters, Hereticks, Apostates, False Teachers, obstinate Schismaticks and Blasphemers are)," for these are "worse and more dangerous then corporal, because they hurt and destroy mens souls, and because the forecited and subsequent texts warrant their punishing of these with death, as wel as those." He then details scripture passages ordering the death of Sabbath breakers, sorcerers and witches and other malefactors, concluding that since heresy and blasphemy are even worse breaches of divine order, they too merit corporal punishment.[48] Others argued that to tolerate Anabaptists and sectarians was the equivalent of tolerating atheism and witchcraft themselves, a point made, for example, by Thomas Edwards in the third part of *Gangraena*.[49]

Accusations of Witchcraft against Baptists and Quakers

Such comparisons between witches and Anabaptists had considerable force. Elmer observes that they occasionally "led to actual accusations of witchcraft being levelled against those suspected of harbouring Baptist views." For example,

---

[48] Prynne, *The sword of christian magistracy supported*, 13, 31.
[49] Edwards, *The third part of gangræna*, 187.

in 1645 the Presbyterian Edward Willan (d.1691) was involved in hearing witch confessions in a Suffolk trial, claiming that "one of the accused 'professed anabaptisme'."[50] Elmer concludes from this that such cases may have inspired ministers to "preach on the joint threat posed to true religion by the activities of apostates such as witches and Baptists."

Many Puritan preachers and writers could not help but use the comparison with demonic witches as a means of striking fear into the hearts of readers with respect to those associated with Anabaptism, and many hearers might simply have focused on the witchcraft accusations. Edwards in 1646 detailed some intriguing stories told to him by his coreligionists, "wholly tending to Libertinisme and Atheisme," including one "Reverend godly Minister" who told him that he had heard one Independent say, "what if I should worship the Sunne or the Moone, as the Persians did, or that Pewter Pot standing by, what hath any man to do with my conscience?" Edwards himself had heard (he claims) "a Sectary plead for a Toleration of Witches, and I urging that argument, that Witches might say, they in their conscience hold the Devill for their God, and thereupon worship him."[51] Such assertions aimed to associate the two forms of apostasy more closely as a means of discrediting the Independents' arguments on behalf of religious toleration, and to make the Independents appear as godless as possible. As noted above with Saltmarsh's critique, not all readers appreciated Edwards' extremes.

Quakers and Witchcraft Accusations

Baptists were not the only ones to suffer from the polemicists' conflation of demonic sects. The Quakers, as

---

[50] Elmer, *Witchcraft*, 128.
[51] Edwards, *The third part of gangræna*, 187.

Elmer has also observed, were frequently accused of witchcraft, and the polemics against them, and only a tiny portion of which we have examined here, made the accusations explicit. Prynne's rhetoric was typical on this point when he fumed,

> Now for our *Quakers* & others better instruction, I shall inform them by way of Caution of these considerable particulars, relating to their *Agonies, Inspirations* and *Revelations*. 1. That the *Devil by Gods permissions frequently doth cause and produce, by his owne immediate power, extraordinary strang Convulsions, Contractions, Distortions, Agonies, Tremblings, Quakings, Shakings, Motions, Jestures of the Bodies, Members, Joints, Nerves Muscels both of Men and women, when, where, and in what manner he pleaseth;* as we see by common experience in such persons as are either *possessed by the Devill himselfe,* or *bewitched by his Instruments;* and by the *Convulsions, Trances, Quakings, Shakings, gestures of Witches, Sorcerers and other, acted or possessed by the Devil;* of which we have many examples in *History* & experience; & one recorded in the Gospel it self. *Mar.* 9. 17. to. 28.[52]

What is particularly notable is that, despite the fact that they themselves were subject to comparisons with witches, some Baptists led the campaign to so demonize the Quakers, perhaps in an effort to project accusations of diabolical doings from themselves onto another target, something seen frequently enough with witch hunters.[53] Similarly, the

---

[52] Prynne, *The quakers unmasked*, 9.
[53] Elmer, *Witchcraft*, 151-2, and esp. "'Saints or Sorcerers': Quakerism, Demonology and the Decline of Witchcraft in Seventeenth-Century

Quaker leader George Fox (1624-1691) in a 1654 tract defending his movement from aspersions of madness and witchcraft, appealed directly to "those that are called Anabaptists," along with Independents, Presbyterians, Levellers, and Ranters to turn to "the light in their Consciences" rather than to their human interpretations of scripture. To the Anabaptists he wrote:

> you take up a command from the letter, and say Christ commands it which Christ did not, you command but the letter commands it, you are not led with the light, which gave forth those commands to observe them, but saith Christ hath commanded them in Scripture, here you are them which use their tongues which the Scripture speaks of, but I have not spoken to them saith the Lord, heer with the light you are comprehended, to be the witches which takes up commands as they did in the Galathians, which the Apostle speaks of which did bewitch them, who drawes from the spirit within them, to harken to your outward commands, them that did observe the commands was led by the spirit, and Christ bid them goe preach, he sent them and bid them goe preach the Gospel to every Creature, they did not goe at the command of the letter, but at the

---

England," in *Witchcraft in Early Modern Europe: Studies in Culture and Belief*, J. Barry, M. Hester, and G. Roberts, eds. (Cambridge, 1996), 145-79. On witch-hunters and deflection, see Waite, *Heresy, Magic, and Witchcraft*, 37-39 on San Bernardino of Siena, and 42-45 on Heinrich Kramer, both of whom projected their own guilt over accusations of malfeasance onto witches; see also Walter Stephens, *Demon Lovers: Witchcraft, Sex, and the Crisis of Belief* (Chicago, 2002).

command of Christ, and they was led by the light which did comprehend the world.[54]

Whether intentional or not, Fox was deflecting the accusations of witchcraft from him and his followers to other sects.

A Large Meeting of Witches, Most of them Quakers and Baptists: Henry Denne vs Thomas Smith, 1659

Despite such efforts to distinguish among the various groups, it appears that the polemicists' strategy of conflation worked. Persecution of Quakers in particular was so intense in large part due to such demonizing polemics, while Baptists and other Independents too suffered from considerable suspicion. The disputes between Independents such as Baptists and the Quakers also contributed to this growing suspicion toward the latter.[55] We can illustrate this with one final example on this demonizing theme: a 1659 screed against Quakers in response to the Baptist Henry

---

[54] George Fox, *A word from the lord unto all the faithlesse generation of the world, who know not the truth, but live in their own imaginations; with a true declaration of the true faith, and in what it doth differ from the worlds imagination: Written in obedience to the lord, that al may see what faith is owned by the saints, and what faith is denied. and also a few words unto all professors of the world, who worship not the true god, but their own imaginations and conceivings instead of the true god: Also a call from god unto all the the world to repentance, that all may turn unto him, lest the lord destroy both root and branch of them that repent not. also a few words unto you that scorne quaking and trembling, which all the holy men of god witnessed that spake forth the scripture, and also the holy men of god justified, and all you denied that scorneth such as witness such things now, as ever was in all the generations of the saints. with a word to those that are called anabaptists, independants, presbyterians, leve* (London: n.p., 1654], 13-14.
[55] T. L. Underwood, *Primitivism, Radicalism, and the Lamb's War: The Baptist-Quaker Conflict in Seventeenth-Century England* (Oxford, 1997); and Crome, "The Münster Rising," 954-55.

Denne's *The Quaker no Papist*, which itself was a rebuttal of the Cambridge scholar Thomas Smith's account of a dispute with some Friends in Cambridge.⁵⁶ After Denne's dispute with Daniel Featley referred to above, Denne remained a Baptist in his ecclesiology while also maintaining a living as parish minister in Cambridgeshire.⁵⁷ Smith had apparently impugned the reputation of the prominent Quaker preacher George Whitehead by calling him a secret papist for his refusal to swear the oath of abjuration, despite Whitehead's strong denial of any affiliation with papacy. On principle Quakers, like Anabaptists, took seriously Jesus's instruction not to swear, a point that Denne uses to suggest that perhaps half of England's population might by Smith's definition be determined to be secret papists.⁵⁸ In defending Whitehead, Denne replied that Smith "would prove *Whitehead* to be a Papist, (a disguised Papist, forsooth; according to that Bedlam-fancy which *Pryn*, and *Baxter*, and the Father of lyes, and this vain man with the rest, go daily sowing in the heads of such people, as they finde apt and willing to be deceived by tales.)"⁵⁹ While also explaining why Whitehead – and by extension any Quaker – was not a secret papist, Denne's tactic was to hurl the accusation of inspiration from "the Father of lyes" back at the Protestant polemicists, naming in particular Prynne and the prominent Puritan theologian Richard Baxter (1615-1691). Denne clearly worried such language was having the intended effect. He critiques his opponents for raising the spectre of Anabaptist Münster to discredit them, for they ignored "our peaceable submissions to the State of *Holland*, our present obedience to our

---

⁵⁶ Henry Denne, *The quaker no papist, in answer to the quaker disarm'd. or, A brief reply and censure of mr. thomas smith's frivolous relation of a dispute held betwixt himself and certain quakers at cambridge* (London: Francis Smith, 1659).

⁵⁷ Campbell, *Windows into Men's Souls*, 161.

⁵⁸ Denne, *The quaker no papist*, 11.

⁵⁹ Denne, *The quaker no papist*, 6.

Governours at home, and our disowning the principles which occasioned those Munster Riots."[60]

Just because rumours that Jesuits were infiltrating various religious groups, "sometimes seeming Anabaptists, sometimes Presbyterians, sometimes Independents, sometimes Quakers, Seekers, Antiscripturists … to carry on their design of working divisions and confusions amongst us both in Church and Commonwealth, that so in time they may bring both to ruine, and upon the ruines build their own Babel again," does not mean they are true, for he cautions that it "ought rather to be examined *by whom* they are spread, and to *what ends*."[61]

Denne's attempts to discredit his critics obviously did not succeed as well as he had hoped, despite the reasonableness of his arguments. Instead, Smith's rejoinder, *A gaag for the quakers*, simply increased the fearmongering to extreme levels. He quotes at length a newssheet account advertising a "strange discovery" of a large meeting of some 200 "witches" near Sherborne in Dorset, "most of them Quakers and Anabaptists." Five of these, two of them women, were committed to jail where they confessed the following: first, "That when the Devill first appeared to, and tempted them to become Witches; He first of all perswaded them; to *renounce their Baptisme* and no wonder, because in it they *renounced the Divel and all his works, with all the sinfull lusts of the flesh*: which they did *Actually renounce before they made a contract with him*."

Second, that the devil frequently appeared to them in "sundry formes" to persuade them to worship him, which they did. Third, that "he instigated them to torment, bewitch and destroy as his and their greatest enemy" a particularly pious minister, a Mr. Lyford, who had been tormented and died from a painful disease, then forcing his

---

[60] Denne, *The quaker no papist*, 16.
[61] Denne, *The quaker no papist*, 18.

successor, Mr. Bamfield, "by their Witchcrafts" to abandon the town. Fourth, the two women confessed to having had sex with the devil "in sundry shapes" but "most commonly in the shape of Mr. *Lyford* and Mr. *Bamfield*, the Ministers of *Sherburne*, whom he and they most hated and endeavoured to destroy."

Finally, the devil had continued to visit all of the imprisoned "witches," possessing their bodies so that they thrashed about in the cell, "*tossing them frequently up & down the prison in a strange manner*, tormenting them with strange fits of convulsions, quakings, shakings in all their joynts, and swellings in their whole bodies, that *their skins are ready to break*, which makes them cry out and roar with great horror, as divers *eye-witnesses of quality attest*." If Mr. Denne remained skeptical, Smith advised that he or the Quakers could visit the accused in the Dorchester goal where "they will be enforced to confess it, and give glory unto God for his discovery of the evillness of the way and sect of Quakers."[62]

Such strange stories conflating Quaker meetings with Anabaptist Münster and demonic witchcraft had an emotional power that reasonable arguments could not easily counteract.[63] Here was presented for the reader evidence that heretical or sectarian witchcraft was returning to England after the Hopkins' trials by means of the Quakers who were also secret Jesuits and brothers to the Anabaptists. But Quakers were not the only victims of such demonizing rhetoric, for our angry lawyer William Prynne added the Jews.

---

[62] Thomas Smith, *A gaag for the quakers, with an answer to mr. denn's quaker no papist* (London: J.C., 1659), unpaginated, "To the Reader."
[63] Smith, *A gaag for the quakers*, fol. A4ʳ, writes, "Reading 'tother day Sleidans relation of your friends affairs at Munster I met with this passage," showing that Sleidanus' account of Münster remained an important source for these writers' efforts to discredit Quakers by association with Anabaptism.

Chapter 6
Anti-Anabaptist Propaganda, 1650-1660

The final decade of the Interregnum period saw polemicists continue their attacks on Christian dissidence, despite this becoming a significant feature of the English landscape. Many Puritans and High Church Anglicans feared that such diversity would reduce allegiance to the state, never mind a single English church. In 1655 they were faced with a new challenge in their efforts to restore religious uniformity in the person of a rabbi from Amsterdam.

William Prynne and the Jews

In 1655 Prynne produced another controversial treatise, a longwinded scandal sheet against Rabbi Menasseh ben Israel's mission to persuade Oliver Cromwell to readmit the Jews to the realm. Ben Israel (1604-1657) was a prominent if controversial rabbi in the vibrant Amsterdam Jewish community who worked very closely with a group of Christian nonconformists who were equally excited about the possibilities of Christian-Jewish collaboration on the eve of the messiah's arrival (or return).[1] In the lead up to the Whitehall Conference to debate the rabbi's request, Prynne set to reading everything he could get his hands on that would help deter his fellow Protestants from pursuing the

---

[1] I discuss this group more fully in Waite, *Jews and Muslims*, 179-96.

path of readmission. The story he tells in his foreword about why he composed this polemic is worth summarizing. He was apparently hanging around Whitehall when he ran into Philip Nye (1595-1672), a leading Independent preacher and Cromwell's advisor on religious matters. In 1644 Nye had co-authored *An Apologeticall Narration* arguing why Calvinists who congregated outside of a Presbyterian national church should be tolerated, although four years later he, like so many others witnessing the religious chaos in this decade, turned away from such broad toleration back to a state-controlled church.² Even so, Nye remained a proponent of an end to religious persecution, and was a strong advocate for the return of the Jews to England. So, it is difficult to imagine Prynne having a civil conversation with Nye, but Prynne describes it as such, telling his readers that Nye related to him that the Whitehall Conference had decided that there was no legal reason not to allow the Jews to reside in the realm.

This infuriated Prynne, for he believed the stories that the English Jews had been "great Clippers and Forgers of Money, and had crucified three or four Children in England," which is why they had been expelled in the first place.³ Here Prynne worries most about the quickly growing

---

² https://en.wikipedia.org/wiki/Philip_Nye; Lamont, *Puritanism*, 24.
³ William Prynne, *A short demurrer to the jewes long discontinued barred remitter into england comprising an exact chronological relation of their first admission into, their ill deportment, misdemeanors, condition, sufferings, oppressions, slaughters, plunders, by popular insurrections, and regal exactions in; and their total, final banishment by judgment and edict of parliament, out of england, never to return again: Collected out of the best historians and records. with a brief collection of such english laws, scriptures, reasons as seem strongly to plead, and conclude against their readmission into england, especially at this season, and against the general calling of the jewish nation. with an answer to the chief allegations for their introduction* (London: for Edward Thomas, 1656), fol. A3ᵛ. He published also a second volume, *The second part of a short demurrer to*

religious diversity and innovation in England, to which the Jews would merely add another unnecessary temptation. To fulfill his goal of convincing the notables at Whitehall, Prynne rummaged through all of the works that he could get his hands on about the history of the Jews in England, and the result is a remarkably uncritical amalgam of Antisemitic myths and illogical comparisons that, as we shall see, astounded some of his coreligionists for its naïve acceptance of all of the hoary stories concocted by medieval Christians to justify forcing Jews to be baptized or robbing and killing them.[4] Prynne's invective, however, was pretty much a scattershot affair because his polemical language against Jews, Independents, Catholics, and Quakers was virtually indistinguishable, and all of it was demonizing.

Prynne's explicit objection to allowing the Jews into England related to the same fear he had about Christian diversity, yet there is an intensity in his invective against the Jews that seems even stronger as he fumed that Jews were merely seeking to "set up their Synagogues of Satan."[5] After his conversation with Nye, during which the latter had doubted that the Jews had ever done anything as evil as the medieval myths would have it, Prynne examined the historical record, concluding that, having with *"wicked*

---

the iewes long discontinued remitter into england. containing a brief chronological collection of the most material records in the reigns of king john, henry 3. and edward 1. relating the history, affaires, state, condition, priviledges, obligations, debts, legal proceedings, justices, taxes, misdemeanors, forfeitures, restraints, transactions, of the jews in, and final banishment out of england, never formerly published in print: With some short usefull observations upon them. worthy the knowledge of all lawyers, scholars, statists, and of such jews who desire re-admission into england (London; Edward Thomas, 1656). See also Waite, *Jews and Muslims*, 187-90, and Waite, "Seventeenth-Century English Writers."
[4] On Jews in England, see David S. Katz, *Philo-Semitism and the Readmission of the Jews to England, 1603-1655* (Oxford, 1982), as well as his *The Jews in the History of England*.
[5] Prynne, *A Short Demurrer*, fol. B2^v.

hands" crucified Christ, they continue to attempt "by their *blasphemies*" to crucify him *"afresh every day,"* constantly praying "for the sudden, universal, total, final subversion, extirpation, perishing of Christs Kingdom, Gospel, and all his Christian Members, which they plot, and continually expect, such is their implacable transcendent malice."[6]

They were, in short, and on his account, a threat to the survival of Christendom. It was therefore "a very ill time to bring in the Jews" as the English remained "dangerously and generally bent to Apostacy, and all sorts of Novelties and Errors in Religion; and would sooner turn Jews, than the Jews Christians."[7] To those of his coreligionists who were arguing that readmitting the Jews would give them the opportunity to hear the true gospel and convert to English Protestantism, Prynne warned, "there being as learned able Protestant Divines in *Holland, Germany, France, Denmarke*, as any in *England*, if they cannot convert them, what hopes have we to do it?"[8] Observing continental affairs, including those in the Dutch Republic from whence Menasseh had arrived in London, Prynne had come to a conclusion similar to Martin Luther who in 1543 had written in his infamous *On the Jews and their Lies* that the Jews would never convert.[9]

Whether or not Luther and Prynne were influenced by the Spanish Inquisition's purity of blood laws which stipulated that Jewish blood was so polluting that even as little as $1/16^{th}$ of it made baptism ineffective, Prynne had certainly come to the conclusion that the Jews would never,

---

[6] Prynne, *A Short Demurrer*, fol. A4^r.
[7] Prynne, *A Short Demurrer*, fol. A3^v. See also Katz, *Philo-Semitism*, 220.
[8] Prynne, *A Short Demurrer*, 110.
[9] Martin Luther, *On the Jews and Their Lies*, in Franklin Sherman, ed., Martin H. Bertram, trans., *Luther's Works*, vol.47, *The Christian in Society* IV (Philadelphia, 1971), 268-78.

or could ever, truly convert.[10] He was clearly terrified about the rapidly increasing religious diversity in England, to which the Jews would merely add another temptation for weak-minded Christians, who would ultimately convert to Judaism on their way to atheism, or worse, Quakerism.[11] As he did with the Quakers, Prynne asserts that Jews were secret Catholic agents:

> The rather, because if extraordinary care be not taken herein, under pretext of Jews, we shall have many hundreds of Jesuites, (who derive both their Name and pedigree from the *Jews* even from *Iesui* and his *family of the Iesuits* Num. 16.44., as some of them affirm in print, though others from other grounds.) of Popish Priests and Friers come over freely into *England* from *Portugal, Spaine, Rome, Italy, Poland,* and other places, under the title, habit, and disguise of Jews, of purpose to undermine our Religion, Church and State, and sow the seeds of Heresie, Blasphemy, Popery, Superstition, Schisms, and Divisions amongst us, they having formerly sent over some of late years amongst us, under the notion and vizard of *converted Jews*, as *Ramsey* the *Scot,* and *Eleazer,* and *Joseph Ben-Isaiah*, all *Jesuitical,* wicked, cheating Impostors.[12]

---

[10] See Jerome Friedman, "Jewish Conversion, the Spanish Pure Blood Laws and Reformation: A Revisionist View of Racial and Religious Antisemitism," *Sixteenth Century Journal* 18 (1987), 3-30.

[11] Prynne, *A Short Demurrer*, 4.

[12] Prynne, *A Short Demurrer*, 89; also 95, where he comments about the popes' allowing them to live in papal jurisdictions: "The reason why they are permitted to live thus under our holy fathers Nose, is forsooth, *an expectation of their conversion, which is a meer pretence, the reason being indeed the benefit hence arising to his Holinesse coffers,* but the hopes of their conversion is small, and the means lesse."

The range of the papacy's plotting is in Prynne's mind incredible, including any religious group, even those persecuted by the Spanish Inquisition and Crown, as secret agents against English Christianity, despite the fact that he also argues that the conversos had not truly converted to Catholicism, but had merely pretended.[13] One of the reasons for their expulsion from Spain, he warned, was that they were succeeding in converting Spanish nobles to the faith, a point he claims had been made also by Menasseh ben Israel.[14]

Furthermore, on his Antisemitic account, the Jews were notorious as poisoners of Christian princes, citing, among others, the trial of Dr. Rodrigo Lopez, the converso physician of Queen Elizabeth who was caught up in a Spanish assassination plot against her in the 1590s. But even when they do not harm Christians physically, Prynne fumes, they do so spiritually, poisoning their faith and culture.[15]

---

[13] *"There being no lesse than one hundred twenty four thousand Jews banished out of Spain, Anno 1492. leaving all their gold, jewels, houses behind them, and paying two duckets a poll to the King for their transportation into Portugal; some of them there seemingly turned Christians, and were baptized, but yet secretly practised their Judaical rites, being Christians only in shew, but not in heart, observing the Passeover, and eating flesh with the Iewes."* Prynne, A Short Demurrer, 113. To portray Jews as secret agents of the Catholic papacy while at the same time not being sincere in their conversion to Catholicism is as specious an argument as they come.

[14] Prynne, *A Short Demurrer*, 118: "And *Frederic.* & *Isabella* banished them out of *Spain* upon this ground, that they induced many of the Nobles in *Andaluzia* to become Jews, as *Manasseh Ben-Israel* himself acknowledged, p. 15.25."

[15] "Yea, *Sedechias* the *Iewish Physician* poysoned the Emperor *Charles the Bald* his body, as well as others in that age and after poysoned other *Christians* souls. What mischiefs then they may doe to mens bodies in *England*, by poysoning of them, (as they did the *English Barons* heretofore, and Dr. *Lopez* a Iew, bribed by the *Spaniard* would have poysoned *Queen Elizabeth* of late whom he professed, he loved as

Any alternative to a single state-mandated Reformed Church was for Prynne diabolical, and it was in that context that he became absolutely apoplectic that Parliament would even consider adding the Jews to the mix.

In 1656 a D.L. responded to Prynne's diatribe, condemning Prynne and his fellows for searching "all the withered and Moth-eaten writers of that Romish faction, and fight only with Popish weapons against the Jews," for the ritual murder accusations and miracle stories Prynne retold were features only of Catholic superstition.[16] D.L. was right: Prynne's use of medieval Catholic Antisemitic myths was irrational for a Protestant, yet reason had not stopped Prynne before, and it did not do so now. Admitting the Jews was for him the last straw in England's descent into religious chaos, as his fellows ran "from one New Sect, Faith, Opinion to another, still seeking after the *newest Faith*, as if they had quite lost the *old*; changing so often, that none know of what Faith or Sect they are." Listing the various sects, he argues that they all lead from one to the other, progressively to "Professed *Atheists*" who make "Christ himself, a *Fable*."[17]

---

well as he did Iesus Christ himself) and what desperate venom they may infuse into their souls by their Iewish Doctrines, Synagogues, and Antichristian Ceremonies, if admitted without, such or upon these restrictions, or any other, let all prudent Christians resolve." Prynne, *A Short Demurrer*, 118. On Lopez, see Waite, *Jews and Muslims*, 26-28.

[16] D. L., *Israels Condition and Cause pleaded; or some Arguments for the Jews Admission into England* (London: P.W., 1656), A3^{r-v}, 2-3.

[17] William Prynne, *Some popish errors, unadvisedly embraced and pursued by our anticommunion ministers wherein is discovered the dangerous effects of their discontinuing the frequent publick administration of the lords supper ...: With a new discovery of some romish emmissaries, quakers ...* (London: for the author, 1658), 2-3. This seems to have been a slightly revised reprint of Prynne's *A new discovery of some romish emissaries, quakers; as likewise of some popish errors, unadvisedly embraced, pursued by our anticommunion ministers. discovering the dangerous effects of their discontinuing the frequent publick administration*

As noted above, for Prynne all new religious groups were secret agent Catholic friars "who turn disguised *Anabaptists* and *Quakers* to undermine our Church, Religion, Ministers, and seduce the people under these disguises."[18] The hazardous bewilderment they are creating will merely "infuse this *Spirit of Giddinesse* into our *intoxicated besotted English brains*." He therefore adds the Jews to this mix of Catholic agents, implying that Menasseh too was an "extraordinary disguised *Missionary of the Pope*" who aimed to ensure that the "*Antichristian Infidel Iews* themselves should *be specially invited to come in and reside amongst us.*"[19] Prynne places responsibility for the ongoing confusion in his homeland squarely at the feet of the Dutch Republic from whence Menasseh had come and where the Anabaptist fanaticism now afflicting England had arisen. He observed that there the Jews were not only tolerated, but they faced no pressure to convert to the Reformed faith, which was one of the purported goals of those at the Whitehall Conference who were supporting Menasseh's recommendations. The currently confused English religious state would do nothing to encourage the conversion of the Jews.[20]

Using stories told by Catholic inquisitors and Jesuits to condemn Anabaptists, Baptists, Quakers, and Jews as Jesuitical, well, that's a bit extreme, as D. L. had observed. Other of Prynne's fellow Puritans condemned him for using nasty Catholic polemics against fellow Christians. Prynne's conviction that Anabaptists, Baptists, Quakers, Catholics, and Jews were all engaged in a single diabolical conspiracy

---

of the lords supper; the popish errors whereon it is bottomed; perswading the frequent celebration of it, to all visible church-members, with their free-admission thereunto; and prescribing some legal regal remedies to redress the new sacrilegious detaining of it from the people, where their ministers are obstinate (London: for the author, 1656).

[18] Prynne, *Some popish errors*, 10.

[19] Prynne, *Some popish errors*, 3, 28.

[20] Prynne, *A Short Demurrer*, 112.

against the church and state in England that came to a head in 1655 with the visit of Rabbi Menasseh ben Israel seems sincere, if illogical. One can only imagine Prynne's bile had he known that Baptists like Henry Jessey and other Christian nonconformists were greatly assisting the rabbi's mission.[21]

Alexander Ross's *Pansebeia*, 1655

Puritans like Pagitt, Featley, and Prynne were not the only opponents of religious diversity in England. High Church Anglicans too opposed dissent from the state church, and this is seen most clearly in the Anglican royalist Alexander Ross' *Pansebeia, or, A view of all religions in the world* of 1652, and the second, post mortem edition of 1655. Here, despite his opposition to Presbyterianism, Ross (1590-1654) pursues a Prynne-like strategy, although relying on continental Protestant writers like Bullinger and Sleidanus to show how each tenet of the Anabaptists had an ancient or medieval heretical forebear. From Arius they deny Christ's divinity, from the Pelagians they deny infant baptism, like the Cathars and Muslims they say that "our righteousnesse depends upon the works of charity and affliction, not upon faith in Christ," like the old Nicolatians they have community of goods, like the Jews they teach that a husband can readily divorce his wife, and that, again like the Muslims,

---

[21] Prynne, *The quakers unmasked*, 20-21, 23. See also Waite, "Seventeenth-Century English Writers." Jessey was also associated with the Fifth Monarchists, although he is considered a moderate. Barrington White, "Henry Jessey in the Great Rebellion," in *Reformation, Conformity and Dissent: Essays in Honour of Geoffrey Nuttall*, R. Buick Knox, ed. (London, 1977), 132-53; and Joshua Caleb Smith, "Whirlwinds, Sudden Death, and an Army of Toads: Baptist Prodigies of the 1660s," in *New Directions in the Radical Reformation: "Thinking Outside the Cages,"* Geoffrey Dipple and Kat Hill, eds. (Leiden: Brill, 2023), 83-114.

a Christian may have many wives.[22] Ross has even increased the number of groups from Featley's 15 to 20 separate sects, excluding Featley's Hemerobaptists and adding six more, including the Denkians, supporters of "Johannes Denck who would have the Devils to be saved."[23] He then uses these definitions to show how English sectarians such as the Brownists hold to one or the other of these noxious heresies.

Interestingly, Ross diverges from Puritan tactics by not associating Anabaptism with witchcraft, which he more or less identifies with pagans, such as the Indigenous Peoples of the Siberian North, whom he claims "are much addicted to witchcraft and idolatry."[24] Even his link between the Quakers and Anabaptists is brief. He writes that "all or most" of the opinions of the Quakers "are Anabaptisticall, and this Sect is the spawn of Anabaptists," whom he notes are divided into numerous factions.[25] He instead emphasizes their pretended visionary authority back in 1520s Germany, beginning with their "author, one *Nicholas Storke* who pretended familiarity with God by an Angel" who promised him an earthly kingdom. Storch apparently then taught Müntzer who led the peasants in a revolt "to maintaine his Masters dreams" which were then taken up by John of Leiden, a dream that crashed to the earth when the city of Münster was captured.

---

[22] Alexander Ross, *Pansebeia, or, A view of all religions in the world with the severall church-governments from the creation, to these times: Also, a discovery of all known heresies in all ages and places, and choice observations and reflections throughout the whole* (London: T.C. for John Saywell, 1655), 362.

[23] Ross, *Pansebeia*, 362-63. His Monstasterienses or Münsterites were more or less a duplication of the Bucheldians. He also lists the *Deo reliciti* who reject "all meanes and relied onely upon God; and the *Semper Orantes*, who pray instead of working for a living.

[24] Ross, *Pansebeia*, 73.

[25] Ross, *Pansebeia*, 387.

The points of doctrine of greatest concern to Ross were Anabaptism's alleged denial of both Christ's humanity – in that he was not the son of Mary – and divinity; its promotion of salvation by one's own merits and of polygamy, easy divorce, and community of goods; and its renunciation of infant baptism, of communion with other churches, and especially of allegiance to a Christian magistracy.[26] And, given Ross' obvious distaste for Islam, he further seeks to discredit this faith by comparison with Anabaptists:

> By Mahuments Law Soothsayers are inprisoned, and yet here are many of that profession. There are here divers Sects of Mahumetans, some like our Anabaptists, condeming all learning, and trusting to Enthusiasmes; others who think by their fasting and good works, that they are so holy and perfect, that they cannot sin. There be some who hold all Religions to be true, because every one takes that to be God which he worships, and they teach that the Heaven with the Planets, Stars, and Elements are one God.[27]

Included at the end of Ross' book is the first English translation, by John Davis, of the Haestens' illustrated text *Abomination of the Foremost Head Heretics*. The translation is fairly consistent with the original, with the exception that the biography of the Prophet Muhammad is reduced from six pages in the Dutch version to only one, but containing even more salacious and scandalous claims than in the

---

[26] Ross, *Pansebeia*, 229.
[27] Ross, *Pansebeia*, 96.

original.[28] This change reflects again Ross's battle against Islam.[29]

The Davis translation frequently satirizes Anabaptist heretics by calling them monsters, making the explicit play on the Münster/Monster alliteration in the biography of Münster's chancellor, Bernhard Knipperdolling: in 1534 "at *Munster* or rather *Monster*, (for so may that place be called from the *monstrous* and portentous pullulation of Anabaptists)," he sneers.[30] The stories included herein emphasize the ecstatic excesses of Anabaptists caught up in the apocalyptic moment, and were clearly intended to act as a warning against modern-day visionaries. For his part, Ross similarly described the Ranters as "a sort of beasts" like the Quakers, although the former practice their lewdnesse in public, while the latter hide theirs behind "pretences of sanctity." This Ranter "monster" regards God, devils, angels, heaven and hell as fictions, Christ as an impostor, and so on. Ross cannot contain his bile, he is so incensed.[31]

Yet the lack of a fully demonizing motif tying Anabaptists and Quakers to witches, is a notable distinction from the polemics of his contemporary Puritan writers. While he does not include any reference to the trials of the Witchfinder General, it is likely that Ross saw these as a distasteful excess caused by Puritan extremists and as harmful to a good social and political order.

---

[28] *Grouwelen der voornaemster hooft-ketteren* (1623), 26-32, compared to John Davis, *Apocalypsis: Or, the Revelation Of certain notorious Advancers of Heresie: Wherein their Visions and private Revelations by Dreams, are discovered to be most incredible blasphemies, and enthusiastical dotages: Together with an account of their Lives, Actions, and* Ends (London: E. Tyler, 1655), 58-59.
[29] See Waite, *Jews and Muslims*, 99.
[30] Davis, *Apocalypsis*, 19.
[31] Ross, *Pansebeia*, 387.

Blome, *The Fanatick History*, 1660

We will conclude our discussion with two very different works from the year of the Restoration of the monarchy, 1660. It helps us here that Andrew Crome has recently published an excellent discussion of Anabaptist polemics (specifically Münster) in Restoration England, so we need not go beyond 1660 in our analysis.[32] The first of these two examples was composed by Richard Blome (d. 1705), an engraver and cartographer who produced highly illustrated works on the geography of Great Britain, its colonies, and "the world," as well as on heraldry and "the gentlemans recreation."[33] Later in his career he sought subscribers for a proposed illustrated edition and translation of Anthony Le Grand's Cartesian philosophy, but that seems not to have gotten off the ground.[34] It is therefore interesting to note that his first publications were on the subject of religious diversity. In 1659 he intervened in a disputation between two Quakers, George Whitehead and George Fox, and "one Universitie man in Cambridge," on August 29, 1659. In this short work, Blome asks 55 questions, most of them leading ones intended to discredit the beliefs of the Friends. These included aspersions that Whitehead was teaching that the

---

[32] Crome, "The Münster Rising."
[33] Basic information on Blome is from https://en.wikipedia.org/wiki/Richard_Blome and from the list of his works in EEBO.
[34] Richard Blome, *Proposals for the printing an entire course or body of philosophy, according to the principles of the famous renate des cartes, wrote in latin by the learned anthony le grand which will now be carefully translated into english by good hands, with large additions and alterations by the said author, and printed in folio, with an illustration of about an hundred ornamental scultptures / by richard blome, dwelling near clare-market in new weld-street, at the house with green pallisado-pails; where proposals are delivered and subscriptions taken for the same, and where they may inspect the said work* (London: R. Blome, 1693).

Bible is not the word of God, that only dreamers and "conjurers" believed in the Trinity, and that the two sacraments were of little worth.³⁵ More scandalously, Blome joined the chorus of anti-Quaker writers associating them with the devil and witchcraft, in his case with insinuations of demonic possession: "Is it not evident that some of you (if not all more or less) are possessed with the Devill," especially when at some Quaker meetings "many men, women and little children, have been strangely wrought upon in their bodies, and brought to fall, foam at the mouth, roar, and swell in their bellies?"³⁶ Given that Quakers were still being prosecuted not only for heresy but also for witchcraft, such accusations had great potential to cause further harm.³⁷

But it is the work that Blome published the following year that we will examine here: *The fanatick history: Or an exact relation and account of the old anabaptists, and new quakers. Being the summe of all that hath been yet discovered about their most blasphemous opinions, dangerous pactises [sic], and malitious endevours to subvert all civil government both in church and state. Together with their mad mimick pranks, and their ridiculous actions and gestures, enough to amaze any sober christian. Which may prove the death & burial of the fanatick doctrine.*³⁸

---

³⁵ Richard Blome, *Questions propounded to george whitehead and george fox &c. who disputed by turnes against one universitie man in cambridge. aug. 29. 1659* (London: n.p., 1659), 2.

³⁶ Blome, *Questions*, 2-3.

³⁷ Elmer, "'Saints or sorcerers';" also John Marshall, "Seventeenth-century Quakers, emotions, and egalitarianism: Sufferings, oppression, intolerance, and Slavery," in *Feeling Exclusion: Religious Conflict, Exile and Emotions in Early Modern Europe*, Giovanni Tarantino and Charles Zika, eds. (London, 2019), 146-64.

³⁸ Richard Blome, *The fanatick history: Or an exact relation and account of the old anabaptists, and new quakers. being the summe of all that hath been yet discovered about their most blasphemous opinions, dangerous pactises [sic], and malitious endevours to subvert all civil government both*

Illustrated with a portrait of King Charles II, to whom the foreword is addressed, Blome claimed that this work was an anonymous one that had come into his hands and that he is simply its publisher. He pleads with the restored king to "stifle" the "Blasphemous tenets, and Heretie [sic] opinions especially by *Anabaptists*, and *Quakers*."[39] In the preface to the work, the author (whether Blome or another), tells the reader that here they have "an exact account and History of the Opinions, Blasphemies, and practises of the *Old Anabaptists* in Germany, which so much infested those States; and the *New Quakers in England*, which have of late so much molested us." That said, the author warns against labelling anything one dislikes "with the brand of *Anabaptist* or *Quaker*," for that merely makes the labels senseless and gives credence to the Quakers when they claim to have been unjustly slandered.[40] The devil can take on many shapes and quote scripture with the best of them.

In this treatise of over 200 pages, the author compares and contrasts "the Old Anabaptist" who had so devastated the German lands, not with the modern Baptists, as one might expect, but with the "New Quaker."[41] This connection is a reflection of the post-Restoration fixation on the dangers of Quakerism and the relative peace made with other sects like the Baptists who were depicted less vigorously as harbingers of ecstatic excess or of rebellion. For Protestants like Blome, the Quakers remained a danger as a means by which the devil could reintroduce Catholicism into the

---

in church and state. together with their mad mimick pranks, and their ridiculous actions and gestures, enough to amaze any sober christian. which may prove the death & burial of the fanatick doctrine. published with the approbation of divers orthodox divines (London: for J. Sims, 1660). There are two known printings of this work, both from 1660.

[39] Blome, *The fanatick history*, fols. A2^{r-v}. The work discusses the disputation at Cambridge in 1659, in which Blome had intervened.

[40] Blome, *The fanatick history*, fols. A3^{r-v}.

[41] Blome, *The fanatick history*, fol. A4^{v}.

realm, since it depreciated scripture and elevated personal experience in ways that sidelined scripture and proper worship so esteemed by Protestants. Anabaptism began, the writer asserts, when Luther "dispelled the dark night of Popery," but inadvertently "raised the foul mist of *Anabaptism*" which found a home in those possessed of "weak and turbulent natures" due to the corruption of their humors. This was an argument based on the very popular theory that humoral corruption, especially the condition known by Galenists as Melancholia, made sufferers susceptible to religious "enthusiasm."

As observed above, in 1656 Henry More had published his *Enthusiasmus triumphatus* explaining the roots of what he considered spiritualistic extremism, such as that propounded by David Joris (George), the Familists, and the Quakers, among others. Such learned humoral theorizing provided the author of our Blome publication with plenty of material from which to fashion his own analysis.[42] The author thus emphasizes the alleged mystical excesses of Anabaptism, which he asserts "lasted not in its strength above ten years" and which continues to cause irritation in England "in obscure corners" only.[43] Like Ross and so many others, he traces the origin of Anabaptism in the mystical radicalism of Nicholas Storch and the other Saxon radicals, especially Thomas Müntzer, who boasted that "they talked

---

[42] Angus Gowland, "The Problem of Early Modern Melancholy," *Past & Present* 191 (2006), 77–120; see also Waite, "The Devil of Delft," 456-63. For an intriguing analysis of enthusiasm and emotions among modern German Protestants, see Monique Scheer, *Enthusiasm: Emotional Practices of Conviction in Modern Germany* (Oxford, 2020). She argues that with their "elimination of mediators between God and the individual soul," they were preoccupied with emotion, something that could certainly also be said of early-modern Protestants, including the English. See Matthew Milner, *The Senses and the English Reformation* (Burlington, VT, 2011).
[43] Blome, *The Fanatick history*, 2.

with God, and God with them, who commanded them to kill all the wicked and make a new World," in the process associating the Wittenberg Reformer Andreas Bodenstein von Karlstadt with the movement, because Karlstadt had advocated for the removal of religious images from churches.[44] Such individuals, Blome implies, relied heavily on dreams as means of divine communication, leading of course to the folly of the Peasants' War, during which Müntzer promised his followers at Frankenhausen that the bullets of the lord's forces would not harm them. Blome laments that Luther's admonitions to not "believe the Sermons of every preacher" since Satan appeared "under the colour of the Gospel" had been ignored to their peril.[45]

Blome then turns to Melchior Hoffman (Hopman) and the Anabaptist kingdom of Münster, claiming that "scarce two years after *Muncer*" Germany was full of Anabaptists, which was a revival of Müntzer's sect under a new name. Their goal was comparable: to take power and destroy the godless. They required community of goods and polygamy, condemned learning, since "ignorant men are the fittest to expound Scripture" and that "everyone may speak as he is inspired by the Holy Ghost."[46] Such policies were put into action by Jan van Leiden and others, which blighted Amsterdam until its magistrates repressed the movement with "fines and imprisonments and wholesome severity," scattering Anabaptists "over the Country, filling all with clamour … threatning ruine and destruction to all that would not adhere to them," and beginning their reign in Münster.[47] Then follows a detailed history of the Münster episode, relying primarily on the Dutch historian Lambertus Hortensius' sensationalistic account *Tumultuum anabaptist-*

---

[44] Blome, *The Fanatick history*, 6-7.
[45] Blome, *The Fanatick history*, 7-15.
[46] Blome, *The Fanatick history*, 16-17.
[47] Blome, *The Fanatick history*, 19.

arum liber unus (Basel, 1548), which praises Amsterdam's magistrates for their strong handling of the Anabaptist affair in contrast to the negligence of Münster's government.[48] Whenever possible, Blome cites examples of ecstatic behaviour on the part of the Anabaptists, such as the chancellor Knipperdolling, who in the court of the pretended king "would ever come out with some *Bedlam* rapture: One time he fell flat to the ground, and creeping upon his hands and feet, he went to several persons of the Assembly, and blowing them in the mouth said, The Father hath sanctified thee, receive the holy Ghost."[49]

After recounting the fall of the kingdom and Van Leiden's execution, Blome turns to the other tumults in the Low Countries, such as the sword spirits and naaktloopers of Amsterdam, and the short-lived uprising in the city in May, 1535. He makes much of the naaktloopers, of course, since their unconventional action was inspired by the ecstatic visions of their prophet "*Theodoret*" who "fell flat to the ground, and prayed with such vehemency, that he scared all the assistants out of their wits. Then rising as it were out of an extasie, I have seen (said he) God in his Majesty, and have spoken with him. I was wrapt up to Heaven, then I descended into Hell," in the end telling his dozen supporters, including several women, to remove themselves from all earthly attachments, including clothing, to proclaim the naked truth (see figure 10).[50]

---

[48] https://gameo.org/index.php?title=Hortensius,_Lambertus_(1500-1574) Blome (*The fanatick history*, 44) also cites the account of the Lutheran Pastor Antonius Corvinus, who had interviewed Van Leiden prior to his execution in 1536. On the sources of Münster, see De Bakker, Driedger, and Stayer, *Bernhard Rothmann*, 9-10.
[49] Blome, *The fanatick history*, 34.
[50] Blome, *The fanatick history*, 51-52.

Figure 10: Diederick Snyder, leader of the Naaktloopers, by Van Sichem, in Haestens, *Historische beschrijvinge ende affbeeldinge der voorneemste hooft ketteren* (Amsterdam: C. Claesz, 1608), plate 11. Courtesy of the Rijksmuseum, Amsterdam, RP-P-1907-3379.

The parallel with the ecstatic actions of a few Quakers, such as James Naylor, Blome exploits without mercy; when he's finished with the Anabaptists, he turns immediately to "our English-Quakers," telling similar stories "All to one and the same end."[51] His description of the origin of the Friends is

---

[51] Blome, *The fanatick history*, 65.

telling: "Of late years, under the Sunshine of *too generall* a toleration, there hath sprung up a sort of people, generally called *Quakers* from the *quaking and trembling* of their bodies, in a *very strange* and *vncouth* manner, when (either really or pretendedly) acted by another spirit then their own."[52] Blome hardly needs to make the comparisons with Anabaptism explicit, for the reader is able to do that quite nicely thanks to his detailed setting of the stage with the chaos caused by Anabaptist enthusiasts who were not adequately suppressed by their government.

Quakers, Blome continues, also relied on "occult revelations" and "the voice of God within them," causing them to disrupt church meetings and allow their women to denude "themselves of all shamefacedness, [and] with *brazen* faces vent their *brain sick phancies* under pretext, of impulsion of the *Holy Spirit*." They too "Go *naked frequently in the streets* exposing their nakedness to publique view."[53] He follows this with detailed stories of infamous Quaker actions by John Gilpin, John Tolderry, and of course James Naylor, all of which were filled with visionary ecstasies, apparitions, physical quaking, and public disrobing at the command of the Spirit that confounded their viewers. So too did apocalyptic claims of becoming one of Christ's judges at the Last Judgement, another obvious comparison with Melchiorite Anabaptism.[54] Naylor's entry into Bristol on horseback while followers sang "holy, holy, holy," was not just a blasphemous parody of Jesus' entry into Jerusalem, but it drew the reader's mind back to the unusual behaviour of Jan van Leiden who similarly saw himself as the new Christ.[55] Blome looks for every single possible case of extreme enthusiasm he can find, such as the alleged 1653 Quaker

---

[52] Blome, *The fanatick history*, 66-67.
[53] Blome, *The fanatick history*, 69-70.
[54] Blome, *The fanatick history*, 91.
[55] Blome, *The fanatick history*, 101.

meeting in North Wales in which the Friends "fell into *great and dreadfull shakings* with such swellings in their bodies, sending out such *shreekings* and *howlings* as not only frighted the beholders, but caused Dogs to bark, swine to cry, and the cattel to run about."[56] He seems particularly concerned about nudity, citing numerous examples of such excess; in Blome's telling, these stories automatically drew the reader's mind back to the naaktloopers of Amsterdam.[57]

Blome's book was noticed on the Continent as well, for in 1701 it was translated into German by the Danzig preacher Benedict Figken, who added a foreword. A variant of Figken's edition was then included in the massive collection of anti-Anabaptist works by Johann Friedrich Corvinus, *Pantheon of Anabaptism and Enthusiasm* (*Anabaptisticum et Enthusiasticum Pantheon*) of 1702.[58] This German edition also included events after 1660, such as the Fifth Monarchist actions in London in early 1661, so the editors were either working from a later edition by Blome, which I cannot find, or added material from other works. In any event, the subtitle of the 1701 edition is perhaps more inflammatory than in Corvinus's version, referring to the Anabaptist/Quaker movements as "gruesome blasphemy, evil acts, rebellion, and murder," which had convulsed many German states, including Münster in Westphalia, and finally

---

[56] Blome, *The fanatick history*, 108.

[57] Blome, *The fanatick history*, 111-19.

[58] Johann Friedrich Corvinus, *Anabaptisticum et enthusiasticum pantheon und geistliches Rüst-Hauss wider die alten Quacker, und neuen Frey-Geiste : welche die Kirche Gottes zeithero verunruhiget, und bestürmet, auch treue Lehrer und Prediger Göttlichen Worts, verachtet, verleumbdet, gelästert und verfolget haben : mit vielen zur Sache dienlichen und nützlichen Kupffern, bloss zu Gottes Ehre und Erhaltun seiner christlichen Kirchen : auch den Geistlichen Weltlichen und Hausstande zur Nachricht, Nutz und besten zusammen getragen und auffgerichtet* (n.p., n.p., 1702). I am thankful to Michael Driedger for alerting me to this work.

now employed and practised in London England.⁵⁹ The major difference between these two variants and that of Blome's original is that the Corvinus version has included images, such as figure 11, depicting the Quaker use of sorcery to bewitch people, especially women, into following them. Such merging of categories such as heresy and witchcraft had already had significant impact in the German lands, as the demonizing of Anabaptists had helped revive the witch-hunts in southwestern Germany in 1562.⁶⁰ We have already noted how such transference of ideas and fears from Anabaptists to alleged witches and back onto dissenters like Quakers had helped inflame witch trials in England as well, along with making life difficult for the Quakers. Corvinus was obviously trying to counteract the growth of Lutheran Pietism, whose proponents, such as Gottfried Arnold in his 1700 *Impartial Church and Heretic History*, had sought to restore the image of Anabaptists and Spiritualists, including David Joris, against the centuries of bad press.⁶¹

---

⁵⁹ [Richard Blome], *Historia Fanaticorvm, Oder eine vollkommene Relation und Wissenschafft/ von denen Schwärmern/ Als Alten Anabaptisten und Neuen Quäkern*, trans. Benedict Figken (Frankfurt am Main: Martin Hermssdorffen, 1701). The version in Corvinus, *Anabaptisticum*, is blander, referring merely to their "blasphemous opinions, dangerous practises, and godless assassinations" that would subvert all governments: "So die Summa ist alles dessen/ was von ihren mehrentheils blasphemischen Opinionen/ gefährlichen Practiken/ und gottlosen Attentaten, alles Civil Guvernement, bydes in der Kirchen/ und in gemeinen Weltwesen zu subvertiren, kund worden/… Publicirit in Londen Anno 1660, mit der Approbation, unterschiedener Englischen Theologen/ Nun aber Dem Vaterland Preussischer Nation, und besonders hiesiger Stadt Dantzig." Both works are available on Google Books.
⁶⁰ Waite, *Eradicating the Devil's Minions*, 144-53.
⁶¹ See Douglas H. Shantz, "David Joris, Pietist Saint: The Appeal to Joris in the Writings of Christian Hoburg, Gottfried Arnold and Johann Wilhelm Petersen," *Mennonite Quarterly Review* 78 (2004), 415-32.

Figure 11: The Quaker and Schwaermer Witchcraft, in Johann Friedrich Corvinus, *Anabaptisticum Et Enthusiasticum Pantheon*, in German translation of Blome, *The fanatick history*, 38. Courtesy of Münchener DigitalisierungsZentrum, https://mdz-nbn-resolving.de/urn:nbn:de:bvb:12-bsb11205321-0.

This example of continental writers reading and translating Blome and other English polemicists is just one of many revealing how the history of English dissent was now shaping continental perspectives. More analysis of this cross-Channel communication would be very helpful. In the meantime, we can make this point: by 1660, English

Protestants like Blome regarded Quakerism as the greatest threat to the survival of the Protestant English state, rather than Baptists, hence they adapted the story of continental Anabaptism to provide a more obvious parallel to the seventeenth-century Spiritualists. It is odd that Blome did not turn to the Spiritualist David Joris with his unusual sexual ethic, alleged approval of polygamy, and visionary claims of messianism; Henry More had done precisely that.[62] Otherwise, Blome's work reflects a significant shift in the strategy of Puritan anti-Anabaptist polemicists, for they were now targeting Quakers much more heavily than Baptists and other sectarian groups.

The Monster of Munster, 1660

We conclude, finally, on a positive note. The clamour of the new religious groups for religious tolerance had an impact. One author in 1660 published *The Gorgon's Head or The Monster of Munster* which takes the monstrous language and turns it on its ("Gorgon") head.[63] Here, the Monster of Munster is not the Münsterites, as Featley and Ross would have it, but the Bishop of Münster and all secular and ecclesiastical powers who would persecute people for their

---

[62] Blome refers to Joris only once, as one of the two "good prophets" that Münsterites allegedly followed: Jan van Leiden and David Joris. Blome, *The fanatick history*, 37. There is another reference in an account of the dispute at Cambridge, August 1659, when T. S. of Christ College disputed with the Quaker George Whitehead; at one point the latter asked the former if any heretics pretended a commission from Christ, to which T.S. responded, "Yes, David George, Socinus, Arius and all the Hereticks I ever read of"; Blome, *The fanatick history*, 152-53. On More and Joris, see Waite, "The Devil of Delft."
[63] John Coffey has noted a few Puritan voices raised against the misuse of Anabaptist history by the heresiographers. Coffey, "'The Last and Greatest Triumph'," 210-13.

religious difference.[64] This interesting work plays on both the German city of Münster and the Irish province of Munster, the latter recently in the news when the Irish rebels surrendered to Cromwell's New Model Army in 1652.

In the author's efforts to dispel the innumerable myths and slander told about Anabaptists, he denies that they held to any truly heretical ideas and were, in the face of persecution and violence, led like sheep to the slaughter. The lies of their opponents were spread precisely because the Monster of Munster had eradicated all of them after Münster's fall, leaving none to correct the misconceptions spread about them. Such lies, the author asserts, were disseminated precisely "to Incense the Multitude." These Anabaptists have instead "been our best and surest friends, and stoutest Warryers in time of Danger," a reference to the Independents who were prominent in Cromwell's army. Fearmongering that Anabaptists would, if left unchecked, "cut the throats" of the English was just one of those lies spread by this Monster who "hath lately crept up into our Pulpits," telling parishioners that the Anabaptists are "more Dangerous and powerful then Inchanters, Conjurors, or Jesuits." Baptists and Quakers are forced to "flie to their Old Denn of Amsterdam."[65]

Our author thus correctly lays blame for the demonizing of the Quakers as witches upon polemical writers and preachers. Why did they have recourse to such a strategy? He concludes that it was the result of the frustration of orthodox preachers who found themselves confounded by

---

[64] *The gorgon's head or the monster of munster cloaked with a lamb's skinn* (London: n.p., 1660). For more on this, see the intriguing essay by Michael Driedger, "Muenster, Monster, Modernity: Tracing and Challenging the Meme of Anabaptist Madness," in Mark Jantzen, Mary S. Sprunger, and John D. Thiesen, eds., *European Mennonites and the Challenge of Modernity over Five Centuries: Contributors, Detractors, and Adapters* (North Newton, KS, 2016), 27-49.

[65] *The gorgon's head*, 2, 8.

the scriptural arguments of the Anabaptists. They therefore turn to violence – to the Monster Persecution – as a means of quieting them.⁶⁶ In the end, the author concludes that England's Anabaptists have no "such unjust, foolish, or ridiculous Principles as are mentioned in that story of Munster," which is nothing but a "romance," like Don Quixote.

Perhaps John of Leiden and Bernhard Knipperdolling were extravagant in their behaviour, but such was the effect of the oppressive siege of the city which led the populace into unusual extremes. It is deeply unfair to charge all Anabaptists with such singular excesses.⁶⁷ While our author went to the opposite extreme of our heresiographers by denying many actual events relating to the Münsterite kingdom, this was perhaps a necessary hyperbole given the weight of polemical exaggeration made against Anabaptists.

---

⁶⁶ *The gorgon's head*, 9.
⁶⁷ *The gorgon's head*, 10.

Conclusion

Written just before Charles Stuart was restored to the throne as Charles II, the *Gorgon's Head* pamphlet is a fitting conclusion to our discussion of anti-Anabaptist polemics. With the Restoration, the religious toleration of the Interregnum period was ended and royal control was restored over religious life, but in a way that was limited by the public's desire for some measure of individuality.[1] While full tolerance would only come after the Glorious Revolution brought by the Dutch William III and the English Queen Mary in 1688, our anti-Anabaptist writers had spent so much time and effort condemning religious diversity that they made it a cause célèbre, one that some readers thought a positive virtue, rather than the diabolical enemy of the state. Thanks to the invective and demonizing rhetoric of the heresiographers, there was no one – certainly neither Dutch Mennonites nor English Baptists – who wished to be called Anabaptist. As Andrew Crome has astutely observed, the Restoration efforts to forgive and forget the calamity of the Civil War made polemicists wary of risking legal action by mentioning the specific groups and events of the last two decades. They could, however, use Anabaptist Münster as a stand-in, knowing that readers had already associated that event with their own Independents, in particular Baptists, Quakers, and the Fifth Monarchists.[2] In 1661 a small group

---

[1] On religious tolerance in the Restoration, see Mark Goldie, "The Theory of Religious Intolerance in Restoration England," in *From Persecution to Toleration: the Glorious Revolution and Religion in England*, Ole Peter Grell, Jonathan I. Israel and Nicholas Tyacke, eds. (Oxford, 1991), 331-368; and from the perspective of the dissenters, Richard L. Greaves, *Deliver Us from Evil: the Radical Underground in Britain, 1660-1663* (Oxford, 1988).

[2] Crome, "The Münster Rising."

of Fifth Monarchists tried to attack the English government, but only captured St. Paul's Cathedral for a couple days. Reminiscent of the Anabaptist assault on Amsterdam's city hall in 1535, this event inspired further attacks on Anabaptism in the English press.[3]

As this study has shown, English writers were profoundly ignorant of the actual history of continental Anabaptism, and certainly of its subsequent development into Mennonite communities that contributed significantly to Dutch society. If and when they read continental works, they did so largely to cherry pick examples they could use to emphasize the worst of the Anabaptists. As a result, these writers brought a distorted version of the beliefs of continental Anabaptists and Spiritualists back to England, with increasing intensity over the course of the seventeenth century. In doing so, they inadvertently provided the discontented reader with plenty of unconventional ideas that, I suggest, inspired innovative approaches to religious, economic, and social relations.

Polemics and Repression

There are several other conclusions to draw from this analysis of polemical works on Anabaptism. First, and most obviously, such literature (and the sermons and tavern conversations that presumably accompanied it) led to profoundly negative consequences for those who were targeted as heretics or Anabaptists. We have observed how some writers, such as William Turner, used the language of disease to inspire fear of religious dissenters, an effective tactic that continues to be used by proponents of conspiratorial thinking about "others," such as Jews and

---

[3] Crome, "The Münster Rising," 955-58.

Muslims.[4] As we have seen, government leaders and civic officials took some of the invective seriously enough to issue edicts against Anabaptists and to act harshly against them and their supposed allies, most especially the Quakers. Words have power, and in this case, the hateful words that we have seen in these works had the power to persuade those in power to act in accordance with the rhetoric. That said, polemicists were never happy enough on this score, as their constant complaints about laxity in prosecution of dissent would indicate. Some of this, as we have noted above, included aspects of victim-blaming, in this case persecuted religious minorities, for social and political crises.

"Anabaptism" as a Polemical Tool to Demonize Diversity

Second, the strategy of conflating groups and beliefs that were separated not only by the English Channel but also by decades or a century in time, further assisted these efforts to shape public opinion on the matter of new religious groups and the problem of religious diversity in the realm. In fact, polemical writers demonized religious diversity itself, associating it with Anabaptism, and hence with disorder and chaos. Well before 1640, Anabaptism had become a polemically loaded term that no one wanted applied to them, and certainly not Baptists. The term came to encompass beliefs and actions that did not pertain even to the original Anabaptists, but which through a process of creative fiction and conflation, became synonymous with anyone critical of the state-supported ecclesiastical hierarchy or of traditional theology relating to baptism, the priesthood, the person of Christ and the Trinity. It was also applied to those who

---

[4] There are many studies about the attacks on Jewish communities in the wake of plague outbreaks; for a recent journalistic comparison, see https://www.nytimes.com/2009/09/01/health/01plague.html.

wanted social, economic, or political change beyond that which the crown or Parliament were willing to grant.

The association with Anabaptism that so many writers made with their current malcontents provoked even more anxiety about dissent and change than would have otherwise been the case. It sharpened differences, increased the volume in arguments, and pushed people into extreme positions as they sought to defend themselves from slanderous charges of Anabaptism or stretched their arguments to make the Anabaptist label fit their opponent. Such extreme propagandizing also made people more liable to believe that change in religion or society would necessarily lead to disorder, violence, and incurring the wrath of God, as had Anabaptism in the sixteenth century, or so the polemicists claimed. They thought it best to cling to the ordered ecclesiastical and political systems in place, or to something as close to them as possible, rather than risking change. All of these were the intended consequences of the writers we have examined here. And to a degree, their hateful discourse worked.

Polemics and Unintended Consequences: Creating the Heresies

Third, in other ways, however, it had effects that would surely have surprised the orthodox had they considered why new religious groups were arising with so many of the heresies that they had been attacking for so long. If our polemicists had been able to reflect clearly upon the state of affairs, they might have noticed that their propaganda was either not working entirely as expected, or was doing the opposite of what it was intended to do. It was, by all appearances, putting those very ideas that the polemicists hated into the minds of some of their readers. In other words, it was inspiring innovation. Decades of polemical description of Anabaptist and Spiritualist novelties, such as rejection of paedobaptism in favour of believer's baptism, or denial of a devil independent from the human conscience, proved an effective means of disseminating new approaches, and not just in theology and ecclesiology.

For example, the Family of Love had been keeping some of these ideas alive in the translated works of Hendrik Niclaes and in their secretive discussions, although it appears that their active presence in England had more or less fizzled out by the 1620s or been morphed into the Seekers. Yet the polemicists did not stop attacking these nonconformist beliefs, thereby keeping them in the public sphere throughout the decades leading into the Civil War. We recall that the Anglican pastor of the English Church in Amsterdam, Henoch Clapham, in 1608 recounted a story of an Englishman who moved from the Brownists to various Anabaptist sects in Holland before finally baptizing himself. This story he told just on the eve of John Smyth doing that very thing, and it is quite possible that Smyth was influenced to take that step by such storytelling.

The concerted attack on the denial of a devil in the natural world that was focused on the demonology of the Spiritualist (and former Anabaptist) David Joris during the 1640s and its sudden appearance in the theology of the Muggletonians, is another such example of this unintended consequence of the polemics, since English readers had no access to Joris's own works, but could read about his ideas in the emotive, if sometimes entertaining, attacks of his enemies. The stories of ecstatic enthusiasm, of those who listened to the Holy Spirit within, and who thereby could find an authoritative voice against the learned clergy and their scripture interpretation, proved enticing, certainly for the Seekers and Quakers. So too did the constant complaints about the sixteenth-century Spiritualists with their invisible church keep the idea in the English consciousness. The parallels that our writers saw between the enthusiastic actions of Anabaptists and Spiritualists and their modern-day Quakers may have, in some ways, been a self-fulfilling prophecy. The personal authority that came from the voice of the Spirit within was, and remains, a powerful inducement to visionary experiences.

Similarly, our writers continued criticizing the socio-economic and political heresies of Anabaptists as a way of putting the brakes on alternative approaches to governance. Anabaptist community of goods remained a source of concern and invective, yet it too appeared in various shapes in the later 1640s, especially in the communitarian dreams of the Levellers and Diggers. New and more egalitarian approaches to social organization that polemicists linked to Anabaptist separatism and renunciation of traditional civic hierarchies may have been inspired by those very linkages.

While most writers focused on the violence of the Anabaptists, many also pointed to their refusal to take up arms and rejection of a Christian magistracy, reminding readers of the non-violence inherent in the teachings of Jesus. Polemicists may have intended their assault on the millenarianism of Melchiorite and Münsterite Anabaptism as a warning that apocalyptic dreams would only result in chaos. But those dreams of a new world order in which the ordinary folk could become God's chosen people proved extremely attractive, as seen with the Fifth Monarchists, and many other millenarian groups since. Anabaptists were also described as overturning the traditional marital order, with their alleged easy divorce for mixed-religion couples or their supposed practice of polygamy. And, most obvious, perhaps, is how polemicists created a religious sect of ecstatic nudists called the Adamites out of single *naaktlooper* incident from 1535, a creation that can still perplex the modern historian.

Over and over again, readers were told of groups of dissenters who disrobed as a means of showing their disdain for the traditional religious and social order, to proclaim the naked truth to the unaware, to show their depreciation of the material world. No surprise, then, that some Ranters and Quakers (and Adamites?) began to perform variations of the polemical descriptions, whether in the grip of ecstatic excitement or as a means of attracting attention. The polemical writers had only themselves to blame for this resurgence of the heretical ideas and behaviours that they had so violently sought to tamp down.

"Anabaptism" and Malleable Religious Identity

Fourth, another apparent observation is that the term and historical content of "Anabaptist" was for these polemicists an extremely flexible one that could be adapted for use against a wide array of targets. Prior to the Civil War, the main one was of course the quite small presence of Flemish Anabaptists in the realm, and the rise of English groups denying infant baptism, practising believer's baptism, and advocating for a separatist church, mostly in the Brownist and Baptist camps. During the Civil War and Interregnum, a vastly expanding number of writers broadened the application of the Anabaptist label to encompass a wide range of new religious movements, in the process further twisting and distorting the history of continental Anabaptism. Furthermore, most writers ignored the transformation of Dutch Anabaptism into various Mennonite groups, all of which explicitly abandoned the apocalyptic ideology, charismatic prophecy, and socio-economic innovation of their Anabaptist predecessors.

Polemicists typically sneered at the divisiveness among the Mennonites, as if that was something distinctive compared to their own situation. Had they actually observed what was happening across the Channel, they would have noticed that conservative Dutch Mennonites had, on the whole, become a self-disciplining and supportive community who cooperated with their largely tolerant government and contributed significantly to the realm's prosperity.[5] The theological innovations of the liberal Doopsgezinden or Waterlanders, not to mention the Collegiants and Socinians, would have given English churchmen plenty of ammunition to use against their own dissenters, but most writers seemed unaware of these developments in any real terms. The Collegiants hardly appear at all in English writings, although the Quaker William Penn describes meeting with some in a description of his travels to Holland in 1677.[6] Instead, polemicists preferred looking to the past, to the most "radical" phase of the Dutch-German Reformation, rather than making contemporary cross-Channel comparisons that would most likely inspire far more interest and imitation than disgust.

As an illustration of the flexibility of terms such as "Anabaptist," Prynne's labelling of Baptists, Quakers, and other Independents as secret agents of the Jesuits to restore Catholicism was not unusual in these anti-heresy diatribes, but it certainly stretched credibility to a breaking point. After the Restoration, writers like Blome could ignore sects like the Baptists entirely by focusing on the ecstatic excesses of some of the Anabaptists to tar the Quakers with the same brush of extremism. The actual history of Anabaptism and its development into a significant group within the Dutch Republic is bypassed entirely, and the Baptists are no longer

---

[5] See Piet Visser, "Mennonites and Doopsgezinden in the Netherlands"; Alastair Hamilton, Sjouke Voolstra and Piet Visser, eds., *From Martyr to Muppy: A Historical Introduction to Cultural Assimilation Processes of a Religious Minority in the Netherlands: the Mennonites* (Amsterdam, 1994); and Zijlstra, *Om de ware gemeente*.
[6] William Penn, *An account of W. penn's travails in holland and germany, anno MDCLXXVII, for the service of the gospel of christ, by way of journal containing also divers letters and epistles writ to several great and eminent persons whilst there* (London: T. Sowle, 1694).

of concern. Quakers, on the other hand, continued to be demonized as secret Catholics and/or as demonic agents.

That such terms were highly adaptable was noted by Christopher Hill in his *The World Turned Upside Down*, when he commented that people "moved easily from one critical group to another, and a Quaker of the early 1650s had far more in common with a Leveller, a Digger or a Ranter than with a modern member of the Society of Friends."[7] Moreover, dissenters had more in common with each other than they did with hardline Protestants and Anglicans like Featley, Prynne, Blome, and Ross. Historians who use labels like "Anabaptist" or "radical" or "Independents" need to keep this flexibility in mind, both for seventeenth-century England and for sixteenth-century "Anabaptists."

Many dissenters in both eras did not see themselves locked into the same kind of hard and fast theological and ecclesial boxes as the nomenclature used by historians might imply. What many of the polemicists seem to have feared most, in fact, was the malleability of religious identity itself, that people could move from one group or set of beliefs to another, that adherence to formal confessions of faith and organizations was not guaranteed. It was disturbing that a person you were arguing with could switch to another group or set of theological beliefs without difficulty, or that they might be harbouring even more unorthodox ideas secretly. It was far more comforting for churchmen to be able to nail down their opponents into fixed confessional categories. They however discovered that this was often impossible, and such elasticity elevated anxiety over religious identity to extreme levels, if Prynne is anything to go by. It would have been easier for such polemicists if dissenters stayed in their own lanes, yet they saw that a prophetic or visionary pronouncement of a charismatic leader could cause some to

---

[7] Hill, *the World Turned Upside Down*, 14.

shift lanes or to run off in unexpected directions. No wonder polemical writers feared chaos.

Historians need to take more seriously this anxiety and that the terms used then – such as "Anabaptist" – had far less precision than scholars might desire. We need more fully to appreciate that people, then and now, could be quite creative and adaptable in the religious ideas that they were considering, and that, when presented with more than one religious option, they could not only compare and contrast the denominations on offer, but pick and choose elements from them to craft new varieties. Even those who remained in the formally approved church might have harboured some ideas that were less than orthodox, or not care all that much about the dissenters among them.

Polemics, Then and Now

Such misuse of history has, unfortunately, become a standard tactic for those engaged in polemical distortions or who search for historical antecedents to serve their particular cause. We see this in the present controversy over the distorted usage of medieval history by far-right wing and White supremacist groups.[8] More obvious is the very strange amalgam of beliefs and prophetic predictions that has come together in the conspiracy world of QAnon and the Freedom Convoys of 2022 and which include many such distortions of previous ideas and myths, including the accusations of global conspiracies and ritual murder levelled for centuries against Jews as well as elements drawn from the early-

---

[8] See, for example, Dorothy Kim, "White Supremacists Have Weaponized an Imaginary Viking Past. It's Time to Reclaim the Real History" *Time*. April 15, 2019. https://time.com/5569399/viking-history-white-nationalists/.

modern witch trials.⁹ And now, Antisemitic tropes are merging with hatred expressed against the LGBTQ and transgender communities.¹⁰

Prynne's recourse to medieval ritual murder myths is merely one example of how these irrational beliefs were and remain an undercurrent of popular culture which could be revived and reimagined over subsequent centuries, laying the groundwork for the Holocaust and continuing to inspire violence against Jews. Perhaps more puzzling are the present elements in QAnon that seem to have been derived from early-modern demonology, including demonic possession and sexual intercourse with demons.¹¹ These too have been reinvigorated within evangelical Christian communities that have maintained belief in a literal devil and his purported machinations, leading to the Satanic Ritual Abuse panics of

---

⁹ Gary K. Waite, "Hate Literature Then and Now," Blog Post, Acadia Centre for Baptist and Anabaptist Studies, Acadia University, Wolfville, NS, April 9, 2022: https://acadiadiv.ca/acbas/2022/hate-literature-then-and-now/. On QAnon, see Mike Rothschild, *The Storm is Upon Us: How QAnon Became a Movement, Cult, and Conspiracy Theory of Everything* (Brooklyn, 2021).

¹⁰ See Nick Logan, "How antisemitic tropes are being used to target the LGBTQ community" CBC. February 5, 2023: https://www.cbc.ca/news/world/antisemitism-transphobia-lgbtq-hate-1.6729223

¹¹ See, for example, reports on the controversial Houston doctor Stella Immanuel who, among other strange things that puzzle reporters, in July 2020 referred to lizard people and alien DNA and claimed that ovarian cysts were caused by sex with demons, https://www.vanityfair.com/style/2020/07/demon-sex-donald-trump; or https://www.thedailybeast.com/stella-immanuel-trumps-new-covid-doctor-believes-in-alien-dna-demon-sperm-and-hydroxychloroquine. Demonic sex was a central part of the demonic witch stereotype, with arguments among demonologists over how incorporeal demons could have sex with humans, many turning to Aristotle's concept of demons shaping the air around them into aerial bodies. See especially Stephens, *Demon Lovers*; and more generally, Clark, *Thinking with Demons*.

the 1980s and 1990s.[12] In those cases, many conservative Christians saw themselves battling against a growth in atheism and assaults against traditional religious values. They preached sermons, published tracts, and produced and disseminated videos on the Satanic dangers of new religious movements, especially Wiccan and other New Age groups.[13] As Debbie Nathan and Michael Snedeker observed with respect to some of the prominent police actors in the phenomenon, their "obsession with endangered children reflected the fact that many were evangelical Christians convinced that Satan was out to conquer the world by turning the younger generation away from God and Jesus." They resorted to alleged proof in the so-called Wicca Letters, which purported to provide evidence of a Satanist plot to "conquer the world by infiltrating day-care centers and corrupting America's preschoolers." The authors suggest that this was a parallel to the infamous *Protocols of the Elders of Zion* which were concocted in the early

---

[12] See, among many other works, James T. Richardson, Joel Best and David G. Bromley, eds., *The Satanism Scare* (New York, NY, 1991). On the long history of belief in a diabolical agency and the end of the world, see, for example, Philip C. Almond, *The Antichrist: A New Biography* (Cambridge, 2020). For an Anthropological comparative approach, see Jean La Fontaine, *Witches and Demons: A Comparative Perspective on Witchcraft and Satanism* (New York, 2016).

[13] A good place to start is David Frankfurter, "Ritual as Accusation and Atrocity: Satanic Ritual Abuse, Gnostic Libertinism, and Primal Murders," *History of Religions* 40 (2001), 352-80, which cites most of the important scholarship on the subject up to 2000; and Richardson, Best, and Bromley, *The Satanism Scare*, which also includes a chapter by the prominent historian of the witch-hunts, Jeffrey Burton Russell on "The Historical Satan," 41-49. On evangelical Christian beliefs and the accusations, see also https://www.ojp.gov/ncjrs/virtual-library/abstracts/one-face-devil-satanic-ritual-abuse-moral-crusade-and-law. See also https://www.vox.com/culture/22358153/satanic-panic-ritual-abuse-history-conspiracy-theories-explained; and https://www.nytimes.com/2021/03/31/us/satanic-panic.html, among numerous journalistic treatments.

twentieth century by Russian police to accuse Jews of plotting the overthrow of Christendom. Unfortunately, this noxious piece of conspiracy thinking remains prominent within Antisemitic circles, and likely provided the role model for the Wicca Letters.[14] The harmful results are now part of the historical record, inspiring the trials of thousands of individuals on charges of satanic abuse of children, as well as increased reports of demonic possession cases and requests for exorcisms.[15]

There are plenty of parallels for historians to examine between the early modern witch panics and the Satanic Ritual Abuse phenomenon, both in terms of the demonological and conspiratorial thinking that lay behind them, and their social dynamics. For example, defending the accused could be dangerous, not only for early-modern writers like Johan Wier, but also for more contemporary ones; the journalist Debbie Nathan cited above, herself once "had the police at her door, on a maliciously false report of child maltreatment, after publishing an article suggesting the innocence of a day-care teacher convicted of ritual abuse."[16] Such conservative Christian groups – unintentionally it seems – followed the demonizing tactics of Prynne et al., and with a similar impact as in the seventeenth century. And, these evangelical propagandists may too have inspired

---

[14] Debbie Nathan and Michael Snedeker, *Satan's Silence: Ritual Abuse and the Making of a Modern American Witch Hunt* (New York, 1995), 129. On the role of Christian Evangelicals in the British cases, see Philip Jenkins, *Intimate Enemies: Moral Panics in Contemporary Great Britain* (New York, 1992), 161-69.

[15] On the exorcisms, see especially Mike Mariani, "American Exorcism" *The Atlantic*. December 2018. https://www.theatlantic.com/magazine/archive/2018/12/catholic-exorcisms-on-the-rise/573943/, which is focused on official Catholic exorcisms, but Charismatic Protestant groups have also emphasized the activity.

[16] Nathan and Snedeker, *Satan's Silence*, ix.

interest in the modern witchcraft that they were condemning (certainly the entertainment industry has taken full advantage of the interest in the occult).

Hate Literature and Violence

Finally, if this study has revealed anything, it is that we need to more carefully examine the role of polemical works on the shaping of public discourse, both in the past and in the present. The works that we have examined here had a profound impact on the people being demonized by shaping the minds of those who demonized them. We have argued here that the anti-Anabaptist attacks, which had obvious negative impacts on English Separatists, also fed into fears of the devil and witchcraft, making the demonic witch stereotype credible by 1644. These publications acted as all forms of hate literature do: to increase fear, anxiety, and distrust of the other. Yet, there were many unintended and unexpected impacts as well, whether in inciting attacks on dissenter groups, or in convincing people of a demonic conspiracy, or in planting challenging ideas of theological, social, economic, and political reform within the minds of readers. What we are observing today, therefore, in the descent of civic discourse into similar kinds of polemical distortions as in the seventeenth century, needs not a crystal ball or a skill in scrying, but an historian's eye to see clearly that such inflammatory language can lead to harmful and violent action, intended or not, or can actually create the enemy that is under attack.

Bibliography

Websites, Databases, and Online Newspapers

https://acadiadiv.ca/acbas/event/zeman-lecture-2021/http://amsterdamnified.ca/project/
https://emodir.hypotheses.org/
https://time.com/5569399/viking-history-white-nationalists/.
https://www.vanityfair.com/style/2020/07/demon-sex-donald-trump
https://www.thedailybeast.com/stella-immanuel-trumps-new-covid-doctor-believes-in-alien-dna-demon-sperm-and-hydroxychloroquine
https://www.ojp.gov/ncjrs/virtual-library/abstracts/one-face-devil-satanic-ritual-abuse-moral-crusade-and-law.
https://www.vox.com/culture/22358153/satanic-panic-ritual-abuse-history-conspiracy-theories-explained
https://www.nytimes.com/2021/03/31/us/satanic-panic.html
https://www.nytimes.com/2009/09/01/health/01plague.html
https://www.theatlantic.com/magazine/archive/2018/12/catholic-exorcisms-on-the-rise/573943/
https://www.cbc.ca/news/world/antisemitism-transphobia-lgbtq-hate-1.6729223

Early English Books Online
Global Anabaptist Mennonite Encyclopedia Online
Wikipedia.org

Printed Primary Sources

Ainsworth, Henry. *A reply to a pretended christian plea for the anti-chistian [sic] church of rome: Published by mr. francis iohnson a°. 1617 wherin the weakness of the sayd plea is manifested, and arguments alleaged for the church of rome, and baptisme therein, are refuted.* Amsterdam: Giles Thorp 1620.

Aylmer, John. *An harborowe for faithfull and trewe subiectes agaynst the late blowne blaste, concerninge the gouernme[n]t of wemen. wherin be confuted all such reasons as a straunger of late made in that behalfe, with a breife exhortation to obedience.* London: John Day 1559.

Anon. *The confession of faith, of those churches which are commonly (though falsly) called anabaptists; presented to the view of all that feare god, to examine by the touchstone of the word of truth: As likewise for the taking off those aspersions which are frequently both in pulpit and print, (although unjustly) cast upon them.* London: n.p., 1644.

Anon. *A catalogue of the several sects and opinions in england and other nations with a briefe rehearsall of their false and dangerous tenents.* London: R.A., 1647.

Anon. *The confessyon of the fayth of the germaynes exhibited to the moste victorious emperour charles the. v. in the councell or assemble holden at augusta the yere of our lorde. 1530. to which is added the apologie of melancthon who defendeth with reasons inuincible the aforesayde confesyon translated by rycharde tauerner at the commaundeme[n]t of his master thomas cromwel chefe secretarie to the kynges grace.* London: Robert Redman, 1536.

Anon. *An Exact Catalogue of all Printed Books and Papers of Various Subjects, Written upon sundry Occasions by William Prynne Esq; a Bencher of the Honourable Society of Lincolns-Inne. Before, During, Since, His Imprisonments.* London: for Michael Sparke, 1643; reprinted for Edward Thomas, by T. Childe and L. Parry, 1660.

Anon. *The gorgon's head or the monster of munster cloaked with a lamb's skinn.* London: n.p., 1660.

Anon. *The institution of a christen man conteynynge the exposytion or interpretation of the commune crede, of the seuen sacramentes, of the .x. commandementes, and of the pater noster, and the aue maria, iustyfication [and] purgatory.* London: Thomas Berthelet, 1537.

Anon. *Obiections: Answered by way of dialogue wherein is proved by the law of god: By the law of our land: And by his maties many testimonies that no man ought to be persecuted for his religion, so he testifie his allegeance by the oath, appointed by law.* n.p.: n.p., 1615.

Anon. *The original [and] sprynge of all sectes [and] orders by whome, wha or were they beganne. translated out of hye dutch in englysh.* London: James Nicolson, 1537.

Anon. *A treuue nyeuu tydynges of the wo[n]derfull worckes of the rebaptisers of mu[n]ster in westuaell how the cete haethe bene wo[n]ne and in what mannar the kinge is taeken, and all their deades and intencyons haethe taeken an ende [et]c. iohu[n] of ley a kinge of nyew iherusalem and of the hoole vniuerall worlde beynghe in the aege of. xxvi. years. aetatis 26.* Antwerp: M. de Keyser, 1535.

B., I. *A bryefe and plaine declaracion of certayne sente[n]ces in this litle boke folowing to satisfie the consciences of them that haue iudged me therby to be a fauourer of the anabaptistes.* London: J. Day, 1547.

Baillie, Robert. *Anabaptism, the true fountaine of Independency, Brownisme, Antinomy, Familisme, and the most of the other errours, which for the time doe trouble the Church of England, unsealed. Also the questions of paedobaptisme and dipping handled from Scripture.* London: for Samuel Gellibrand, 1647.

Bakewell, Thomas. *A iustification of two points now in controversie with the anabaptists concerning baptisme: The first is, that infants of christians ought to be baptized, with grounds to prove it, and their objections answered. with a briefe answer to master tombes twelve doubtfull arguments against it in his exercitation about infants baptisme. also a briefe answer to captaine hobsons five arguments in his falacy of infants baptisme, being (as he saith) that which should have beene disputed by him, and mr. knowles, and some others; against mr. calamy and mr. cranford. the second point is, that the sprinckling the baptized more agreeth with the minde of christ then dipping or plunging in or under the water: With grounds to prove it, and a briefe auswer [sic] to what they have to say against it.* London: for Henry Shepard and William Ley, 1646.

Barlow, William. *A dyaloge describing the originall grou[n]d of these lutheran faccyons, and many of theyr abusys, compyled by syr wyllyam barlow chanon.* London: William Rastell, 1531.

Becke, E. *A brefe confutatacion of this most detestable, [and] anabaptistical opinion, that christ dyd not take hys flesh of the blessed vyrgyn mary nor any corporal substaunce of her body for the maintenaunce whereof ihone bucher otherwise called ihone of kent most obstinately suffered and was burned in smythfyelde, the .ii day of may. anno domini M.D.L.* London: John Day and William Seres, 1550.

Becon, T. *The iewel of ioye.* London: John Daye and William Seres, 1550.

Benefield, Sebastian. *A commentary or exposition vpon the first chapter of the prophecie of amos deliuered in xxi. sermons in the parish church of meysey-hampton in the diocesse of glocester.* London: Iohn Hauiland, 1629.

Bernard, Nathaniel. *Esoptron tes antimachias, or, A looking-glasse for rebellion being a sermon preached upon sunday the 16 of iune 1644, in saint maries oxford, before the members of the two houses of parliament.* Oxford: Leonard Lichfield, 1644.

Bernard, Richard. *Plaine euidences the church of england is apostolicall, the separation schismaticall. directed against mr. ainsworth the separatist, and mr. smith the se-baptist: Both of them seuerally opposing the booke called the separatists schisme. by richard bernard, preacher of the word of god at worsop.* London: T. Snodham, 1610.

Blome, Richard. *Questions propounded to george whitehead and george fox &c. who disputed by turnes against one* universitie man in cambridge. aug. 29. 1659. London: n.p., 1659.

_____. *The fanatick history: Or an exact relation and account of the old anabaptists, and new quakers. being the summe of all that hath been yet discovered about their most blasphemous opinions, dangerous pactises [sic], and malitious endevours to subvert all civil government both in church and state. together with their mad mimick pranks, and their ridiculous actions and gestures, enough to amaze any sober christian. which may prove the death & burial of the fanatick doctrine. published with the approbation of divers orthodox divines.* London: for J. Sims, 1660.

_____. *Proposals for the printing an entire course or body of philosophy, according to the principles of the famous renate des cartes, wrote in latin by the learned anthony le grand which will now be carefully translated into english by good hands, with large additions and alterations by the said author, and printed in folio, with an illustration of about an hundred ornamental scultptures / by richard blome, dwelling near clare-market in new weld-street, at the house with green pallisado-pails; where proposals are delivered and subscriptions taken for the same, and where they may inspect the said work.* London: R. Blome, 1693.

[Blome, Richard]. *Historia Fanaticorvm, Oder eine vollkommene Relation und Wissenschafft/ von denen Schwärmern/ Als Alten Anabaptisten und Neuen Quäkern*, trans. Benedict Figken. Frankfurt am Main: Martin Hermssdorffen, 1701.

Bodin, Jean. *On the Demon-Mania of Witches*, Jonathan L. Pearl, ed., Randy A. Scott, trans. Toronto, 1995.

Braght, Thieleman J. van. *Martyrs Mirror: The Story of Seventeen Centuries of Christian Martyrdom, from the Time of Christ to A.D. 1660*, trans. Joseph F. Sohm. Scottdale, PA, 1938.

Bullinger, Heinrich. *A moste sure and strong defence of the baptisme of children, against [the] pestiferous secte of the anabaptystes. set furthe by that famouse clerke, henry bullynger: & nowe translated out of laten into englysh by ihon veron senonoys.* Worcester: John Oswen, 1551.

——. *A most necessary & frutefull dialogue, betwene [the] seditious libertin or rebel anabaptist, & the true obedient christia[n] wherin, as in a mirrour or glasse ye shal se [the] excellencte and worthynesse of a christia[n] magistrate: & again what obedience is due vnto publique rulers of all th[os]e [that] professe christ yea, though [the] rulers, in externe & outward thinges, to their vtter dampnatyon, do otherwyse then well: Translated out of latyn into englishe, by iho[n] veron senonoys*. Worcester: John Oswen, 1551.

Busher, Leonard. *Religions peace or A reconciliation, between princes & peoples, & nations (by leonard busher: Of the county of gloucester, of the towne of wotton, and a citticen, of the famous and most honorable city london, and of the second right worshipfull company) supplicated (vnto the hygh and mighty king of great brittayne: Etc: And to the princely and right honorable parliament) with all loyalty, humility and carefull fidelity*. Amsterdam: n.p., 1614.

——. *Religions peace: Or, A plea for liberty of conscience. long since presented to king james, and the high court of parliament then sitting, / by leonard busher citizen of london, and printed in the year 1614. wherein is contained certain reasons against persecution for religion, also a designe for a peaceable reconciling of those that differ in opinion*. London: for John Sweeting, 1646.

Byfield, Richard. *Temple Defilers Defiled, Wherein a True Visible Church of Christ is Described ... Delivered in two Sermons Preached at the Lecture in Kingston Upon Thames*. London: John Field, for Ralph Smith, 1645.

——. *A short treatise describing the true church of christ, and the evills of schisme, anabaptism and libertinism ... delivered in two sermons*. London: for Ralph Smith, 1653.

Calvin, John. *A short instruction for to arme all good christian people agaynst the pestiferous errours of the common secte of anabaptistes*. London: John Daye and William Seres, 1549.

Carion, J. *The thre bokes of cronicles, whyche iohn carion (a man syngularly well sene in the mathematycall sciences) gathered wyth great diligence of the beste authours that haue written in hebrue, greke or latine whervnto is added an appendix,* conteynyng all such notable thynges as be mentyoned in cronicles to haue chaunced in sundry partes of the worlde from the yeare of christ. 1532. to thys present yeare of. 1550. gathered by iohn funcke of nurenborough. whyche was neuer afore prynted in englysh. London: S. Mierdman, 1550.

Clapham, Henoch. *Antidoton or a soueraigne remedie against schisme and heresie: Gathered to analogie and proportion of faith, from that parable of tares. matth.13. aug.ep.3.nullorum disput.&c. we ought to haue no men their disputations (although men catholike and praise worthie) in that count as we haue the canonicall scriptures: So that it should be vnlawfull for vs to improue and refuse some things in their writings, if happily we finde that they thought otherwise then the truth hath. such a one am I in other mens writings, and so would I haue others to vnderstand of my writings.* London: Felix Kingston, 1600.

———. *Errour on the right hand, through a preposterous zeale acted by way of dialogue. betweene 1 mal-content and flyer. 2 flyer and anabaptist. 3 anabaptist, & legatine-arrian. 4 flyer and legatine-arrian. 5 flier, legaine-arria[n] & familist. 6 flyer and familist. 7 flyer and mediocritie. whereto is also added, certaine positions touching church and antichrist: As without the true holding thereof, it is impossible for a zelous soule, to auoyde either schisme or faction.* London: W. White, 1608.

———. *Errour on the left hand, through a frozen securitie howsoeuer hot in opposition, when satan so hears them. acted by way of dialogue. betw. 1 malcontent and romanista. 2 mal-content romanista & libertinus. 3 malcontent and libertinus. 4 malcontent and atheos. 5 malcontent and atheoi. 6 malcontent & the good & bad spirit. 7 malcontent and mediocrity.* London: N. Okes, 1608.

Cloppenburg, Johannes. *Gangraena Theologiae Anabaptisticae, Dat is: Cancker van de leere der Weder-dooperen: Ontdeckt uyt hare eygene Schriften: [tot bewijs dat hare Bekentenisse A° 1624. Uytgegeven/ enckel bedecking der schande is.] Met een Teghen-gift, der ghesonde Woorden Godes.* Amsterdam: for Hans Walschaert, 1625.

Clyfton, Richard. *The plea for infants and elder people, concerning their baptisme, or, A processe of the passages between M. iohn smyth and richard clyfton wherein, first is proved, that the baptising of infants of beleevers, is an ordinance of god, secondly, that the rebaptising of such, as have been formerly baptised in the apostate churches of christians, is utterly unlawful, also, the reasons and objects to the contrarie, answered : Divided into two principal heads, I. of the first position, concerning the baptising of infants, II. of the second position, concerning the rebaptising of elder people.* Amsterdam: Gyles Thorp, 1610.

Cooper, Thomas. *The mystery of witch-craft discouering, the truth, nature, occasions, growth and power thereof. together with the detection and punishment of the same. as also, the seuerall stratagems of sathan, ensnaring the poore soule by this desperate practize of annoying the bodie: With the seuerall vses therof to the church of christ. very necessary for the redeeming of these atheisticall and secure times.* London: Nicholas Okes, 1617.

_____. *Sathan transformed into an angell of light expressing his dangerous impostures vnder glorious shewes. emplified [sic] specially in the doctrine of witchcraft, and such sleights of satan, as are incident thereunto. very necessary to discerne the speciplague raging in these dayes, and so to hide our selues from the snare thereof.* London: Barnard Alsop, 1622.

Corvinus, Johann Friedrich. *Anabaptisticum et enthusiasticum pantheon und geistliches Rüst-Hauss wider die alten Quacker, und neuen Frey-Geiste : welche die Kirche Gottes zeithero verunruhiget, und bestürmet, auch treue Lehrer und Prediger Göttlichen Worts, verachtet, verleumbdet, gelästert und verfolget haben : mit vielen zur Sache dienlichen und nützlichen Kupffern, bloss zu Gottes Here und Erhaltun seiner christlichen Kirchen : auch den Geistlichen Weltlichen und Hausstande zur Nachrict, Nutz und besten zusammen getragen und auffgerichtet.* N.p., n.p., 1702.

Coverdale, Miles. *A confutacion of that treatise, which one iohn standish made agaynst the protestacion of D. barnes in the* yeare. M.D.XL. wherin, the holy scriptures (peruerted and wrested in his sayd treatise) are restored to their owne true vnderstonding agayne.* Zurich: C. Froschauer, 1541.

Davis, John. *Apocalypsis: Or, the Revelation Of certain notorious Advancers of Heresie: Wherein their Visions and private Revelations by Dreams, are discovered to be most incredible blasphemies, and enthusiastical dotages: Together with an account of their Lives, Actions, and* Ends. London: E. Tyler, 1655.

Denison, Stephen. *The doctrine of both the sacraments to witte, baptisme, and the supper of the lord. or A commentary vpon the 16. verse of the 22. of the acts of the apostles: And vpon a great part of the 11. chapter of the former epistle to the corinthyans: To wit, from the beginning of the 23. verse vnto the ende of the chapter. deliuered in sundry sermons by stephen denison preacher of gods word at kree-church, London.* London: Augustine Mathewes for Robert Mylbourne, 1621.

——. *The white wolfe, or, A sermon preached at pauls crosse, feb. 11 being the last sonday in hillarie tearme, anno 1627, and printed somewhat more largely then the time would permit at that present to deliuer wherein faction is vnmasked, and iustly taxed without malice, for the safetie of weake christians: Especially, the hetheringtonian faction growne very impudent in this citie of late yeeres, is here confuted.* London: George Miller, 1627.

Denne, Henry. *Antichrist unmasked in two treatises. the first, an answer unto two pædobaptists, dan. featly, D.D. and stephen marshall, B.D. the arguments for childrens baptisme opened, and answered. the second, the man of sinne discovered in doctrine; the root and foundation of antichrist laid open.* London: n.p., 1645.

——. *The quaker no papist, in answer to the quaker disarm'd. or, A brief reply and censure of mr. thomas smith's frivolous relation of a dispute held betwixt himself and certain quakers at Cambridge.* London: Francis Smith, 1659.

Eachard, John. *The axe, against sin and error; and the truth conquering. A sermon on matthew 3. 10. now also the ax is laid to the root of the trees, therefore every tree, that bringeth not forth good fruit, is hewn down, and cast into the fire. at which, a christian confessed, she was converted; and because it did good to her, desired it might be preached again at her funerall, that it might do good to others, ... wherein are shewed the causes of the sword upon england, and on the lutherans, and the remedies that must be used, before the judgements cease.* London: Matthew Simmons, 1646.

Edwards, Thomas. *The first and second part of gangræna, or, A catalogue and discovery of many of the errors, heresies, blasphemies and pernicious practices of the sectaries of this time, vented and acted in england in these four last years also a particular narration of divers stories, remarkable passages, letters: An extract of many letters, all concerning the present sects: Together with some observations upon and corollaries from all the fore-named premisses.* London: T.R. and E.M. for Ralph Smith, 1646.

_____. *The third part of gangræna. or, A new and higher discovery of the errors, heresies, blasphemies, and insolent proceedings of the sectaries of these times; with some animadversions by way of confutation upon many of the errors and heresies named. ... briefe animadversions on many of the sectaries late pamphlets, as lilburnes and overtons books against the house of peeres, M. peters his last report of the english warres, the lord mayors farewell from his office of maioralty, M. goodwins thirty eight queres upon the ordinance against heresies and blasphemies, M. burtons conformities deformity, M. dells sermon before the house of commons; ... as also some few hints and briefe observations on divers pamphlets written lately against me and some of my books.* London: for Ralph Smith, 1646.

Elizabeth I. Single page broadsheet: England and Wales, Sovereign (Elizabeth I), *By the quene the quenes maiestie vnderstandyng that of late tyme sundrye persons beyng infected with certayne daungerous and pernicious opinions in matters of religion, contrary to the faith of the church of christe, as anabaptistes ...* London: Rycharde Jugge and John Cawood, 1560.

Etherington, John. *A description of the church of christ, with her peculiar priuiledges, and also of her commons, and entercommoners with some oppositions and answers of defence, for the maintenance of the truth which shee professeth: Against certaine anabaptisticall and erronious opinions, verie hurtfull and dangerous to weake christians. maintained and practised by one master iohn smith, sometimes a preacher in lincolneshire, and a companie of english people with him now at amsterdam in holland. whome he hath there with himselfe rebaptised.* London: W. Stansby, 1610.

[_____.] *A discouery of the errors of the english anabaptists as also an admonition to all such as are led by the like spirit of error. wherein is set downe all their seuerall and maine points of error, which they hold. with a full answer to euery one of them seuerally, wherein the truth is manifested. by edmond iessop who sometime walked in the said errors with them.* London: W. Iones for Robert Bird, 1623.

Featley, Daniel. *Katabaptistai kataptūstoi the dippers dipt, or, the anabaptists duck'd and plung'd over head and eares, at a disputation in southwark: Together with a large and full discourse of their 1. original. 2. severall sorts. 3. peculiar errours. 4. high attempts against the state. 5. capitall punishments, with an application to these times.* London: for Nicholas Bourne, 1645.

Fox, George. *A word from the lord unto all the faithlesse generation of the world, who know not the truth, but live in their own imaginations; with a true declaration of the true faith, and in what it doth differ from the worlds imagination: Written in obedience to the lord, that al may see what faith is owned by the saints, and what faith is denied. and also a few words unto all professors of the world, who worship not the true god, but their own imaginations and conceivings instead of the true god: Also a call from god unto all the the world to repentance, that all may turn unto him, lest the lord destroy both root and branch of them that repent not. also a few words unto you that scorne quaking and trembling, which all the holy men of god witnessed that spake forth the scripture, and also the holy men of god justified, and all you* denied that scorneth such as witness such things now, as ever was in all the generations of the saints. with a word to those that are called anabaptists, independants, presbyterians, leve. London: n.p., 1654.

Glanvill, Joseph. *Saducismus triumphatus, or, Full and plain evidence concerning witches and apparitions in two parts ... With a letter of Dr. Henry More on the same subject and an authentick but wonderful story of certain Swedish witches done into English by Anth. Horneck*. London: for J. Collins and S. Lownds, 1681.

[Haestens, Henrick Lodewijcxsoon van]. *Grouwelen der voornaemster hooft-ketteren die haer in dese laeste tijden soo in Duytslandt, als oock in dese Nederlanden opgheworpen hebben, haer leven, leere, begin ende eynde, enz. Mits-gaders haere af-beeldingen*. Leiden: Henrick Lodewijcxsoon van Haestens, 1607.

Hall, Edward. *The vnion of the two noble and illustre famelies of lancastre [and] yorke, beeyng long in continual discension for the croune of this noble realme with all the actes done in bothe the tymes of the princes, bothe of the one linage and of the other, beginnyng at the tyme of kyng henry the fowerth, the first aucthor of this deuision, and so successiuely proceadyng to the reigne of the high and prudent prince kyng henry the eight, the vndubitate flower and very heire of both the sayd linages*. London: Richard Grafton, 1548.

Hall, Thomas. *The font guarded with XX arguments. containing a compendium of that great controversie of infant-baptism, proving the lawfulness thereof; as being grounded on the word of god, agreeable to the practice of all reformed churches; together with the concurrent consent of a whole jury of judicious and pious divines. occasioned partly by a dispute at bely in worcestershire, aug. 13. 1651. against joseph paget, dyer. walter rose, and john rose. butchers of bromesgrove. john evans a scribe, yet antiscripturist. francis loxly, sho-maker. here you have the question fully stated, ... with a word to one collier, and another to mr. tombs in the end of the book*. London: R.W. for Thomas Simmons, 1652.

Henry VIII. Single page broadsheet: England, Sovereign (Henry VIII), *A proclamation concerninge heresie*. London: Thomas Berthelet, 1535.

—— Single page broadsheet, England and Wales, Sovereign (Henry VIII). *The kynges most royall maiestie being enfourmed*. London: Thomas Berthelet, 1538.

Hill, Edmund. *A quartron of reasons of catholike religion, with as many briefe reasons of refusal*. n.p.: English Secret Press], 1600.

Hooper, John. *A godly confession and protestacion of the christian fayth, made and set furth by ihon hooper, wherin is declared what a christia[n] manne is bound to beleue of god, hys kyng, his neibour, and hymselfe*. London: John Daye, 1550.

Hopkins, Matthew. *The Discovery of Witches: in Answer to several Queries, lately delivered to the Judges of Assize for the County of Norfolk*. London: for R. Royston, 1647.

Hortensius, Lambertus. *Tumultuum anabaptistarum liber unus*. Basel: Johann Oporinus, 1548.

——. *Het Boeck van den Oproeren der Weder-dooperen*. Enkhuizen: Jacob Lenaertsz Meyn, 1614.

Huggarde, Miles. *The displaying of the protestantes, [and] sondry their practises, with a description of diuers their abuses of late frequented newly imprinted agayne, and augmented, with a table in the ende, of all suche matter as is specially contained within this volume. made by myles huggarde seruant to the quenes maiestie*. London: Robert Caly, 1556.

Israel, Jonathan, ed. *Spinoza: Theological-Political Treatise*. Cambridge, 2007.

Jackson, John. *The soule is immortall, or, certaine discourses defending the immortalitie of the soule against the limmes of sathan to wit, saducees, anabaptists, atheists and such like of the hellish crue of aduersaries*. London: W.W., 1611.

Jewel, John. *An apologie, or aunswer in defence of the Church of England concerninge the state of religion vsed in the same. Newly set forth in Latin, and nowe translated into Englishe*. London: Reginald Wolf, 1562.

Johnson, Francis. *A brief treatise conteyning some grounds and reasons, against two errours of the anabaptists 1. the one, concerning baptisme of infants. 2. the other, concerning anabaptisme of elder people.* Amsterdam: G. Thorp, 1609.

Joye, G. *The exposicion of daniel the prophete gathered oute of philip melanchton, iohan ecolampadius, chonrade pellicane [and] out of iohan draconite. [et] c. by george ioye. A prophecye diligently to be noted of al emprowrs [and] kinges in these laste days.* Antwerp: A. Goinus, 1545.

Knox, John. *An answer to a great number of blasphemous cauillations written by an anabaptist, and aduersarie to gods eternal predestination. and confuted by iohn knox, minister of gods worde in scotland. wherein the author so discouereth the craft and falshode of that sect, that the godly knowing that error, may be confirmed in the trueth by the euident worde of god.* Geneva: John Crespin 1555.

L., D. *Israels Condition and Cause pleaded; or some Arguments for the Jews Admission into England.* London: P.W., 1656.

Latimer, Hugh. *The seconde [seventh] sermon of maister hughe latimer which he preached before the kynges maiestie [with?]in his graces palayce at westminster, ye xv. day of marche [-xix daye of apryll], M.ccccc.xlix.* London: John Day and Wylliam Seres, 1549.

Leland, John. *The laboryouse iourney [and] serche of iohan leylande, for englandes antiquitees geuen of hym as a newe yeares gyfte to kynge henry the viij. in the. xxxvij. yeare of his reygne, with declaracyons enlarged: By iohan bale.* London: S. Mierdman, 1549.

Lessius, Leonardus. *A consultation what faith and religion is best to be imbraced ... and translated into english by W.I.* Saint-Omer: English College Press, 1618.

Luther, Martin. *Against the Robbing, Murdering Hordes of Peasants,* http://zimmer.csufresno.edu/~mariterel/against_the_r obbing_and_murderin.htm.

____. *On the Jews and Their Lies.* Pp. 268-78 in *Luther's Works*, vol.47, *The Christian in Society*. IV Franklin Sherman, ed., Martin H. Bertram, trans. Philadelphia, 1971.

More, Henry. *An antidote against atheisme, or, An appeal to the natural faculties of the minde of man, whether there be not a God.* London: Roger Daniel, 1653.

———. *Enthusiasmus triumphatus, or, A discourse of the nature, causes, kinds, and cure, of enthusiasm* .... London: J. Flesher, 1656.

More, Thomas. *The second parte of the co[n]futacion of tyndals answere in whyche is also confuted the chyrche that tyndale deuyseth. and the chyrche also that frere barns deuyseth. made by syr thomas more knight.* London: William Rastell, 1533.

Naogeorgus, Thomas. *The popish kingdome, or reigne of antichrist, written in latine verse by thomas naogeorgus, and englyshed by barnabe googe.* London: Henrie Denham, for Richarde Watkins, 1570.

Ormerod, Oliver. *The picture of a puritane: Or, A relation of the opinions, qualities, and practises of the anabaptists in germanie, and of the puritanes in england Wherein is firmely prooued, that the puritanes doe resemble the anabaptists, in aboue fourescore seuerall things ... wherunto is annexed a short treatise, entituled, puritano-papismus: Or a discouerie of puritan-papisme.* London: Edward Allde for Nathaniel Fosbroke, 1605.

Osiander, Andreas. *The coniectures of the ende of the worlde, translated by george ioye.* Antwerp: S. Mierdman, 1548.

Pagitt, Ephraim. *Heresiography, or, A discription of the hereticks and sectaries of these latter times.* London: W. Wilson for John Marshall and Robert Trot, 1645.

Payne, J. *Royall exchange to suche worshipfull citezins, marchants, gentlemen and other occupiers of the contrey as resorte therevnto. try to retaine, or send back agayne. the contents ys after the preface. sene and allowed here.* Haarlem: Gilis Romaen, 1597.

Penn, William. *An account of W. penn's travails in holland and germany, anno MDCLXXVII, for the service of the gospel of christ, by way of journal containing also divers letters and epistles writ to several great and eminent persons whilst there.* London: T. Sowle, 1694.

Perkins, William. *A discourse of the damned art of witchcraft so farre forth as it is reuealed in the scriptures, and manifest by true experience. framed and deliuered by M. william perkins, in his ordinarie course of preaching, and now published by tho. pickering batchelour of diuinitie, and minister of finchingfield in essex. whereunto is adioyned a twofold table; one of the order and heades of the treatise; another of the texts of scripture explaned, or vindicated from the corrupt interpretation of the aduersarie.* Cambridge: Cantrel Legge, 1610.

Pontanus, Johan Isaksson. *Historische Beschrijvinghe der seer wijt beroemde Coop-stadt Amsterdam.* Amsterdam: Judocus Hondius, 1614.

Prynne, William. *A Soveraigne Antidote to Prevent, Appease, and Determine our Unnaturall and Destructive Civill Wars and Dissentions.* London: A.N., for Richard Lowads, 1642.

———. *The popish royall favourite: Or, A full discovery of his majesties extraordinary favours to, and protections of notorious papists, priests, jesuits, against all prosecutions and penalties of the laws enacted against them; notwithstanding his many royall proclamations, declarations, and protestations to the contrary. as likewise of a most desperate long prosecuted designe to set up popery, and extirpate the protestant religion by degrees, in this our realme of england, and all his majesties dominions. manifested by sundry letters of grace, warrants, and other writings under the kings owne signe-manuall, privy-signet, his privy-councels, and secretary windebanks hands and seals, by divers orders and proceedings in open sessions at newgate, in the kings bench, and elsewhere ... / collected and published by authority of parliament.* London: for Michael Spark Senior, 1643.

———. *Independency examined, vnmasked, refuted, by twelve new particular interrogatories: Detecting both the manifold absurdities, inconveniences that must necessarily attend it, to the great disturbance of church, state, the diminution, subversion of the lawfull undoubted power of all christian magistrates, parliaments, synods: And shaking the chiefe pillars, wherwith its patrons would support it.* London: F.L., for Michael Sparke Senior, 1644.

———. *A fresh discovery of some prodigious new wandring-blasing-stars, & firebrands, stiling themselves new-lights, firing our church and state into new combustions. divided into ten sections, comprising severall most libellous, scandalous, seditious, insolent, uncharitable, (and some blasphemous) passages; published in late unlicensed printed pamphlets, against the ecclesiasticall jurisdiction and power of parliaments, councels, synods, christian kings and magistrates, in generall; the ordinances and proceedings of this present parliament, in speciall: The nationall covenant, assembly, directory, our brethren of scotland, presbyterian government; the church of england, with her ministers, worship; the opposers of independent novelties; ... whereunto some letters and papers lately sent from the sommer-islands, are subjoyned, relating the schismaticall, illegal, tyrannicall proceedings of some independents there.* London: John Macock, 1645.

_____. *New presbyterian light springing out of independent darkness. or VI. important new queries proposed to the army, and their friends and party of the houses; concerning the late ordinance for repeal of the new militia of london, setled by an ordinance of both houses, when full and free, for an whole year, (not yet one quarter expired;) and other late repeals of ordinances and votes; and the high declaration against the intended petition and engagement of the londoners and others, for the speedy settlement of the kingdomes peace: Occasioned by the debates thereof in the common councel in the guildhal on saturday last, the 24 of this instant iuly. discovering the dangerous consequences of repealing ordinances and votes, and the independents, sectaries, and armies plots, to blast the honour, justice, and reputation of this parliament, thereby to dissolve it and all others in it; their false pretences of peace, when they intend nought lesse; and their strange injustice and malice against presbyterians, which will end in their own dishonour and downfall.* London: n.p., 1647.

_____. *The levellers levelled to the very ground. wherein this dangerous seditious opinion and design of some of them; that it is necessary, decent, and expedient, now to reduce the house of peeres, and bring down the lords into the commons house, to sit and vote together with them, as one house. and* the false absurd, grounds whereon they build this paradox, are briefly examined, refuted, and laid in the dust. London: T.B. for Michael Spark, 1648.

———. A brief memento to the present unparliamentary juncto touching their present intentions and proceedings to depose and execute, charles stuart, their lawful king. London: n.p., 1649.

———. A vindication of Wiliam prynne esquire from some scandalous papers and imputations, newly printed and published, to traduce and defame him in his reputation. London: n.p., 1649.

———. The sword of christian magistracy supported, or, A vindication of the christian magistrates authority under the gospell, to punish idolatry, apostacy, heresie, blasphemy, and obstinate schism, with corporall, and in some cases with capitall punishments. London: R.I. for John Bellamy, 1653.

———. The quakers unmasked, and clearly detected to be but the spawn of romish frogs, jesuites, and franciscan fryers; sent from rome to seduce the intoxicated giddy-headed english nation. by an information newly taken upon oath in the city of bristol, jan. 22. 1654. and some evident demonstrations. … London: for Edward Thomas, 1655.

———. A new discovery of some romish emissaries, quakers; as likewise of some popish errors, unadvisedly embraced, pursued by our anticommunion ministers. discovering the dangerous effects of their discontinuing the frequent publick administration of the lords supper; the popish errors whereon it is bottomed; perswading the frequent celebration of it, to all visible church-members, with their free-admission thereunto; and prescribing some legal regal remedies to redress the new sacrilegious detaining of it from the people, where their ministers are obstinate. London: for the author, 1656.

———. A short demurrer to the jewes long discontinued barred remitter into england comprising an exact chronological relation of their first admission into, their ill deportment, misdemeanors, condition, sufferings, oppressions, slaughters, plunders, by popular insurrections, and regal exactions in;

and their total, final banishment by judgment and edict of parliament, out of england, never to return again: Collected out of the best historians and records. with a brief collection of such english laws, scriptures, reasons as seem strongly to plead, and conclude against their readmission into england, especially at this season, and against the general calling of the jewish nation. with an answer to the chief allegations for their introduction. London: for Edward Thomas, 1656.

____. *The second part of a short demurrer to the iewes long discontinued remitter into england. containing a brief chronological collection of the most material records in the reigns of king john, henry 3. and edward 1. relating the history, affaires, state, condition, priviledges, obligations, debts, legal proceedings, justices, taxes, misdemeanors, forfeitures, restraints, transactions, of the jews in, and final banishment out of england, never formerly published in print: With some short usefull observations upon them. worthy the knowledge of all lawyers, scholars, statists, and of such jews who desire re-admission into England.* London; Edward Thomas, 1656.

____. *Some popish errors, unadvisedly embraced and pursued by our anticommunion ministers wherein is discovered the dangerous effects of their discontinuing the frequent publick administration of the lords supper ...: With a new discovery of some romish emmissaries, quakers ...* London: for the author, 1658.

[Reeve, John]. *A Transcendent Spiritual Treatise.* London: for the authors, [1651].

Richardson, Samuel. *Some briefe considerations on doctor featley his book, intituled, the dipper dipt, wherein in some measure is discovered his many great and false accusations of divers persons, commonly called anabaptists, with an answer to them, and some brief reasons of their practice.* London: n.p., 1645.

Ross, Alexander. *Pansebeia, or, A view of all religions in the world with the severall church-governments from the creation, to these times: Also, a discovery of all known heresies in all ages and places, and choice observations and reflections throughout the whole*. London: T.C. for John Saywell, 1655.

Saltmarsh, John. *Groanes for liberty presented from the presbyterian (formerly non-conforming) brethren, reputed the ablest and most learned among them, in some treatises called smectymnuus, to the high and honorable court of parliament in the yeare 1641, by reason of the prelates tyranny. now awakened and presented to themselves in the behalf of their now non-conforming brethren. with a beam of light, discovering a way to peace. also some quæres for the better understanding of mr edwards last book called gangræna. with a parallel betweene the prelacy and presbytery*. London: for Giles Calvert, 1646.

Sarcerius, Erasmus. *Co[m]mon places of scripture ordrely and after a co[m]pendious forme of teachyng set forth with no litle labour, to the gret profit and help of all such studentes in gods worde as haue not had longe exercyse in the same ... translated in to englysh by rychard tauerner*. London: John Byddell, 1538.

Sleidanus, Johannes. *A Famouse Cronicle of Oure Time, Called Sleidanes Commentaries Concerning the State of Religion and Common Wealth, during the Raigne of the Emperour Charles the Fift, with the Argumentes Set before Euery Booke, Conteyninge the Summe Or Effecte of the Booke Following. Translated Out of Latin into Englishe, by Ihon Daus. here Vnto is Added also an Apology of the Authoure*. London: John Daie, 1560.

Smith, Nigel, ed. *A Collection of Ranter Writings: Spiritual Liberty and Sexual Freedom in the English Revolution*. London, 2014.

Smith, R. *A bouclier of the catholike fayth of christes church conteynyng diuers matters now of late called into controuersy, by the newe gospellers. made by richard smith, doctour of diuinitee, [and] the quenes hyghnes reader of the same I her graces vniuersite of oxford*. London: Rychard Tottell, 1554.

Smith, Thomas. *A gaag for the quakers, with an answer to mr. denn's quaker no papist*. London: J.C., 1659.

Smyth, John. *Paralleles, censures, observations. Aperteyning: to three several writinges, 1. A lettre written to Mr. Ric. Bernard, by Iohn Smyth. 2. A book intituled, the Seperatists schisme published by Mr. Bernard. 3. An answer made to that book called the Sep. Schisme by Mr. H. Ainsworth. Whereunto also are adioyned. 1. The said lettre written to Mr. Ric. Bernard divided into 19. sections. 2. Another lettre written to Mr. A.S. 3. A third letter written to certayne bretheren of the separation.* Middelburg: R. Schilders, 1609.

Stephens, Nathaniel. *A precept for the baptisme of infants out of the new testament. where the matter is first proved from three severall scriptures, that there is such a word of command. secondly it is vindicated, as from the exceptions of the separation, so in special from the cavils of mr. robert everard in a late treatise of his intituled baby-baptisme routed.* London: T.R. and E.M. for Edmund Paxton, Nathanaell Webb and William Grantham, 1651.

Taylor, J. *Religions Enemies: With a Brief and Ingenious Relation, as by Anabaptists, Brownists, Papists, Familists, Atheists and Foolists, Sawcily Presuming to Tosse Religion in a Blanquet.* London, 1641.

Terry, John. *The reasonablenesse of wise and holy truth: And the absurditie of foolish and wicked errour.* Oxford: John Lichfield and William Wrench, 1617.

Torshell, Samuel. *The three questions of free iustification. christian liberty. the use of the law explicated in a briefe comment on st. paul to the galatians, from the 16. ver. of the second chapter, to the 26. of the third. by sam. torshell pastor of bunbury in cheshire* (London: I. Beale, for H. Overton, 1632).

Turner, William. *A Perseruatiue, Or Triacle, Agaynst the Poyson of Pelagius Lately Renued, ... by the Furious Secte of the Annabaptistes ...* London, S. Mierdman, 1551.

Whitgift, John. *The defense of the aunswere to the admonition against the replie of T.C. by iohn Whitgift doctor of diuinitie. in the beginning are added these. 4. tables. 1 of dangerous doctrines in the replie. 2 of falsifications and* vntruthes. 3 of matters handled at large. 4 A table generall. London: Henry Binneman, 1574.

Widdowes, Giles. *The schysmatical puritan A sermon preached at witney concerning the lawfulnesse of church-authority, for ordaining, and commanding of rites, and ceremonies, to beautifie the church.* Oxford: John Lichfield, 1630.

Wied, Herman van. *A simple, and religious consultation of vs herman by the grace of god archebishop of colone, and prince electour. [et] c. by what meanes a christian reformation, and founded in gods worde, of doctrine, administration of the deuine sacramentes, of ceremonies, and the hole cure of soules, and other ecclesiastical ministeries may be begon among men committed to our pastorall charge, vntil the lorde graunt a better to be appoynted either by a free, and christian cou[n]sayle, general, or national, or elles by the states of the empire of the natio[n] of germanie, gathered together in the holye gost.* London: John Daye, 1547.

Wilkinson, W. *A confutation of certaine articles deliuered vnto the familye of loue with the exposition of theophilus, a supposed elder in the sayd familye vpon the same articles. by william wilkinson maister of artes and student of diuinitye. hereunto are prefixed by the right reuerend father in god I.Y. byshop of rochester, certaine notes collected out of their gospell, and aunswered by the fam. by the author, a description of the tyme, places, authors, and manner of spreading the same: Of their liues, and wrestyng of scriptures: With notes in the end how to know an heretique.* London: Iohn Daye, 1579.

Secondary Sources

Almond, Philip C. *The Antichrist: A New Biography.* Cambridge, 2020.

Atherton, Ian, and David Como. "The Burning of Edward Wightman: Puritanism, Prelacy and the Politics of Heresy in Early Modern England," *English Historical Review,* 120 (2005), 1215–1250.

Bakker Willem de, and Gary K. Waite, "Rethinking the Murky World of the Post-Münster Dutch Anabaptist

Movement, 1535-1538: A Dialogue between Willem de Bakker and Gary K. Waite." *Mennonite Quarterly Review* 92 (2018), 47-91.

Bakker, Willem de, Michael Driedger, and James M Stayer. *Bernhard Rothmann and the Reformation in Münster, 1530-35.* Kitchener, ON, 2009.

Blickle, Peter. *The Revolution of 1525: The German Peasants' War from a New Perspective,* trans. Thomas A. Brady, Jr., and H.C. Erik Midelfort. Baltimore, 1981.

Brock, Michelle D. "Internalizing the Demonic: Satan and the Self in Early Modern Scottish Piety." *Journal of British Studies* 54 (2015), 23-43.

Burrage, Champlin. "The Antecedents of Quakerism." *The English Historical Review* 30 (1915), 78-90.

Buys, Ruben. *Sparks of Reason: Vernacular Rationalism in the Low Countries, 1550–1670.* Hilversum, 2015.

____. "'Without Thy Self, O Man, Thou Hast No Means to Look for, by Which Thou Maist Know God': Pieter Balling, the Radical Enlightenment, and the Legacy of Dirck Volckertsz Coornhert." *Church History and Religious* Culture 93 (2013), 363–83.

Cameron, Euan. *Enchanted Europe: Superstition, Reason, & Religion, 1250-1750.* Oxford, 2010.

Campbell, Kenneth L. *Windows into Men's Souls: Religious Nonconformity in Tudor and Early Stuart England.* Lanham, MA, 2012.

Clark, Stuart. *Thinking with Demons: The Idea of Witchcraft in Early Modern Europe.* Oxford, 1997.

Coffey, John. "'The Last and Greatest Triumph of the European Radical Reformation'? Anabaptism, Spiritualism and Anti-Trinitarianism in the English Reformation." In Heal and Kremers, *Radicalism and Dissent,* 201-24.

____. *Persecution and Toleration in Protestant England, 1558-1689.* Harlow, 2000.

Coggins, James R. *John Smyth's Congregation: English Separatism, Mennonite Influence and the Elect Nation.* Scottdale, PA, 1991.

Como, David R. "The Family of Love and the Making of English Revolutionary Religion: The Confession and

'Conversions' of Giles Creech." *Journal of Medieval and Early Modern Studies* 48 (2018), 553-598.

____. *Blown by the Spirit: Puritanism and the Emergence of an Antinomian Underground in Pre-Civil-War England.* Stanford, 2004.

Cressy, David. *Travesties and Transgressions in Tudor and Stuart England: Tales of Discord and Dissension.* Oxford, 1999.

Crome, Andrew. "The Münster Rising, Memories of Violence, and Perceptions of Dissent in Restoration England." *The Historical Journal* 65 (2022), 946-68.

Davies, Catharine. *A Religion of the Word: The Defence of the Reformation in the Reign of Edward VI.* Manchester 2003.

Dipple, Geoffrey. "The Spiritualist Anabaptists." In Roth and Stayer, *A Companion to Anabaptism and Spiritualism*, 357-97.

Driedger, Michael. "Muenster, Monster, Modernity: Tracing and Challenging the Meme of Anabaptist Madness." Pp. 27-49 in *European Mennonites and the Challenge of Modernity over Five Centuries: Contributors, Detractors, and Adapters.* Mark Jantzen, Mary S. Sprunger, and John D. Thiesen, eds. North Newton, KS, 2016.

____. "Against 'the Radical Reformation': On the Continuity between Early Modern Heresy-Making and Modern Historiography," in Heal and Kremers, *Radicalism and Dissent*, 139-61.

____. "Response to Graeme Hunter: Spinoza and the Boundary Zones of Religious Interaction." *The Conrad Grebel Review* 25 (2007), 21-28.

____, et al., eds. *Spiritualism in Early Modern Europe*, special double issue of *Church History and Religious Culture* 101/2-3 (2021), https://brill.com/view/journals/chrc/101/2-3/chrc.101.issue-2-3.xml.

____, and Gary K. Waite, with contributions from Francesco Quatrini and Nina Schroeder, "From 'the Radical Reformation' to 'the Radical Enlightenment'?: The Spectre and Complexities of Spiritualism in England, Germany, and the Low Countries." In Driedger et al., *Spiritualism in Early Modern Europe*, 135-166.

____, and Johannes C. Wolfart. "Reframing the History of New Religious Movements," *Nova Religio* 21 (2018), 5–12.

Duffy, Eamon. *Fires of Faith: Catholic England under Mary Tudor*. New Haven, CT, 2009.

Duke, Alastair. "Martyrs with a Difference: Dutch Anabaptist Victims of Elizabethan Persecution." *Dutch Review of Church History / Nederlands Archief Voor Kerkgeschiedenis* 80 (2000), 263–81.

Dunthorne, Hugh. *Britain and the Dutch Revolt, 1560-1700*. Cambridge, 2013.

Early, Jr., Joe. *The Life and Writings of Thomas Helwys*. Macon, GA, 2009.

Elmer, Peter. *Witchcraft, Witch-Hunting, and Politics in Early Modern England*. Oxford, 2016.

____. "'Saints or Sorcerers': Quakerism, Demonology and the Decline of Witchcraft in Seventeenth-Century England." Pp. 145-79 in *Witchcraft in Early Modern Europe: Studies in Culture and Belief*, J. Barry, M. Hester, and G. Roberts, eds. Cambridge, 1996.

Euler, Carrie. "Anabaptism and anti-Anabaptism in the early English Reformation, defining Protestant heresy and orthodoxy during the reign of Edward VI." In Marshall and Loewenstein, eds., *Heresy, Literature and Politics*, 40-58.

Fauth, Dieter. "Kirchmeyer, Thomas." In *The Oxford Encyclopedia of the Reformation*. Hans J. Hillerbrand, ed., 4 vols. Oxford, 1996, 2: 378.

Fix, Andrew. *Prophecy and Reason: The Dutch Collegiants in the Early Enlightenment*. Princeton, 1991.

____. "Mennonites and Collegiants in Holland, 1630-1700." *Mennonite Quarterly Review* 64 (1990), 160-77.

Frankfurter, David. "Ritual as Accusation and Atrocity: Satanic Ritual Abuse, Gnostic Libertinism, and Primal Murders." *History of Religions*, 40 (2001), 352-80.

Friedman, Jerome. *The Battle of the Frogs and Fairford's Flies: Miracles and the Pulp Press during the English Revolution*. London, 1993.

____. "Jewish Conversion, the Spanish Pure Blood Laws and Reformation: A Revisionist View of Racial and Religious

Antisemitism." *Sixteenth Century Journal* 18 (1987), 3-30.

Frijhoff, Willem. "Religious Toleration in the United Provinces: From 'Case' to 'Model.'" Pp. 27-52 in *Calvinism and Religious Toleration in the Dutch Golden Age*. Ronnie Po-Chia Hsia and Henk van Nierop, eds. Cambridge, 2002.

Gaskill, Malcolm. *Witchfinders: A Seventeenth-Century English Tragedy*. Cambridge, MA, 2005.

Gibson, Marion. *Reading Witchcraft: Stories of Early English Witches*. London, 1999.

Goertz, Hans-Jürgen. "Karlstadt, Müntzer and the Reformation of the Commoners, 1521-1525." In Roth and Stayer, *A Companion to Anabaptism*, 1-44.

Goldie, Mark. "The Theory of Religious Intolerance in Restoration England." Pp. 331-68 in *From Persecution to Toleration: the Glorious Revolution and Religion in England*. Ole Peter Grell, Jonathan I. Israel and Nicholas Tyacke, eds. Oxford, 1991.

Gowland, Angus. "The Problem of Early Modern Melancholy." *Past & Present* 191 (2006), 77–120.

Greaves, Richard L. *Deliver Us from Evil: the Radical Underground in Britain, 1660-1663*. Oxford, 1988.

Gregory, Brad S. "Anabaptist martyrdom, Imperatives, Experience, and Memorialization." In Roth and Stayer, *A Companion to Anabaptism*, 467-506.

Grell, Ole Peter. *Calvinist Exiles in Elizabethan and Stuart England*. Abingdon, 1996.

Hamilton, Alastair. *The Family of Love*. Baden-Baden, 2003.

____, Sjouke Voolstra and Piet Visser, eds. *From Martyr to Muppy: A Historical Introduction to Cultural Assimilation Processes of a Religious Minority in the Netherlands: the Mennonites*. Amsterdam, 1994.

Heal, Bridget and Anorthe Kremers, eds. *Radicalism and Dissent in the World of Protestant Reform*. Göttingen, 2017.

Hessayon, Ariel. "Early Modern Communism: The Diggers and Community of Goods." *Journal for the Study of Radicalism* 3 (2009), 1-50.

Hill, Christopher. "Censorship and English Literature." Pp. 32-71 in *The Collected Essays of Christopher Hill*, vol. 1,

    Writing and Revolution in Seventeenth-Century England. Amherst, MA, 1985.

____. "John Reeve and the Origins of Muggletonianism." Pp. 64-110 in *The World of the Muggletonians*, Christopher Hill, Barry Reay, and William Lamont, eds. London, 1983.

____. *Milton and the English Revolution.* New York, 1977.

____. *The World Turned Upside Down: Radical Ideas During the English Revolution.* London, 1972.

Horst, Irvin B. *The Radical Brethren: Anabaptism and the English Reformation to 1558.* Nieuwkoop, 1972.

Israel, Jonathan. *Radical Enlightenment: Philosophy and the Making of Modernity, 1650-1750.* Oxford, 2001.

Hughes, Ann. *Gangraena and the Struggle for the English Revolution.* Oxford 2004.

Hunt, Lynn, Margaret C. Jacob, and Wijnand Mijnhardt. *The Book that Changed Europe: Picart & Bernard's Religious Ceremonies of the World.* Cambridge, MA, 2010.

Hunter, Graeme. *Radical Protestantism in Spinoza's Thought.* Aldershot, 2005.

Hutton, Ronald. *The Witch: A History of Fear, from Ancient Times to the Present.* New Haven, CT, 2017.

Jenkins, Philip. *Intimate Enemies: Moral Panics in Contemporary Great Britain.* New York, 1992.

Kaplan, Benjamin J. *Reformation and the Practice of Toleration: Dutch Religious History in the Early Modern Era.* Leiden, 2019.

____. *Muslims in the Dutch Golden Age: Representations and Realities of Religious Toleration.* Amsterdam, 2007.

____. *Calvinists and Libertines: Confession and Community in Utrecht, 1578-1620.* Oxford, 1995.

Karabela, Mehmet. *Islamic Thought Through Protestant Eyes.* London, 2021.

Katz, David S. *The Jews in the History of England, 1485-1850.* Oxford, 1994.

____. *Philo-Semitism and the Readmission of the Jews to England, 1603-1655.* Oxford, 1982.

Kennel, Maxwell. *Postsecular History: Political Theology and the Politics of Time.* Cham, 2022.

_____. "Postsecular History: Continental Philosophy of Religion and the Seventeenth Century Dutch Collegiant Movement." *Studies In Religion/ Sciences Religieuses* 56 (2017), 406-32.

Klötzer, Ralf. "The Melchiorites and Münster." In Roth and Stayer, *A Companion to Anabaptism and Spiritualism*, 217-56.

Kolakowski, Leszek. "Dutch Seventeenth-Century Anticonfessional Ideas and Rational Religion: the Mennonite, Collegiant and Spinozan Connections." James Satterwhite, trans. *Mennonite Quarterly Review* 64 (1990), 259-97 and 385-416.

Kooi, Christine. *Reformation in the Low Countries, 1500-1620.* Cambridge, 2022.

_____. *Calvinists and Catholics during Holland's Golden Age: Heretics and Idolaters.* Cambridge, 2012.

_____. "Paying off the Sheriff: Strategies of Catholic Toleration in Golden Age Holland." Pp. 87-102, in *Calvinism and Religious Toleration in the Dutch Golden Age*, R. Po-Chia Hsia and Henk van Nierop, eds. Cambridge, 2002.

Kors, Alan C. *Atheism in France, 1650-1729*, vol. 1, *The Orthodox Sources of Disbelief.* Princeton, NJ, 1990, 2016.

La Fontaine, Jean. *Witches and Demons: A Comparative Perspective on Witchcraft and Satanism.* New York, 2016.

Lake, Peter. *The Boxmaker's Revenge: "Orthodoxy", Heterodoxy' and the Politics of the Parish in Early Stuart London.* Manchester, 2009.

Lamont, William M. *Puritanism and Historical Controversy.* Montreal, 1996.

Lee, Jason. *The Theology of John Smyth: Puritan, Separatist, Baptist, Mennonite.* Macon, GA, 2003.

Levack, Brian P. *The Witch-Hunt in Early Modern Europe*, 4th ed. London, 2016.

_____. *Witch-Hunting in Scotland: Law, Politics and Religion.* New York, 2008.

Levelt, Sjoerd, Esther van Raamsdonk, and Michael Rose, eds. *Anglo-Dutch Connections in the Early Modern World.* Abingdon, 2023.

Loewenstein, David. *Treacherous Faith: The Specter of Heresy in Early Modern English Literature and Culture*. Oxford, 2013.

____. *Representing Revolution in Milton and His Contemporaries: Religion, Politics, and Polemics in Radical Puritanism.* Cambridge, 2001.

Ludlow, Morwenna. "Why was Hans Denck Thought to be a Universalist?" *Journal of Ecclesiastical History* 55 (2004), 257-74.

Machielsen, Jan. *Martin Delrio: Demonology and Scholarship in the Counter-Reformation.* Oxford, 2015.

Marsh, Christopher W. *The Family of Love in English Society, 1550-1630.* Cambridge, 1994.

Marshall, John. "Seventeenth-century Quakers, emotions, and egalitarianism: Sufferings, oppression, intolerance, and Slavery." Pp. 146-64 in *Feeling Exclusion: Religious Conflict, Exile and Emotions in Early Modern Europe*, Giovanni Tarantino and Charles Zika, eds. London, 2019.

____. *John Locke, Toleration and Early Enlightenment Culture* (Cambridge, 2006).

____, and David Loewenstein, eds. *Heresy, Literature and Politics in Early Modern English Culture.* Cambridge, 2006.

Marshall, Peter. *Heretics and Believers: a History of the English Reformation.* New Haven, CT, 2017.

Miller, William Cook. "Theodora Wilkin's *Wandering Soul*: Spiritual Adaptation in an Anglo-Dutch context." In Driedger et al., *Spiritualism in Early Modern Europe*, 357-75.

Milner, Matthew. *The Senses and the English Reformation.* Burlington, VT, 2011.

Mulsow, Martin. *Enlightenment Underground: Radical Germany, 1680-1720*, trans. H. C. Erik Midelfort. Charlottesville, 2015.

Nadler, Steven. *Spinoza: A Life.* Cambridge, 1999.

Nathan, Debbie and Michael Snedeker. *Satan's Silence: Ritual Abuse and the Making of a Modern American Witch Hunt.* New York, 1995.

Oberman, Heiko A. *Luther: Man between God and the Devil.* New Haven, 1989.

Packull, Werner O. *Hutterite Beginnings: Communitarian Experiments during the Reformation.* Baltimore, 1999.

Parker, Charles H. *Faith on the Margins: Catholics and Catholicism in the Dutch Golden Age.* Cambridge, MA, 2008.

Peter, Rodolphe, Martin Rothkegel und William H. Brackney. *Clemens Ziegler. Christoph Freisleben, Leonhard Freisleben. Leonard Busher* [Bibliotheca Dissidentium 30]. Baden-Baden/Bouxwiller, 2016.

Pollmann, Judith. *Catholic Identity and the Revolt of the Netherlands, 1520-1635.* Oxford, 2011.

Quatrini, Francesco. *Adam Boreel (1602–1665): A Collegiant's Attempt to Reform Christianity.* Leiden, 2021.

Rabb, Theodore K. "The Editions of Sir Edwin Sandys's 'Relation of the State of Religion.'" *Huntington Library Quarterly* 26 (1963), 323–36.

Richardson, James T., Joel Best, and David G. Bromley, eds. *The Satanism Scare.* New York, NY, 1991.

Roth John D., and James M. Stayer, *A Companion to Anabaptism and Spiritualism, 1521-1700.* Leiden, 2007.

Rothschild, Mike. *The Storm is Upon Us: How QAnon Became a Movement, Cult, and Conspiracy Theory of Everything.* Brooklyn, 2021.

Scheer, Monique. *Enthusiasm: Emotional Practices of Conviction in Modern Germany.* Oxford, 2020.

Schroeder, Nina. "Art and Heterodoxy in the Dutch Enlightenment: Arnold Houbraken, the Flemish Mennonites, and Religious Difference in *The Great Theatre of Netherlandish Painters and Painteresses* (1718–1721)." In Driedger et al., *Spiritualism in Early Modern Europe*, 324-56.

____. "Heretics and Martyrs: Picturing Early Anabaptism in Visual Culture of the Dutch Republic." Ph.D. diss., Queen's University, 2018.

Scribner, Robert W. *Popular Culture and Popular Movements in Reformation Germany.* London, 1988.

_____. *For the Sake of Simple Folk: Popular Propaganda for the German Reformation.* Cambridge, 1981.

Shantz, Douglas H. "David Joris, Pietist Saint: The Appeal to Joris in the Writings of Christian Hoburg, Gottfried Arnold and Johann Wilhelm Petersen." *Mennonite Quarterly Review* 78 (2004), 415-32.

Sharpe, James. *Witchcraft in Early Modern England.* Harlow, 2001.

_____. *Instruments of Darkness: Witchcraft in England, 1550-1750.* London, 1996.

Smith, Joshua Caleb. "Whirlwinds, Sudden Death, and an Army of Toads: Baptist Prodigies of the 1660s." Pp. 83-114 in *New Directions in the Radical Reformation: "Thinking Outside the Cages."* Geoffrey Dipple and Kat Hill, eds. Leiden: Brill, 2023.

Smith, Nigel. "To Network or Not to Network: Art, the Literary, and 'Invention' in Early Modern European Radical Religion." In Driedger et al., *Spiritualism in Early Modern Europe,* 376-98.

_____. *Literature and Revolution in England, 1640-1660.* New Haven, 1997.

_____. *Perfection Proclaimed: Language and Literature in English Radical Religion, 1640-1660.* Oxford, 1989.

Snyder, C. Arnold. "Swiss Anabaptism: The Beginnings, 1523-1525." In Roth and Stayer, *A Companion to Anabaptism,* 45-82.

_____. *Anabaptist History and Theology: An Introduction.* Kitchener, 1995.

Sprunger, Keith and Mary Sprunger, "The Church in the Bakehouse: John Smyth's English Anabaptist Congregation at Amsterdam, 1609-1660." *Mennonite Quarterly Review* 85 (2011), 219-58.

Stayer, James M. "Swiss-South German Anabaptism, 1526-1540." In Roth and Stayer, *A Companion to Anabaptism,* 83-118.

_____. *The German Peasants' War and Anabaptist Community of Goods.* Montreal and Kingston, 1991.

Stephens, Walter. *Demon Lovers: Witchcraft, Sex, and the Crisis of Belief.* Chicago, 2002

Swetschinski, Daniel M. *Reluctant Cosmopolitans: The Portuguese Jews of Seventeenth-Century Amsterdam*. Oxford, 2000.

Taber, Andrew. "'You May Be What Devil You Will': Depictions of Dutch Religious Plurality in English Print, 1609-1699." MA Thesis, University of New Brunswick, 2018.

Underwood, T. L. *Primitivism, Radicalism, and the Lamb's War: The Baptist-Quaker Conflict in Seventeenth-Century England*. Oxford, 1997.

Valente, Michaela. *Johann Wier: Debating the Devil and Witches in Early Modern Europe*. Amsterdam, 2022.

____. "'Against the devil, the subtle and cunning enemy': Johann Wier's *De praestigiis daemonum*. Pp. 103-18 in *The Science of Demons: Early Modern Authors Facing Witchcraft and the Devil*. Jan Machielsen, ed. London, 2020.

Veen, Mirjam van. "Dutch Anabaptist and Reformed Historiographers on Servetus' Death: Or How the Radical Reformation Turned Mainstream and How the Mainstream Reformation Turned Radical." In Heal and Kremers, *Radicalism and Dissent*, 162-72.

Visser, Piet. "Mennonites and Doopsgezinden in the Netherlands, 1535-1700." In Roth and Stayer, *A Companion to Anabaptism and Spiritualism*, 299-345.

____. "Stad van verdraagzaamheid? Amsterdam als vrijhaven voor andersdenkenden." Pp. 19-39 in *Spinoza als gids voor een vrije wereld*, Cis van Heertum, ed. Amsterdam, 2008.

____. "'Blasphemous and pernicious': the role of printers and booksellers in the spread of dissident religious and philosophical ideas in the Netherlands in the second half of the seventeenth century." *Quaerendo* 26 (1996), 303-26.

Voltmer, Rita. "Debating the Devil's Clergy. Demonology and the Media in Dialogue with Trials (14th to 17th Century)." In *Religions* 10 (2019), 648, https://doi.org/10.3390/rel10120648.

Voolstra, Sjouke. *Het Woord is Vlees Geworden: De Melchioritisch-Menniste Incarnatieleer*. Kampen, 1982.

Waardt, Hans de. "Inflating the Prestige of Demons: Johan Wier's Role-Playing." In Driedger, et al., *Spiritualism in Early Modern Europe*, 234-62, https://brill.com/view/journals/chrc/101/2-3/article-p234_6.xml.

Waite, Gary K. "Seventeenth-Century English Writers on Dutch Nonconformists: the Cases of David Joris (George) and Menasseh ben Israel." Pp. 225-34 in Levelt, Van Raamsdonk, and Rose, *Anglo-Dutch Connections in the Early Modern World*.

_____. "Hate Literature Then and Now." Blog Post, Acadia Centre for Baptist and Anabaptist Studies, Acadia University, Wolfville, NS, April 9, 2022: https://acadiadiv.ca/acbas/2022/hate-literature-then-and-now/

_____. "The Devil of Delft in England: the Reception of the Dutch Spiritualist David Joris in 17th-Century English Polemics." *Church History and Religious Culture* 101 (2021), 429-95, https://brill.com/view/journals/chrc/101/4/article-p429_1.xml

_____. "Spiritualism and Rationalism in Early Modern Europe: The Case of David Joris." In Driedger et al., *Spiritualism in Early Modern Europe*, 263-285.

_____. "Sixteenth-Century Spiritualists." Pp. 543-58 in the *T&T Clark Handbook of Anabaptism*, Brian C. Brewer, ed. London, 2021.

_____. *Jews and Muslims in Seventeenth-Century Discourse: From Religious Enemies to Allies and Friends*. London, 2019.

_____. "'Turning Turke the Anabaptist Way': Muslims, Jews, Christian Spiritualists, and Polemical Discourse in the Dutch Republic, c. 1570 to c. 1630." Pp. 73-94 in *Global Reformations: Transforming Early Modern Religions, Societies, and Cultures*, Nicholas Terpstra, ed. London, 2019.

_____. "Knowing the Spirit(s) in the Dutch Radical Reformation: From Physical Perception to Rational Doubt, 1536-1690." Pp. 23-54 in *Knowing Demons, Knowing Spirits in*

the Early Modern Period. Michelle D. Brock, Richard Raiswell, and David R. Winter, eds. Basingstoke, 2018.

_____. "The Drama of the Two Word Debate among Liberal Dutch Mennonites, c. 1620-1660: Preparing the Way for Baruch Spinoza?" In Heal and Kremers, *Radicalism and Dissent*, 118-36.

_____. "Naked Harlots or Devout Maidens? Images of Anabaptist Women in the Context of the Iconography of Witches in Europe, 1525-1650." Pp. 17-51 in *Sisters: Myth and Reality of Anabaptist, Mennonite, and Doopsgezind Women ca 1525-1900*, Mirjam van Veen et al., eds. Leiden, 2014.

_____. "Sixteenth Century Religious Reform and the Witch-Hunts." Pp. 485-506 in *The Oxford Handbook of Witchcraft in Early Modern Europe and Colonial America*. Brian P. Levack, ed. Oxford, 2013.

_____. "Demonizing Rhetoric, Reformation Heretics and the Witch Sabbaths: Anabaptists and Witches in Elite Discourse." Pp. 195-219 in *The Devil in Society in the Premodern World*, Richard Raiswell and Peter Dendle, eds. Toronto, 2012.

_____. "Apocalyptical Terrorists or a Figment of Governmental Paranoia? Re-evaluating the Religious Terrorism of Sixteenth-Century Anabaptists in the Netherlands and Holy Roman Empire, 1535-1570." Pp. 105-25 in *Grenzen des Täufertums / Boundaries of Anabaptism: Neue Forschungen*, Anselm Schubert, Astrid von Schlachta, and Michael Driedger, eds. Gütersloh, 2009.

_____. *Eradicating the Devil's Minions: Anabaptists and Witches in Reformation Europe, 1535-1600*. Toronto, 2007.

_____. *Heresy, Magic and Witchcraft in Early Modern Europe*. Basingstoke, 2003.

_____. "'Man is a Devil to Himself': David Joris and the Rise of a Sceptical Tradition towards the Devil in the Early Modern Netherlands, 1540-1600." *Nederlands Archief voor Kerkgeschiedenis / Dutch Review of Church History*, 75 (1995), 1-30.

Walsham, Alexandra. *Charitable Hatred: Tolerance and Intolerance in England 1500-1700*. Manchester, 2006.

_____. "'Frantick Hacket': Prophecy, Sorcery, Insanity, and the Elizabethan Puritan Movement," *Historical Journal*, 41 (1998), 27-66.

Weeks, Andrew. *The Radical Enlightenment in Germany: A Cultural Perspective*, ed. Niekerk. Leiden, 2018.

White, Barrington. "Henry Jessey in the Great Rebellion." Pp. 132-53 in *Reformation, Conformity and Dissent: Essays in Honour of Geoffrey Nuttall*, R. Buick Knox, ed. London, 1977.

Williams, George H. *The Radical Reformation*, 3rd ed. Kirksville, MO, 1992.

Zijlstra, Samme. *Om de ware gemeente en de oude gronden: Geschiedenis van de dopersen in de Nederlanden 1531-1675*. Hilversum, 2000.

_____. *Nicolaas Meyndertsz van Blesdijk. Een bijdrage tot de Geschiedenis van het Davidjorisme*. Assen, 1983.

Index of Proper Names

Adam (Adamites), 51, 64, 94-96, 99, 104, 108, 142, 190
Ainsworth, Henry, 68
Angel, Mr. of Leicester, 138-39
Anon, A Catalogue of the Severall Sects and Opinions in England, 110-11
Anon, An Exact Catalogue of all Printed Books, 112-13
Anon, A true nyeuu tydyinges, 44
Anon, Obiections: Answered by way of dialogue, 72n33
Anon, The Confession of Faith, of those Churches, 87, 97n36
Anon, The confession of the fayth of the germaynes, 46
Anon, The Gorgon's Head, 182-85
Anon, The institution of a christen man, 48n15
Anon, The original [and] sprynge of all sectes, 48n15
Arnold, Gottfried, 180
Aylmer, John, 53-54
Baillie, Robert, 82, 101-106
Bakewell, Thomas, 150
Bamfield, Mr. (minister of Sherborne), 158
Barlow, William, 42-43
Bastwick, John, 112
Batenburg, Jan van (Batenburgers), 85, 105
Baxter, Richard, 36, 156
Beek, Jan Lucas van der, 92, 95
Bellarmine, Robert, 137-38
Benefield, Sebastian, 78n51
Bernard, Jean Frederic, 95
Bernard, Nathaniel, 148-49
Bernard, Richard, 69-70
Blesdijk, Nicolaas Meyndertsz van, 102
Blome, Richard, 170-82, 192-93
Bodin, Jean, 121
Boucher, Joan (Joan of Kent), 27, 51, 53

Bres, Guy de, 102
Browne, Robert, 37
Bull, John, 97-98
Bullinger, Heinrich 3, 27, 35, 48, 83, 86, 102, 167
Burton, Henry, 112
Busher, Leonard, 72-74
Byfield, Richard, 135-38, 144
Calvin, John, 35, 48-49, 100, 129
Carion, J., 50-51
Cartwright, Thomas, 37
Cassander, Georgius, 102
Charles I, King, 94, 113
Charles II, King, 18, 173, 185
Charles V, Holy Roman Emperor, 103
Clapham, Henoch, 66-71, 189
Clifton, Richard, 69
Cloppenburg, Johannes, 82-83, 102, 105
Clyfton, Richard, 145
Coffey, John, 14, 17, 19
Como, David, 19, 38
Cooper, Thomas, 146-47
Coornhert, Dirck Volckhertsz, 52
Corvinus, Johann Friedrich, 179-81
Coverdale, Miles, 48-49
Cressy, David, 94
Crome, Andrew, 18-20, 84, 171, 185
Cromwell, Oliver, 20, 38, 107, 119, 122, 159, 183
Davis, John, 169-70
Denck, Hans, 46, 168
Denham, Henrie, 59
Denison, Stephen, 77-78
Denne, Henry, 97, 155-58
Descartes, René, 8, 11
Dircksz, Barend, 93, 95
D.L., Israels Condition, 165-66

Driedger, Michael, 19
Dury, John, 63
Eachard, John, 142-44
Eder, George, 3
Edward VI, King, 28, 35-36, 48
Edwards, Thomas, 20-22, 24, 49n18, 65, 81-83, 95-96, 103, 151-52
Elizabeth I, Queen, 36, 38, 54, 73, 164
Elmer, Peter, 134-35, 138, 140, 144, 148, 151-53
Etherington, John, 69, 76-78
Euler, Carrie, 18-19
Evans, Arise, 108
Everard, Robert, 138
Faber, Johann, 3
Farnham, Richard, 97-98
Featley, Daniel, 13-14, 20, 41-42, 63, 81, 89-92, 96-98, 100-101, 140, 156, 167-68, 182, 193
Figken, Benedict, 179
Fox, George, 154-55, 171
Foxe, John, 94
Francis (St.), 123
Gallus, Carolus, 3
Gibson, Marion, 147-48
Gilpin, John, 178
Glanvill, Joseph, 139
Googe, Barnabe, 59
Grebel, Conrad, 30-31
Hacket, William, 66
Haestens, Hendrik van, 56, 102-103
Hall, Edward, 61
Hall, Joseph, 79n51
Hall, Thomas, 140-42
Hartlib, Samuel, 63
Helwys, Thomas, 13
Henry VIII, King, 36, 44, 47-48, 61

Hessayon, Ariel, 88
Hill, Christopher, 193
Hill, Edmund Thomas, 64-65
Hoffman, Melchior, 17, 27, 32, 44, 145, 175
Hooper, John, 27-29
Hopkins, Matthew, 130-31, 133, 138, 144, 149, 158, 170
Hortensius, Lambertus, 83, 85, 93, 95, 102, 105, 175-76
Huggarde, Miles, 53
Hughes, Ann, 19-20, 24
Hut, Hans, 30
I.B., A bryefe and plaine declaracion of certayne sente[n]ces, 61n5
Israel, Menasseh ben, 63, 121-122, 159, 162, 164, 166-67
Jackson, John, 69n27
James I (James VI of Scotland), King, 72-73, 131
Jessey, Henry, 63, 167
Jessop, Edmund, 76-77
Jewell, John, 62
Johnson, Francis, 68
Joris, David, 11-12, 17, 25-26, 34, 47, 49, 52, 56, 59, 91-92, 99-100, 102, 105, 132, 140, 174, 180, 182, 189
Joye, George, 49
Karlstadt, Andreas Bodenstein von, 30, 175
Kennel, Maxwell, 9
Kett, Robert, 28
Knipperdolling, Bernhard, 55-56, 101, 170, 176, 184
Knox, John, 28, 53
Kors, Alan C., 22
Kramer, Heinrich (Malleus Maleficarum), 3, 148
Lamont, William, 36
Latimer, Hugh, 16n4
Legate, Bartholomew (brothers), 67, 150
Leiden, Jan van 1, 11, 31-32, 45, 55-56, 65, 78, 85, 91, 97-98, 101, 105, 145, 168, 175-76, 184
Leland, John, 61-62

Lessius, Leonardus, 90
Lilburne, John, 117
Lindanus, William, 124-25
Locke, John, 8
Loewenstein, David, 19
Lopez, Dr. Rodrigo, 164
Luther, Martin, 1, 23, 78, 85, 103, 132-33, 138, 162, 174-75
Lyford, Mr. (minister of Sherborne), 157-58
Marshall, John, 122-23
Mary, Queen, 36, 53
Matthijs, Jan, 32, 56
Melanchthon, Phillip, 103
More, Henry, 63, 139, 174, 182
Muggleton, Lodowicke (Muggletonians), 36, 99-100, 189
More, Thomas, 43, 102
Muhammad, 56, 103, 169
Mulsow, Martin, 23
Müntzer, Thomas, 30, 32, 44, 49, 56, 65, 85, 92, 103-104, 168, 174-75
Naogeorgus, Thomas (Kirchmeyer), 59-61, 129
Nathan, Debbie, 196-97
Naylor, James, 177-78
Niclaes, Hendrik, 17, 52, 56, 67, 189
Nye, Philip, 160-61
Ormerod, Oliver, 2-4, 65-66
Osiander, Andreas, 49, 86
Pagitt, Ephraim, 81, 83-89, 149, 167
Payne, J., 145n37
Penn, William, 192
Perkins, William, 145-46
Picart, Bernard, 94-95
Pontanus, Johan Isaksson, 86
Prynne, William, 36, 75, 82-83, 106-128, 151, 153, 156, 158-67, 192-93, 195, 197
Quixote, Don, 184

Richardson, Samuel, 98, 101
Robbertsz le Canu, Robbert, 58
Ross, Alexander, 167-70, 174, 182, 193
Rothmann, Bernhard, 55, 100, 104
Saltmarsh, John, 20-22
Sarcerius, Erasmus, 46-47
Schoenmaker, Harmen (Herman van 't Sant), 32, 56
Schroeder, Nina, 19
Schwenckfeld, Caspar von (Schwenckfeldians), 53, 62, 140
Scot, Reginald, 21-22, 127
Serrarius, Peter, 63
Servetus, Michael, 49, 56, 100
Sichem, Christoffel van, 56
Simons, Menno, 17, 34, 83, 105
Sleidanus, Johannes, 55, 83, 102, 105, 119, 167
Smith, Nigel, 19
Smith, R., 53n27
Smith, Thomas, 155-58
Smyth, John, 13, 35, 57, 68-71, 74, 78-79, 189
Snedeker, Michael, 196
Snyder, Diederick (Diederick Sartor), 56, 176-77
Spinoza, Baruch, 8-11
Stearne, John, 130
Stephens, Nathaniel, 138-39
Storch, Nicolaus (Nicholas Storke), 168, 174
Terry, John, 74-75
Tolderry, John, 178
Torshell, Samuel, 78-79
Turner, William, 51-54, 63, 186
Twisck, Pieter Jansz, 72-73
Tyndale, William, 43
Waardt, Hans de, 126-27
Walsham, Alexandra, 5, 24
Whitehead, George, 156, 171
Whitgift, John, 37

Widdowes, Giles, 75-76
Wied, Herman von, 49-50, 133
Wier, Johan, 21-22, 124-27, 197
Wilkinson, W., 144n37
Willan, Edward, 152
Willemsz, John, 85
William III, King, and Queen Mary, 185
Williams, George H., 25, 37
Winstanley, Gerald, 88-89
Ziegler, Clemens, 47
Zwingli, Ulrich, 30-31